NEXT-LEVEL
Healthcare Employees

Improving the Performance of a Good Team

Laura Hills, D.A.

978-1-960762-03-0 Print
978-1-960762-04-7 eBook
Published by **American Association for Physician Leadership, Inc.**
PO Box 96503 | BMB 97493 | Washington, DC 20090-6503

Website: www.physicianleaders.org

13 8 7 6 5 4 3 2 1

Copyedited, typeset, indexed, and printed in the United States of America

PUBLISHER
Nancy Collins

PRODUCTION MANAGER
Jennifer Weiss

DESIGN & LAYOUT
Carter Publishing Studio

COPYEDITORS
Karen Doyle
Pat George

For Sandy Kirschenbaum
and Jean Hills Bailey,
my next-level sisters-in-love

TABLE OF CONTENTS

ACKNOWLEDGMENTS

First, I would like to thank Nancy Collins for her steadfast belief in me year after year and for once again championing and guiding me through a book project. Thank you, Nancy, for making this book possible and for continuing to be an uplifting presence in my life. I am grateful to have witnessed the amazing things that you have accomplished in publishing. You stand as a role model for excellence and inspire that same excellence in others. I am honored and grateful to be one of your authors.

Next, I would like to thank Dr. Marcel Frenkel for giving me the opportunity in 1998 to write about staff development in *The Journal of Medical Practice Management.* Neither of us could have foreseen that this would become a 25-year writing gig for me (and we're still going strong), but how lucky for me that it's turned out that way. You are and always will be one of my heroes.

My sincere thanks go, too, to the talented team that has supported my writing for many years and that has made this book possible. My phenomenal copy editor Karen Doyle has ensured that my writing has its snap, crackle, and pop. Thank you, Karen, for your astute author's queries, for your excellent suggestions, and for catching my errors. A debt of gratitude goes, too, to the extraordinary Jennifer Weiss, who provides the production support for my writing. Thank you, Jen, for the countless things you do to ensure that everything chugs along smoothly through the production process. And to the "Other Laura" in my life, the fabulous Laura Carter, thank you again for once again spinning my Word document straw into design gold. This is our fifth book together and it doesn't get old, does it? It is always, always a treat to work with you.

Additionally, I wish to thank the American Association for Physician Leadership for believing in me, for publishing another of my books, and for all you do to provide physicians with the knowledge and skills required to become better leaders. We share the same passion for and commitment to this work and I am thrilled once again to have the opportunity to work with you. As professional associations go, AAPL is aces.

Finally, I wish to thank my husband Cornell Hills for his enthusiastic support of anything and everything I want to do. Forget Paris, Baby. Baltimore is the most beautiful city in the world, thanks to you.

ABOUT THE AUTHOR

PHOTO BY STEVE BRANAGAN

Laura Hills, D.A., has accomplished many things over a distinguished 40-year career but defines herself first and foremost as an educator. Her passion is to teach professionals how to lead and develop others, build better relationships, and communicate more effectively. She is well known for her programs, books, and articles, and notably is a columnist for AAPL's *Healthcare Administration Leadership & Management Journal* and the *Journal of Medical Practice Management* since 1998.

Hills has grounded her work in a rigorous academic foundation. She holds a Doctor of Arts in higher education with a focus on adult learning and leadership and wrote and published her award-winning dissertation on leadership legacies. She lives in Baltimore, Maryland, with her husband Cornell Hills and is the mother of three adult daughters.

Also by Dr. Laura Hills

Hills, L. *The Problem Employee: How to Manage the Employees No One Wants to Manage.* Washington, DC: American Association for Physician Leadership, 2021.

Hills, L. *They'll Eat Out of Your Hand If You Know What to Feed Them: The 30 Essential Communication Skills that Give Highly Successful Career Professionals Their Edge.* Fairfax, Virginia: Blue Pencil Publishing, 2014.

Hills, L. *Lasting Female Educational Leadership: Leadership Legacies of Women Leaders.* Amsterdam and New York: Springer, 2013.

Hills, L. *Climbing Out of a Rut: Four Steps and 101 Secrets to Supercharging Your Career and Finding Greater Fulfillment and Reward in What You Do Every Day.* Fairfax, Virginia: Blue Pencil Publishing, 2012.

Sachs-Hills, L. *How to Recruit, Motivate, and Manage a Winning Staff: A Medical Practice How-to Guidebook.* Phoenix, Maryland: Greenbranch Publishing, 2004.

Sachs, L. *The Professional Practice Problem Solver.* New York: Prentice-Hall, 1991.

Sachs, L. *Do-It-Yourself Marketing for the Professional Practice.* New York: Prentice-Hall, 1986.

PREFACE

I have been writing about healthcare management for more than 40 years. In that time, a great deal of my work has been problem–solution focused. In fact, two of my books have the word *problem* in their title.

There's nothing wrong with a problem–solution focus, and in fact, I would be among the first to argue that there is everything right about it. Facing challenges in our work and in our lives is an inevitable part of our human experience. We are always going to have problems, so naturally, we are always going to be on the lookout for strategies that will help us solve them and walk away from them with the fewest bumps and bruises possible. I have been very fortunate to provide my readers with effective solutions to their most challenging employee management problems, and if fortune smiles on me, I will continue to do so.

This book, however, does not focus on problems, but on opportunities. It suggests that healthcare leaders can and must strive to bring out excellence in *all* of their employees, including the good ones. It argues that when it comes to the people who work in a healthcare organization, good enough is not good enough. It encourages healthcare leaders to believe that every employee deserves to be their best and that every healthcare organization deserves to have excellent employees, not just good ones.

In my experience, the majority of people who work in healthcare organizations are good employees. They don't cause problems and they are capable people who know their jobs and who get along with one another, at least for the most part. They are dependable and they want to make a difference.

But also, in my experience, those good employees are the ones who don't squeak, so they don't get much of the management oil. It is so easy to overlook good employees and even take them for granted. Healthcare leaders are busy and often are stretched thin. They spend a lot of their time dealing with not only the day-to-day operations of their organizations, but also the problems that come knocking on their doors. However, leadership requires more than problem-solving, more than keeping everything humming along. It also requires healthcare leaders to inspire, guide, support, and encourage their employees to level up their performance, and that means *all* of their employees, not just the ones who are clamoring for attention. That's what this book is about.

Good parents love all of their children equally. Likewise, healthcare leaders must show the love equally to all of their employees, not just to those who make a ruckus. In the pages that follow, you will learn how to show the love to your good employees. You will read about the specific strategies you can use to motivate them and inspire them to be more. You will learn a positive, strengths-based approach to leading others that can lift everyone higher.

And while I can't guarantee that every strategy will improve the performance of every good employee, I am confident that the strategies you learn will significantly improve your batting average. In my experience, helping even one good employee reach for that next level and attain it will be extremely gratifying and well worth the effort.

Dr. Laura Hills
Baltimore, Maryland

Part 1:

Next-Level Healthcare Employees

The Big Picture

"If you'll not settle for anything less than your best, you will be amazed at what you can accomplish in your lives."

– Vince Lombardi

Creating a stellar team is one of the hardest things a healthcare leader can do, for three reasons.

First, you may have employees who are satisfied with their adequate performance and who hold fast to the idea that good enough is good enough. Such employees may be unmotivated and unwilling to change.

Second, you may have external pressures working against you, such as limited resources, problem employees, understaffing, or an HR mess you've inherited from a predecessor.

And third, you may have employees who *want* to improve but who have trouble doing so because change is often complex, hard, and unpleasant. Employees who seek to improve their performance must disrupt comfortable, familiar habits while simultaneously fostering new, possibly unfamiliar ones. They may be filled with self-doubt, lack needed skills, falter, and backslide.

Megan Call[1] warns, " [Changing behavior] takes time — usually longer than we prefer." In some cases, the change employees aspire to is so painful and takes so much effort and time that they give up, reverting to their more comfortable good but not stellar performance.

Although creating a stellar healthcare team is one of the hardest things a healthcare leader can do, it is also one of the most important. Everything that happens in your healthcare organization relies on the people who work in it. In fact, your employees are your most valuable asset — more so than the building you sit in or the equipment you use.

The quality of your professional services and the very reputation of your healthcare organization depend on your employees. As eLearning Partners[2] shares, "Employees champion your business and determine the success or failure of it."

Healthcare leaders can and should be grateful for their good employees. However, they cannot afford to allow good-level performance to slide by unnoticed and unchanged year after year because they are too busy putting out fires or racing to keep up with a punishing workload. A stellar healthcare team must be every leader's goal.

It's up to you to set the bar high. It's also your job to identify what next-level performance looks like for your employees individually and as a team, and then, help them get there.

Ideally, a stellar team begins at recruitment. Every healthcare leader wants to hire job candidates who have the potential to become stellar employees, and there is merit in seeking the best of the best. Yet while hiring the best talent helps stack the deck in your favor, that strategy alone will not ensure stellar performance from your healthcare team. Even the most promising job candidates can plateau or become jaded once on the job if we are not careful with them. Talent and motivation need to be nurtured.

It's hard for new hires to hang onto their rookie enthusiasm and work ethic when they are surrounded by coworkers who do a good job but who don't seek to improve, or who have just-OK working relationships with one another. Tim McKinnon[3] explains, "Employees can become uninspired, distracted or frustrated if we don't develop a positive and collaborative work environment for them." Certainly, they will be unlikely to reach their full potential and may learn to settle, as others have, for good-enough performance.

Those new hires who hang onto their desire and passion before being stellar performers won't remain long in an organization that doesn't foster that excellence within them. When they're ready to seek greener pastures, another employer will be all too happy to encourage and help them improve if you and your organization can't or won't.

Most healthcare organizations have good employees. They may even have some stellar ones. But imagine if you could help your good employees ramp up their performance to the next level. Imagine a healthcare organization where *every* employee is continuously improving, striving ever upward to achieve higher and higher levels of performance. As the HR and employment engagement website Hppy[4] contends, "It is your *responsibility* to take [your employees] from good to great." Doing so benefits your employees but also your healthcare organization and every patient you serve.

THE BENEFITS OF A CONTINUOUSLY IMPROVING HEALTHCARE TEAM

Your employees will be most receptive to leveling up their performance if you take the time to prepare them for the task. Without preparation, they may dig in their heels about what you ask of them or be afraid that their jobs may be in jeopardy. Some may placate you by telling you that they want to improve their performance but not do so in spirit or deed. Be transparent about your motives. Naturally, your employees will suspect that you want them to improve their performance for the sake of your organization. Admit to them that this is true. Your organization *will* enjoy many benefits from their improved performance, such as increased productivity and profitability, lower costs, more efficient operations, fewer errors, lower turnover, and higher quality. These are the outcomes every healthcare leader seeks, so be unapologetic about it.

However, help your employees *also* see that your goal as a leader is to develop them professionally and to help them succeed. Share with them the benefits that *they* will enjoy both personally and professionally by bringing their performance to the next level. As Nawras Skhmot[5] argues, "Knowing the benefits of the process can provoke action, allow for proper allocation of resources, and inspire everyone to put in the hard work necessary to pull off a successful program."

Before proceeding, be sure that your employees see that, as Kevin Nye[6] suggests, becoming next-level employees "benefits everyone, not just the business." Specifically, describe what your employees stand to gain if they level up their performance. Here are five of those benefits described in detail, with several more listed later. Explore these with your employees, but also ask them what they think they will enjoy when they bring their performance up to the next level.

1. **Better work environment:** Problems can be solved and the work environment can get better. But do your employees believe this? Have they experienced it? Nothing more clearly demonstrates to employees that

the work environment can improve than leaders who take action, have high expectations, and work continuously to make things better for the people they lead. Be a continuously improving leader and show your employees how bringing their performance to the next level makes the work environment better for everyone.

2. **Greater happiness:** Employees will enjoy working in a better work environment and logically, Nye says, "better working environments result in happier employees." Continuous improvement, when undertaken without inordinate pressure, ultimately makes employees' jobs easier, not harder. It can increase morale, a sense of wellbeing, and happiness about work.
3. **Less fault-finding and conflict:** Employees who are happy are far less likely than employees who are unhappy or neutral in their feelings to find fault with others. Happy employees are less likely to nitpick, spread gossip, or complain about coworkers. They usually don't dwell on negative thoughts for long and are less likely to act on them. As well, happy employees are less likely to take the bait and engage in a fight when a coworker provokes them. In short, Nye says, "happier employees are less likely to create conflict with others."
4. **Better relationships with coworkers:** Happy employees are more likely to form strong teams. They generally believe that obstacles are easier to overcome if they work together. They believe, too, that creativity flourishes through collaboration and that achieving goals as a team is extremely gratifying. They find that victories are sweeter when they are won together. Happy employees also find it easier to stay motivated and true to their individual next-level paths when the whole team is doing the same. James Milsom[7] suggests that "continuous improvement acts as the glue" that helps employees develop stronger bonds and work collaboratively.
5. **Opportunities for advancement:** Of course, you cannot promise your employees that improving their performance will guarantee them promotions and raises. However, you can tell them that setting and achieving higher performance goals will be reflected positively in their performance reviews. And, as the team at Indeed[8] suggests, employees who produce quality work and continue to improve "are more likely to have greater job security."

There are many more benefits that employees will enjoy by leveling up their performance. For example, they may feel that they take more pride in their work, that work is more interesting, and that they are developing new skills and gaining new knowledge. They may find that their confidence is increasing as they master new skills, and that it is exciting to work toward becoming the best version of themselves.

There is something naturally appealing about self-improvement. Allison Greco[9] shares, "I am an absolute sucker for a before and after. I love watching home improvement shows. It's amazing to see the big reveal at the end and see how all of that hard work paid off to create something absolutely beautiful." So, too, will your employees enjoy seeing their progress and results.

If you doubt the allure of self-improvement, take a look at the number of self-help resources in a bookstore or online. In fact, think for a moment about why you are reading this book right now. Aren't you reading it because you want to improve or expand your approach to managing your good employees and to add new tools for your leadership toolkit?

Your good employees are no different. They, too, will be attracted to self-improvement activities, provided that they see them as such. Therefore, help your employees appreciate that taking their performance to the next level, from good to stellar, will indeed be a gratifying self-improvement effort.

APPLY THE "I+1" PRINCIPLE TO EMPLOYEE PERFORMANCE IMPROVEMENT

The i+1 Principle is a learning theory developed by linguist Stephen Krashen[10] in the 1970s. It suggests that learning is most effective when we meet a learner's current level and add just one level of difficulty, like the next rung on a ladder. Phil Western[11] suggests that although Krashen developed his i+1 Principle for those striving to learn a new language, "We're talking about more than just language here; this applies to anything you decide to do."

I'd like to share with you an example of how Krashen's i+1 Principle worked in my own life to illustrate how you can use it to help your employees improve their performance. I enjoy playing jazz standards and classic Broadway show tunes on the piano. Several years ago, in an effort to improve my playing, I decided to listen again and again to recordings of the greats like Art Tatum, Oscar Peterson, Marian McPartland, Errol Garner, and Mary Lou Williams. However, my playing got no better, no matter how many times I listened to a song or how hard I tried to figure out what these incredible pianists were doing.

Then one day, I stumbled upon recordings of standards played by a pianist I'd never heard of (and probably most people haven't). He was a cocktail pianist at a hotel lounge. His playing was very enjoyable and just a little bit better than mine. I listened to his recordings repeatedly and determined what he was doing that made his playing better than mine. Pretty soon, with more listening and practice, I pulled myself up to his level for one song, then another, and another, until my overall playing improved.

There is no way that at my level of playing at that time or even now, I could begin to understand how to play like Oscar Peterson. His intricate runs and improvisations were and are unfathomable to me and certainly beyond my technical ability. But playing like that relatively unknown cocktail pianist was something I could achieve because he was only a little better than me. In Krashen's terms, his playing was +1, or one level above mine. Peterson's playing, on the other hand, was probably +1,000.

If we ask employees to ramp up to Oscar Peterson-level employee performance, we'll be asking for a miracle. Too ambitious a goal can overwhelm them and they may react to it by deciding that it is impossible. However, if we ask them to level up just one level, as Krashen suggests, such a goal will seem reasonable and within their reach. When they make it to that next level, they can set their sights on the level one step higher and achieve it, too. Then they can move on to the next level and the next and the next.

Employees who are continuously applying Krashen's i+1 Principle to their self-improvement enjoy many successes along the way that reinforce their efforts. They also learn a strategy that they can use to improve their performance throughout their careers.

Your job is to help your employees identify their +1s, give them the support and time they need to work toward them, troubleshoot and guide them when needed, and reinforce and reward their efforts and accomplishments. Your job also is to inspire your employees to set their sights high and to work toward them step by step. As Muhammad Ali[12] wrote toward the end of his life, "I have learned to live my life one step, one breath, and one moment at a time....I am still learning."

HOW TO CREATE A NEXT-LEVEL CULTURE IN YOUR ORGANIZATION: 10 STRATEGIES

Different things can motivate employees to improve their performance. Hppy suggests, "Anything from positive reinforcement to providing methods of professional development and upward mobility can have a desirable impact on employee development." However, what motivates improvement for one employee may not work for another.

The common denominator in every stellar healthcare team, though, is a leader who creates a next-level culture, one who envisions, describes, motivates, supports, and reinforces next-level performance for everyone. Here are 10 strategies that you can use to create that culture within your organization:

1. **Start with yourself.** Oliver Goldsmith[13] famously wrote in 1832, "People seldom improve when they have no other model but themselves to copy." His words ring true today. What are you doing to level up your own performance? For instance, what books are you reading, courses are you taking, conferences are you attending, or new skills are you learning? Are you working with a leadership coach or a mentor? Do you meet regularly with other leaders to share best practices? Have you been the subject of a 360-feedback review? Martin Webster[14] suggests, "You must become the change you want to see in your team or organization." Commit to leveling up your own performance and share your next-level goals, strategies, and progress with your employees.
2. **Involve your employees in defining stellar performance.** When it comes to your team's performance, you ultimately will be the person to set the bar where it needs to be. However, your employees will take to the idea of leveling up more willingly if they have been part of the bar-setting process. Andrew Horlick[15] explains, "By getting employees actively involved in a change that impacts them directly, you will provide them with an increased sense of control, build their commitment to the change, and reduce the amount of resistance that is likely to occur."

   Hold one or more staff meetings to engage your staff in a discussion about what stellar performance looks like. Where have they seen it both inside and outside your healthcare organization? Then ask them to identify ways that their good performance falls short of that definition of stellar. Ask them to identify obstacles that they believe stand in the way of their achieving higher levels of performance.

Asking and answering these questions together will encourage your employees to feel ownership of the process. That can feel very empowering as they embark on their leveling-up journey.

3. **Emphasize the importance of soft skills.** For decades, there's been a strong emphasis on technical or hard skills in the workplace. Job candidates often are hired because of their training, credentials, certifications, technical knowledge, and experience. However, Olive Keogh[16] says, "hard skills get you hired, soft skills could get you fired." That's because soft skills, though usually harder to define and measure than hard skills, are just as critical. Explore with your employees the ways that leveling up their performance may require them to improve their hard skills, soft skills, or very possibly, both.
4. **Focus on what they are already doing well.** It's all too easy to dwell on our shortcomings. Help your employees begin their leveling-up efforts by taking stock of their strengths. Hppy suggests, "Your goal here is to build your employees up." A strengths-based approach to self-improvement allows employees to capitalize on what they already do well. Be generous with your well-deserved compliments. Hppy says, "Complimenting employees is a simple way to make employees feel empowered and invested."
5. **Establish the first achievable i+1 goal.** You may work with employees one-on-one to establish the first goal that they will tackle individually. You may also establish the first goal that your team will tackle together. In either case, agree to goals that are i+1, or only one level up from where employees are now. Stick to a behavioral goal that is easy to describe, observe, and measure. Make it specific. For instance, being friendlier to patients is too large and too unclear a goal. Making eye contact and smiling at the beginning of every patient interaction is a more manageable and measurable goal.
6. **Go for a quick win.** Ideally, employees should achieve their first goal in no more than one month. Margaret Reynolds[17] explains, "Quick wins seem like the antithesis of long-term performance improvement. Yet strategic leaders realize that quick wins are in their arsenal of tactics because it helps them achieve the Holy Grail of business leadership

— sustainable long-term performance." Keep in mind that the setting of the first goal presents a tender moment in the self-improvement process. Leveling-up with this kind of focus and intention may be a new experience for your employees, and they may not feel sure about it. Don't allow them to be too ambitious. Quick wins, especially at the beginning, are what Reynolds calls the "#1 way to keep the momentum going in the right direction."

7. **Establish a precise strategy for achieving the first goal.** Work with your employees to figure out how they will work toward achieving their first goal. There may be more than one way to go about it, or it may be that a combination of strategies will work best. The key here is to explore the options and involve your employees not only in the "what to do" but also in the "how to do." Are they going to take an online course, read a book, shadow a more-experienced employee, or practice a new skill at least 30 minutes a day? Are they going to document a behavioral change? For example, if they are trying to make it a habit to smile and make eye contact with every patient, how are they going to track their progress patient by patient, day by day?
8. **Establish a deadline.** When will your employees reach their first goals? One week? Two? One month? Choose a "Goldilocks" deadline for the goal — not too soon, not too late, but just right. Scott Young[18] suggests, "Parkinson's Law states that tasks expand to fill the time given to them. By setting a strict deadline in advance, you can cut off this expansion and focus on what is most important." Don't give your employees so much time that they lollygag, but also don't give them so little time that they become stressed or give up. Young explains, "Robots can work without sleep, relaxation, or distractions. Your employees aren't robots." Therefore, don't schedule your deadline with the expectation that your employees can work 16-hour days to meet it. As Young says, "Death marches aren't healthy."
9. **Establish metrics or other assessment methods.** How will you determine that your employees have achieved their goals? Will they have to demonstrate a new skill they learned or show you precisely how their behavior has indeed changed? Keep in mind that it is not adequate that they completed the strategy that they set forth, such as reading a book or attending a program. Those are learning goals, not performance goals.

   If they have done what they said they would do but they have not achieved their performance goals, you will need to work with them to figure out why and determine next steps. It may be that the goal was too ambitious or that the learning strategies were not adequate. Or it may be that there was an obstacle standing in their way. A smaller goal, additional learning strategies, and more practice time may be needed. If so, reset the goal and strategy, and come up with a new deadline. Keep up with the employee's progress the next time around and troubleshoot as needed.

10. **Celebrate successes.** When employees achieve their goals, it may be tempting to jump immediately into the next ones. Take a beat before they do. Celebrate and reinforce your employees' accomplishments, even if they were small. Teresa Amabile and Steven Kramer[19] suggest, "When we think about progress, we often imagine how good it feels to achieve a long-term goal or experience a major breakthrough. These big wins are great — but they are relatively rare. The good news is that even small wins can boost inner work life tremendously."

    Reinforce the good work your team has done and make an effort to follow up with each of your employees individually. Amabile and Kramer warn, "The power of progress is fundamental to human nature, but few managers understand it or know how to leverage progress to boost motivation." Talk with your staff about the sheer joy there is in progress. Congratulate them on their good work. Give them credit for achieving their goals or for trying if they did not quite achieve them.

Some goals will be achieved and require no follow-up. For instance, earning a certification is a one-and-done goal. Once the employee earns it, it's done. However, behavioral changes require further assessments to ensure that the employee keeps up the new behavior and doesn't backslide. Establish a follow-up assessment schedule and continue it until you and the employee are certain that the new behavior has become a habit.

WHAT MORE CAN YOU DO TO CREATE A STELLAR HEALTHCARE TEAM?

The focus of this introduction has been on helping your employees level up from good to stellar through goal setting and accountability. However, there is much more that a healthcare leader can do to create a stellar team. The chapters in Part 2 of this book describe effective strategies that you can use to improve the performance of a good healthcare team.

That said, professional development is not a spectator sport. Your employees must be accountable for their own professional development and play an active role in it. They must work collaboratively with their teammates and with you to level-up their performance, and they must be willing to do the work. Simply put, you can't do all the work for them, nor should you try to. At the end of the day, it is what they learn, what they practice again and again, what they strive for, and what they achieve that will determine whether they improve or stagnate. The powerful combination of the individual work employees do plus the additional creative and strategic efforts of a good leader are what is necessary to transform a good employee into a stellar one.

When you ask your good employees to improve their performance, remember that it's a big ask. Many employers would be thrilled to have good employees and would be happy to settle for good performance. Asking good employees to become better may not be met with triple cartwheels. Have patience, keep at it, and don't let your employees lull you into that "good-enough" trap. Stay firm in your commitment. See the potential in your employees— it's there if you look hard enough. Then, stay with it. The only way you will ever create a stellar team is if you believe that it is possible and if you are willing to be the catalyst for change.

PART 1 BONUS FEATURE

10 BARRIERS TO CREATING A STELLAR HEALTHCARE TEAM

Even highly motivated employees who want to improve their performance may hit some roadblocks along the way. Stuart Hearn[20] identifies 10 barriers that employees often face when attempting to level-up their performance and suggests how you can overcome them.

The Barrier	The Problem	What to Do
Poor work/life balance	Healthcare organizations that encourage a first-in/last-out culture and lunches at desks are doing their employees a great disservice. Leveling up requires focus and energy. Employees need time away from work to rest and recuperate.	Be a leader who "walks the walk," Hearn says. Model good work/life balance. Leave work at a reasonable time. Take your full annual vacation. Don't work through lunch. Then, encourage your employees to do the same.

Toxic work environment	Many problems can create a toxic work environment such as bullying, overworking, and unfairness in the way employees are treated. Toxicity will eat away at employees and be a powerful distraction from their efforts to improve.	Take a hard line with toxic behavior and do not allow it. Be certain that your management policies are administered fairly and consistently. Do not allow anyone to overwork or overstress your employees, or to treat them in any way less than with complete respect.
Lack of community	Employees spend a great deal of their time at work. They need to feel social bonds and that they are part of a well-functioning team.	Facilitate team-building activities and organize social events for your employees. Do not allow exclusionary behaviors from cliques or individuals.
Too much red tape	Is it a trial to get even the simplest task completed? Are your employees bogged down by rules and complicated procedures? Red tape can be a huge obstacle to your employee's productivity and improvement.	Keep simplicity at the heart of your work processes. Intervene when you identify a rule or process that is needlessly difficult and seek ways to eliminate or streamline it.
Complicated software	Employees who are constantly struggling to navigate your software will become frustrated. Their productivity and performance will suffer and their patience will be stretched thin.	Make user-friendly, intuitive software a priority. Hearn suggests that you opt for "simple and effective tools" that your employees will enjoy using.
Few one-on-ones	Employees want to feel that they are individuals, not part of a herd. They crave one-on-one time to discuss their problems, questions, feedback, and professional development.	Develop a system of regular one-on-one performance conversations. Coach employees to ensure that they are "engaged and enthusiastic," Hearn says.
Few development opportunities	Employees who believe that they are in a dead-end job are likely to become demotivated. Hearn says, "This will likely result either in an employee who isn't contributing as much as they have the potential to, or in an employee who will jump ship to explore opportunities elsewhere."	Offer clear pathways for personal and career advancement, as well as ongoing training and development opportunities both inside and outside your healthcare organization.

Lack of clarity	Employees cannot aspire to being stellar performers if they don't know what stellar looks like. They won't know what to do if you don't tell them what's expected of them.	Work collaboratively with your employees to determine their performance goals and the best strategies for achieving them. Be clear about your expectations for their current performance and for their leveling up.
Lack of alignment with your organization's goals	Employees who do not understand how and why their efforts are relevant to the organization won't be motivated to improve. They won't be able to see how their next-level performance will contribute to the greater good or make anything better.	Be transparent with your employees about your organization's goals. Help them to connect what they do day in and day out to the bigger picture. Also help them to establish personal and team goals that align with your organization's goals.
Lack of employee recognition and reward	Even the most engaged employees can become demotivated and frustrated if their efforts go unacknowledged. Recognition is a huge driver for employee improvement.	Create recognition moments for your employees. A simple thank-you card or social event can provide a needed opportunity for you to recognize your employees' leveling up efforts and achievements. Never underestimate the power of a simple word of recognition. Praise and thanks can be hugely reinforcing, Hearn says.

Part 2:

How to Take Your Good Employees to the Next Level

CHAPTER 1

Customer Service 101: An Introduction for Healthcare Employees

Your patients' perceptions of your healthcare organization usually are as good as their most recent interactions with you. Even loyal patients who have been satisfied with or enthusiastic about the quality of care they have received from you can sour the moment they have a bad exchange with a member of your staff.

Keep in mind that patient perception is the key. According to the Practice Builders blog,[1] "When consumers judge the quality of healthcare, perception is more important than reality. And your patients' perceptions are most often based on how well they're treated." In fact, customer service often influences patients' perceptions of you more than the quality of your clinical care, which is much harder for them to assess. That's why customer service directly relates to patient retention and referral rates, as well as to the reputation of your healthcare organization in your community.

That puts a lot of pressure on every employee, including the good ones. Each of them has the potential to foster, build, or destroy goodwill with your patients, and it takes only a moment for the good or the damage to be done. For this reason, it is essential that every employee share your consistent vision for customer service and have proper training. This chapter provides an introduction to customer service for you to share with your employees to help them achieve next-level performance.

WHO ARE YOUR CUSTOMERS?

We typically don't use the word *customer* in healthcare organizations. Nonetheless, *customers* is an apt description of the individuals your organization serves. According to the Tutorials Point customer service tutorial,[2] a customer is anyone who is provided with a good, product, service, or idea. "Financial transactions may or may not be part of this provision," the tutorial suggests. Overall, your healthcare organization has many customers; however, these customers can be divided into two categories:

1. **Internal customers.** According to Tutorials Point, internal customers are customers who are directly connected with your healthcare organization and are often working within it (e.g., employees, departments, owners, and shareholders). Board members are also internal customers for healthcare organizations that are governed by a board.
2. **External customers.** Clearly, patients are external customers of the healthcare organization. But so, too, are their families and friends when they visit your facilities or otherwise interact with you. Referring physicians and other providers also are external customers because they want to know that the patients they refer to you are treated well, and they may interact with you personally. Pharmacies and insurance carriers with whom you interact also may be considered to be your external customers because they require information from you and timely responses to their questions.

Tutorials Point suggests that any organization that is able to satisfy its internal customers is better equipped to satisfy its external customers. Therefore, your employees must take very seriously their responsibilities both to the internal and the external customers of your organization.

WHAT IS CUSTOMER SERVICE?

Customer service is everything an employee in your healthcare organization does to take care of your customers' needs and to solve their problems. It begins the moment your employee connects with a customer and it continues even after a customer's needs are met. Every employee, department, or division that takes customer requests, processes them, addresses their concerns and problems, and acts as an interface on behalf of your healthcare organization is a customer service provider. Every healthcare organization that has customers automatically has customer service. The question is, how good is that customer service?

15 CHARACTERISTICS OF GOOD CUSTOMER SERVICE

Customers want and often expect good customer service. They are looking for two things, according to George Root,[3:] "a combination of well-trained employees and an efficient system." Customers want to encounter knowledgeable and professional customer service representatives who use an efficient system to resolve their issues. When that winning combination is in place, Root says, customers will be satisfied and organizations will be more likely to retain them and their business.

Good customer service generally has the following 15 characteristics. Some of these are explored in detail in the remaining chapters of this book.

1. **Responsiveness.** When customers enter your healthcare organization, leave a phone message, or e-mail you, how long does it take for you or one of your employees to acknowledge them? As EA Consulting blog[4] warns, "One of the most dreaded customer experiences is waiting to be serviced or even just to be acknowledged!"

   Furthermore, when issues arise, how long is it before the situation is addressed and a resolution is provided to the customer? Allen says, "The responsiveness clock is ticking in your customer's head while waiting to be serviced or to receive a reply to inquiry." A slow response time is not a component of good customer service and it often makes bad situations worse.
2. **Knowledge.** Every employee who represents your healthcare organization should know a great deal about it, including what your organization does and why, how you do it, who does what, and your basic policies and procedures. Any employee who doesn't know this information is not ready to serve your customers. Marta[5] suggests, "Being knowledgeable communicates trust."

   Of course, every employee can't be expected to know how to answer every question or how to address every problem beyond the basics. Wild cards will show up every now and then that you could not possibly have anticipated. However, employees who don't know the answer to a specific question or problem should not try to bluff their way through it. According to Marta, "It's better for service employees to admit they don't know the answer at the moment and to make an effort to find the right answer." This type of honesty is sure to increase customer loyalty.

3. **Clear-cut policies and procedures.** Every healthcare organization needs established policies and procedures for handling the problems and requests it is likely to encounter. Likewise, your employees must know these policies and procedures and be able to implement them.

   Record-keeping and follow-up are extremely important. Therefore, you need to establish procedures for recording customer requests, problems, and complaints, as well as the steps your employees have taken to resolve them. Employees also should be on the lookout for recurring customer service problems and bring them to your attention so you can work together to fix them.
4. **Reliability.** Good customer service includes being punctual and doing whatever you have promised to do to serve customers, whether it be to provide information, call back, make an adjustment to their account, or keep an appointment. Tutorials Point suggests, "Changes or cancellations later in the day can be harmful to you and your organization's reputation."
5. **A personal chord.** Good customer service is a personal experience. It is an opportunity for your employee to humanize your customers' experiences with your healthcare organization. It is a chance to make customers feel that they are valued as people, not just for the healthcare services they need and the dollars they represent.

   Respectfully calling customers by their name is a good start to personalizing the experience, Tutorials Point suggests. However, there are other good ways to strike a personal chord such as by offering customers a warm and genuine smile, an expression of care, a compliment, and a sincere apology when one is warranted.

   Be mindful that customer service is always customer-centric. Gregory Ciotti[6] warns, "Make sure you're getting to the problem at hand quickly; customers don't need your life story or to hear about how your day is going."
6. **Empathy.** Empathy is essential to good customer service. It allows your employees to keep their cool even when an irrational customer shouts at them for a mistake they did not make. However, creating empathy means more than being nice. Marta explains, "Being empathic means having a natural understanding of the other's point of view."

Empathy helps customer service representatives deal with all types of customers no matter their anxiety or anger levels, Marta says. (See Chapter 8 for more information on developing your employees' empathy.)

7. **Courtesy.** Courtesy goes a long way with customers, especially when they are unhappy with something you've done. However, courteous words alone are not enough. Allen suggests, "Body language and facial expressions also contribute to the courtesy factor." Therefore, your employees must not only sound courteous and look courteous to customers face to face, they also must use a courteous tone on the phone and in writing.

   This is true even when customers are discourteous to them. Your employees must stay above the fray. In challenging customer service situations, your employees must exercise a great deal of self-control. Teach your employees that courtesy is not a luxury or a nicety; it is a requirement of the job.
8. **Good language skills.** Your employees speak with people who may be non-native speakers of English, who have hearing or cognitive difficulties, who are upset and not communicating clearly, or who have other communication challenges. Marta suggests, "Good service employees are sensitive to language style and can tailor their style to each individual customer."

   That means that in the interest of good customer service, employees may need to speak more carefully, more slowly, more simply, or even more loudly to accommodate some of your customers. They must be sensitive, perceptive, and accommodating to each customer's individual communication needs.
9. **Positivity.** Your customers create perceptions about you and your healthcare organization based upon the way you say things. According to Laura Hills,[7] "When healthcare employees learn to reframe negative ways of communicating into sincere, positive ones, they may not change the basic situation or problem; rather, they will change the way that they and others look at it."

   Of course, all communication with your customers must be sincere or they will see through it. Your communication with your customers can never be patronizing. When communication *is* sincere and positive, the payoff can be huge.

   Ciotti readily admits, "Sounds like fluffy nonsense, but your ability to make minor changes in your conversational patterns can truly go a long way in creating happy customers." How can an employee use more positive language? In many ways.

For example, an employee may tell a patient that there is no opening in the doctor's schedule for three weeks. Or the employee can say, "You're in luck. Dr. Anderson has an opening in her schedule on Tuesday the 21st at 2:00 pm. We can schedule that now, and I can also put you on a call list in case we have a cancellation between now and then." (See Chapter 10 for more information on teaching your employees how to reframe negatives into positives.)

10. **Patience.** Your employees' patience is extremely important to your customers, who often reach out for support and help when they are confused and frustrated. They do not want your employees to rush them as they are telling their tales of woe, to cut them off, or to jump ahead to the wrong conclusions.

    Ciotti suggests, "Be sure to take the time to truly figure out what they want — they'd rather get competent service than be rushed out the door!" Fortunately, even though both nature and nurture have conspired to make us impatient, the situation is not hopeless. Patience can be learned. (See Chapter 12 for more information on developing your employees' patience.)

11. **Acting skills.** One of the most important roles your employees play in your healthcare organization is professional, capable, polite, and upbeat customer service representative. They must not deviate from this role even when they are stressed and challenged.

    Circumstances outside of our control can and do creep into our usual routine. Your employees must learn to expect it. Monkey wrenches will be thrown into their schedules. Equipment will malfunction. They won't feel their best. The weather will be a downer. They may have been stuck in traffic on your way to work. And some days they'll be greeted with what Ciotti calls "barnacle" customers: those people who seem to want nothing else but to pull them down.

    Nonetheless, your employees can't give in to these challenges. Ciotti's advice: "Every great customer service rep will have those basic acting skills necessary to maintain their usual cheery persona in spite of dealing with people who may be just plain grumpy."

    Teach your employees how to keep negativity from derailing them from their customer service role. They must not break character. Just as in theater, the show must go on. (See Chapter 9 for more information on teaching your employees how to be better actors.)

12. **Perceptiveness.** What works well for one customer may not work well for another. Your employees must be able to read each individual and to make an educated guess about what is going to be most effective. As your employees interact with your customers, Ciotti suggests, teach them to "look and listen for subtle clues about their current mood, patience level, personality, etc." Teach your employees to give customers their full attention, to notice their words and phrases, posture, body language, facial expressions, and gestures. Teach them to hone their observation and listening skills.

    Lorette[8] says, "Instead of planning an answer or retort as the customer is speaking, listen with the goal of comprehension." As well, teach your employees to make notes and to summarize your customers' words back to them to ensure understanding.

13. **Good questions.** Customers will express themselves and their needs to you however they will. It is up to your employees to get at the heart of what is troubling them. Lorette suggests, "Quality questions help to uncover the actual needs, goals, objectives, and concerns of the customers." For example, if a customer complains that your services are "expensive," your employee can ask her what she means. Of course, your employee must do this in a sincere, nonjudgmental way, expressing genuine concern and curiosity. Your employee could say simply, "It is a considerable sum. Please, tell me, how do you mean *expensive*?" Then let the customer answer.

    The customer may mean that she will have trouble paying your fee and that she needs a payment plan. She may be sad that your fee will use up the funds she had put aside for a vacation or a purchase. She may think that your fees are higher than those of other providers, even if this is not true. She may not understand the services well enough to know why they cost what they do. Or your employee may find that there is something else at play.

    Your employees will be able to help your customers with their concerns or problems only if they know more precisely what they are. Thoughtful, sincere, curious questions will help them to get there.

14. **Consistency.** Why do you keep going to your favorite restaurants, stores, gas stations, or hotels? It's because you like what you get every time you go there. The same is true of a healthcare organization.

Customers who like what you do and who appreciate knowing what to expect every time they interact with you will keep coming back to you. This is true even when they have a choice of providers available to them. In fact, Allen suggests, consistency is "the glue that holds it all together." It is what creates long-term customers.

Therefore, your customers must be able to depend on your employees and your healthcare organization to provide the same high level of service every time they choose or need to use your services. This must be true no matter how busy your organization is, how understaffed it may be, who is having a bad day, or who on your staff is interacting with them. When consistency is added to other good customer service characteristics, Allen says, "long-term retention is usually the result."

15. **Optimism.** Optimistic employees truly believe that they can provide great service. Therefore, Ian Landsman[9] says, they try harder and end up providing better experiences that their customers notice and appreciate.

    Your genuinely optimistic employees are those who are invested in helping your organization grow, and they believe that it can. They care about each customer's experience, Landsman says. They firmly believe that what your healthcare organization does, along with the support they provide, can result in a positive experience. They don't jump to negative conclusions. They assume that problems can be solved.

    But they're not all rainbows and unicorns. Optimistic employees live in the real world, too. As Landsman suggests, "They balance their optimism with honesty, giving members of the public and your internal team real answers that help everyone make progress." Ultimately, because optimistic employees go into every customer service encounter believing that it will turn out well, they usually are right.

20 TIPS FOR EXCELLENT CUSTOMER SERVICE

What exactly does good customer service look like in action? Here are 20 tips for providing good customer service in your healthcare organization from Business Training Works.[10] See how many of them you are currently implementing and which ones your good employees can add to level up their customer service skills.

1. **Smile.** Smile when you greet your customers in person and on the phone. Callers will hear the smile in your voice.

2. **Greet appropriately.** Use age-appropriate greetings. Err on the side of formality when you don't know the person or their greeting preferences. Avoid calling your customers *guys* when you don't know them, as in, "How are you guys doing today?
3. **Be proactive.** Don't wait in silence or look blankly at a customer. Ask how you may be of service.
4. **Stay visible and available.** Don't ignore or look away from customers. However, don't hover over them either if they need space to complete paperwork, talk privately with a family member or friend, or do other personal things.
5. **Don't avoid customers.** Don't turn away, walk away, begin to make a phone call, or duck beneath your desk when a customer approaches you. Make eye contact, even if you must end a conversation with a colleague, put aside paperwork, or take your eyes away from your computer screen and your hands off the keyboard to do so.
6. **Prioritize.** Patients are the customers who always come first in the healthcare organization. As well, the patient standing in front of you takes precedence over the one who calls you on the phone (except in an emergency).
7. **Don't judge a book by its cover.** All of our customers deserve good customer service from you, regardless of their age or appearance.
8. **Be professional.** Leave food and beverages in the breakroom or cafeteria. Check your appearance to be sure that it is clean and tidy. Do not chew gum. Keep your work area clean and organized.
9. **Be discreet.** Customers don't want to hear about your personal problems or your complaints. Don't overstep the boundaries of your relationships with them.
10. **Remove yourself.** Make personal calls only when you are on a break and out of customers' earshot.
11. **Own the answer.** The correct answer is never "I don't know" unless you immediately add to it, "but I will find out for you."
12. **Get them what they want.** If a customer asks you for a brochure, paperwork, or something else that is not easily at hand, excuse yourself and go get it. Don't tell customers to get what they want themselves or to pick it up on their way out.
13. **Pay attention:** Learn to read body language and also to read between the lines when customers speak or write to you. Notice when it looks

or sounds like customers can use your help. It's always better to ask if they do rather than to leave them struggling on their own.

14. **Politely move forward.** Don't let chatty customers monopolize your time if other customers are waiting for your attention.
15. **Get help.** Ask your colleagues for backup support if you have many customers who need your attention at once.
16. **Be sensitive.** If a customer's credit card is declined, ask if there is another form of payment they would like to use. Don't discuss a patient's payment issues, finances, or medical issues with them in front of others.
17. **Guard confidentiality.** Never discuss customers in front of other customers or even in front of staff members who do not need to be privy to the information.
18. **Ensure quality.** Inspect paperwork and anything else you give to a customer to be sure that it is correct and complete.
19. **Ask.** Make sure customers have everything they need before they leave your office or hang up the phone.
20. **End well.** Smile again as you say *goodbye*. When appropriate, thank the customers. Make sure they leave feeling good about their experience with you.

CHAPTER 1 BONUS FEATURE

THE CARP METHOD: HANDLING CUSTOMER COMPLAINTS IN FOUR STEPS

Good customer service relies on giving attention and credence to every customer complaint you receive. Here is Robert Bacal's[11] four-step method that you can use to be sure that you are consistent in how you process customer complaints. You can remember it with the acronym CARP:

C: Control the situation. Let the complaining customer know that they have your full attention and that you want to help. However, don't take the customer's bait. Assert your control by behaving in ways that demonstrate that the customer's attempts to provoke you or to make you angry or defensive will not work with you.

A: Acknowledge the situation. It is important that the angry customer see that you understand their emotional state and the situation. Two techniques to apply here are empathy and active listening. Repeat what the complaining customer has told you to be sure you have everything right. Let the customer know that you do indeed understand what they are telling you.

R: Refocus the conversation. Sometimes angry customers simply want to vent. Once you feel they've done enough of that, help them transition from dealing with their emotions to dealing with the actual problem at hand.

P: Problem solve. Problem-solving can be fostered by getting and giving information, suggesting possibilities, offering choices, appearing to be helpful, and following through.

CHAPTER 2

How to Create an Ownership Mentality within Your Team

Do you feel frustrated by your good employees' reluctance to take charge or to make quick decisions? Do you wish your employees cared about their work as much as you care about yours? Do you sometimes find even good employees coasting, slacking, cutting corners, or simply not giving their work their best effort?

If so, and you are wondering how to get your employees to take ownership of their work, you're not alone. According to Halley Bock,[1] "A culture of personal accountability, where employees possess the freedom to make appropriate decisions and the courage to take ownership, is the single most powerful, most desired, and least understood characteristic of a successful work environment."

It's easy to see why we would want employees to take ownership of their work. Those who do are self-reliant, accurate, productive, energetic, and enthusiastic. They are the employees who do what needs to be done, often without your having to ask them. And when you do ask them, they won't say *no*. In fact, they will be willing to do whatever it takes for the sake of your healthcare organization and the patients you serve. As de Haaf[2] says, "From tireless days and sleepless nights to unpleasant decisions and difficult problems to resolve, [they'll] do what you think is right. [They'll even] take out the garbage if they have to."

We can tell employees to develop an ownership mentality about their work. "Owning the problem," "being the owner of the project," "you've got to really own it," and similar phrases are very easy off the lips and have become well-used workplace jargon. But such words can ring hollow. Typically, we take care of what we actually own; we don't take care of what we believe belongs to someone else. If your employees don't feel that they actually own their work, no well-intentioned catch phrases will get them to do it.

Fortunately, there is a great deal that you can do to help your employees develop an ownership mentality about the work they do in your healthcare organization every day.

WHAT IS AN OWNERSHIP MENTALITY?

Many people, including your good employees, assume that "think like an owner" is a thinly veiled code for "do more work." However, an ownership mentality does not always lead to more work. In fact, an employee who has an ownership mentality invests time and resources in training, establishing systems, and solving problems that reduces work in the long run.

Having an ownership mentality means that an employee does what's best in the moment but also has an eye to what's going to happen next and what's going to be best down the road. Neil Ducoff[3] suggests, "You need to invest the time, energy and resources to educate employees on what ownership thinking looks like, feels like and performs like." It is up to you as a leader in your organization to clarify for your employees the boundaries and limits of ownership thinking, Ducoff adds. This may require an investment in time, training, and coaching.

TEN WAYS TO CREATE AN OWNERSHIP MENTALITY

Although employees do not literally own the healthcare organization in which they work, it is possible to encourage, create, and foster ownership thinking. Here are 10 strategies healthcare leaders can use to get their employees to think more like owners:

1. **Hire employees who already think like owners.** You may be able to save yourself a lot of effort and headaches simply by designing your recruiting process to screen for the qualities of a good "owner" employee. As de Haaf suggests, "These [qualities] could include an entrepreneurial spirit, self-starting mentality, responsible or self-accountable mindset, big picture awareness, and a take-initiative attitude." In fact, you may want to give special consideration to a job applicant who has owned their own business. Entrepreneurs are likely to understand what it is like to be an owner and have an owner's mindset, de Haaf says.
2. **Make every job the most important job in your healthcare organization.** Many of us have heard the story of the NASA custodian who told President Kennedy that his job was to help put a man on the moon. A

lesser-known example of ownership thinking comes from the famous director Stanislavski, who once said, "Theater begins at the cloakroom." By this, Stanislavski meant that audiences begin to experience the magic of theatrical productions the moment they step into a theater and interact with its employees — from the box office attendant to the coatroom attendant to the ticket taker to the ushers who show them their seats.

Likewise, every employee who works in your healthcare organization must regard their job as most important and essential to your mission to serve your patients. Louis Efron[4] suggests, "All great leaders [and managers] help every employee see the importance of their role in the larger mission of their organization." Therefore, it is essential that you believe and communicate to your employees that your front desk receptionist does much more than check in your patients and answer your telephone. Like the custodian whose job it was to put a man on the moon, your receptionist's job is to help to provide every patient with the highest-quality healthcare possible. Be sure to help them to see the job in this way and regard it that way yourself.

3. **Don't take the monkey.** We all experience the "monkey on our back" at work. That's the serious and annoying problem that won't go away. Employees often assume that because healthcare leaders are more senior to them and more highly paid, it is their responsibility to solve problems and make decisions. They arrive at their boss's doors ready to give them the monkeys on their backs. However, taking the monkey can be dangerous.

   Antoinette Oglethorpe[5] warns, "For leaders, there is the strong temptation to help their employees by taking on their problems and solving them for them. But taking their monkeys is nothing more than rescuing them." Instead, Oglethorpe suggests that leaders invest the little extra time that is needed to help their employees take the initiative and to handle their monkeys themselves, the way that an owner would.

4. **Delegate the right way.** Employees won't take ownership of their work if they are not sure that they should. They may not take ownership if they feel that they need to check in with you before taking every action. As well, they won't take ownership if they're afraid of making a decision that you won't like and that will get them into trouble.

   Delegation requires much more than assigning projects. Bock suggests, "It's also about clearly communicating where the decision-making power lies and allowing your employees to hold themselves able to take responsibility for their results." Delegating the right way isn't for the faint of heart, Bock warns. It requires a lot of time and energy on your part to communicate your expectations to those around you. It also requires you to let go of some control. Eventually, however, delegating the right way will yield an environment of ownership that is not paralyzed by fear, Bock says, and is worth the investment.

5. **Collect and act on employee feedback.** Lots of employers survey their employees. Unfortunately, many don't use this feedback or if they do, they use it in ways that are not transparent to their employees. As de Haaf suggests, "If you want your employees to be owners, then let them know that their voices are heard and can actually create change." Tell your employees and clearly demonstrate to them that you value and are using their feedback.
6. **Express confidence in your employees' abilities.** Let your employees know what strengths, skills, and positive qualities you see in them. Then, link those positive qualities to the tasks or problems at hand. For example, you may say, "You're a wonderful listener and you have a knack for defusing tension and anger. This is going to be very helpful to you and make you very effective when you call Mrs. Nguyen today." Recognizing and identifying your employees' useful qualities can build their confidence and self-esteem. As well, as Oglethorpe suggests, it can enhance your relationship with them and encourage them to take ownership of their work.
7. **Be explicit.** Tell employees that you are going to step back and let them do their jobs. Charpentier[6] suggests, "Remember that the individual staff member knows his particular job better than anyone else and remind all your employees of this on a regular basis." When you cease efforts to manage and begin to lead, Charpentier says, you allow your team to do its job. Like student pilots who have made their first solo flights, your employees will become more comfortable with this form of independence. Charpentier adds, "Assure them, though, that you're there as a safety net, should they need assistance. As they grow, they'll assume ownership of their jobs naturally, just as the student pilot begins to take on greater challenges."
8. **Reinforce and reward employees who take ownership.** In general, healthcare leaders are likely to see more of the employee behaviors that they reinforce and fewer of the behaviors that they don't. You don't want your employees' emerging ownership thinking to die on

the vine. Marcus Erb[7] warns, "Nothing can quell people's desire to give extra than not feeling recognized." Therefore, be on the lookout for opportunities to reinforce and reward your employees' ownership behaviors. Praise and recognize them at staff meetings. Identify ownership behaviors that you'd like to see more of and make them part of your staff's regular performance and salary reviews.

9. **Empower employees to think and act like owners.** Patients who are upset about a policy may ask to speak with someone higher up. Unfortunately, that person sometimes ends up giving them exactly what they wanted in the first place, reversing what an employee has told them.

   Why put your employee and your patients through that painful exercise? Give your employees the authority and leeway to work with your patients to resolve their issues directly, without patients having to go over their heads to get what they want. Randi Busse[8] suggests, "Watch how efficient and effective things become when we push decisions down to their lowest possible level and cut the tape required to get everything but the major decisions done."

10. **Model and teach ownership thinking.** You undoubtedly do things every day in your healthcare organization that demonstrate ownership thinking. But do your employees know about them? If they do, do they know why you do them? Repurpose your own moments of ownership thinking as lessons for your employees. Ask and encourage them to share their examples of ownership thinking, too. Doing so regularly will help you to develop a culture of ownership within your team.

GUIDING EMPLOYEES AWAY FROM A RESCUE MENTALITY

Employees sometimes avoid ownership of their problems because they are hoping that someone will rescue them and fix things for them. John Coleman[9] calls this a "silver bullet from an unexpected source" and says, "One of the most common momentum killers I've seen in my professional life is our propensity to wait for someone else to act, take initiative, assume blame, or take charge. But very often, no help comes." Taking responsibility is the first step in developing a healthy sense of self, Coleman says. We internalize the idea of taking responsibility when we realize that no one is coming to our rescue, he says.

An ownership mentality begins when we develop a belief or habit of mind that we, as individuals, own our work outcomes, even when we're working with others. Ownership doesn't always mean that we have authority over a project or problem, nor does it mean that we shouldn't involve others. But it does mean that we own the obligation to take action and deliver results. The ownership of this obligation may be lacking for employees who have been previously coddled, Coleman warns.

Coleman suggests three lessons that you can teach to your employees to help them develop this belief and habit of ownership:

1. **Fault and responsibility are not the same thing.** Fault is backward-looking; responsibility looks forward. Employees may be responsible for a situation or problem, even if it's not their fault. Blame becomes far less important than finding the solution. Refocus employees who point fingers at one another. Ask them what they're going to do to solve the problem.
2. **You must be proactive.** Employees who own their work identify problems when they are small and nip them in the bud. According to Coleman, "The most productive people and those most likely to succeed are those who are proactive about finding and solving problems, and comfortable acting with increasing autonomy and decreased oversight." Think of leaders whom you admire who declined to wait for help and instead pioneered solutions. Encourage your employees to think that way.
3. **Taking ownership helps others.** Appeal to your employees' altruism. Help them understand the link between their ownership of their work and the quality of the healthcare you deliver to your patients. Show them how their work contributes to the quality of their coworkers' work life. Help them see how owning their work matters beyond them in the larger picture of your healthcare organization.

ACCOUNTABILITY VERSUS OWNERSHIP

Healthcare organizations need to hold employees accountable for fulfilling the terms of their job descriptions. They also need to hold employees accountable for behaving in ways that are consistent with the organization's values and mission. However, accountability is not the same thing as ownership. According to Joe Tye,[10] "Great organizations are characterized by people holding themselves and each other accountable for their attitudes and behaviors as well as their performance because they have pride of ownership."

Accountability, Tye explains, is doing what you're supposed to do because someone else expects it of you. Accountability, Tye says, springs from the extrinsic motivation of reward and punishment and is only "the baseline, the price of entry" for your employees. On the other hand, ownership is doing what needs to be done because *you* expect it of *yourself*. It springs from the intrinsic motivation of pride and engagement. Tye adds, "It's important to distinguish those things for which people can be held accountable by holding their feet to the fire, and those things for which they cannot be held accountable but which must be accomplished through personal ownership."

You can hold employees accountable for complying with your healthcare organization's rules, showing up on time, treating people with respect, and meeting deadlines. But you can't hold them accountable for working with passion, caring, putting their hearts into their work, or thinking entrepreneurially. These thoughts and behaviors come only from pride of ownership, Tye says.

DO YOU CREATE AN OWNERSHIP MENTALITY?

Three key factors are essential if you want to develop an ownership mentality among your employees: transparency, clear and quantifiable goals, and a stake in the outcome. John Spence[11] has created a simple four-question quiz to help you figure out where your healthcare organization stands on these three factors. Rate your performance in each of the following statements on a scale from 1 to 10, with 10 being "We are excellent at this — truly world-class" and 1 being "We are terrible at this — we don't do this at all."

1. We openly share critical information about our healthcare organization with our entire team. If there is news, they hear it first from us.
2. Everyone in our healthcare organization has very clear, specific, and measurable performance objectives.
3. We generously reward (in both money and praise) those employees who demonstrate a true ownership mentality and who consistently meet or exceed their performance objectives.

4. We deal decisively and effectively with employees who are mediocre and/or who do not consistently meet their performance objectives.

According to Spence, any score below 7 is cause for concern. He adds, "A score lower than a 5 is probably a major issue."

CHAPTER 2 BONUS FEATURE

WHY TALENTED EMPLOYEES DON'T TAKE OWNERSHIP

What's the top reason that talented employees don't take ownership of their work? It is not laziness, low self-esteem, or a poor work ethic, as some may think. According to Eric Shannon,[12] the culprit is *blame*.

Blame is easy to recognize when it's stated obviously, Shannon says. Clearly, we know that an employee is blaming someone else if they say overtly, "I didn't do it. It's Jennifer's fault." Blame can be a little less obvious to us when an employee more subtly blames a coworker, as in, "I was late because Eduardo couldn't finish his part on time." Still, we can see the blame fairly easily. However, blame is the hardest to see when employees blame something that seems plausibly out of their control.

For example, imagine that an employee arrives to your office one morning a half hour late for work. They could blame the traffic or the weather, and that may seem plausible. But is that the whole story? The employee could have said, "I should have listened to the weather report and allowed more time to get here this morning." Or they could have said, "I cut things too close. I now know that I will need to allow a little more slack in my commute." Such statements are not blaming and suggest that the employee is taking ownership of their behavior, Shannon says.

Healthcare leaders can model a less-blaming way of thinking for their employees by framing their own remarks from an owner's perspective. For example:

Instead of saying:	Say:
The landlord hasn't sent the new lease yet.	I haven't received the lease from the landlord yet. I will follow-up.

We are behind schedule because Dana is on vacation.	I failed to plan well with my team for Dana's absence.
I didn't have enough time.	I didn't schedule my time well enough to finish. I was distracted by other things.
I had too many things I had to do today and couldn't get to it.	I made other tasks my priority today. I will take care of this first thing tomorrow.
The patient showed up 25 minutes late.	I allowed the patient's lateness to throw a monkey wrench into our schedule. That won't happen again.

Shannon suggests that blame subverts the process of our own ownership. As soon as we blame, we remove the need for ourselves to be in charge. Blame places the requirements for us to do our work, to meet our obligations, or to improve ourselves on someone else's shoulders. "Blame makes us victims of our environment, rather than masters of the universe," Shannon says.

CHAPTER 3

Improving Your Workplace Experience to Increase Employee Productivity and Engagement

Customer experience has been a popular strategy for forward-thinking organizations for decades. Jeanne Meister[1] says, "Businesses have long recognized the importance of delivering a differentiated and engaging experience for their customers." A much newer approach for organizations is to focus attention as well on the *employees'* experience.

For example, according to Accenture,[2] "Leading companies are starting to realize that delivering great [customer experience] is easier when you have a strong workplace experience . . . creating an environment and a culture that enables and encourages employees to collaborate, develop their skills and be more productive."

Of course, every business outcome starts with your employees, from productivity and efficiency to talent retention, innovation, and growth. That is not a new idea. However, what is new about the concept of workplace experience is that it combines technology, operations, culture, and interpersonal experience in a holistic way. Victoria Fitoussi[3] suggests that continuously managing your employees' workplace experience creates "a culture of happiness and high performance, and an environment in which employees want to work and succeed." Organizations where employees have a positive workplace experience are the ones where the customers' positive experiences can also flourish, according to Fitoussi.

Today, a great employee workplace experience is much more than a nicety; according to research, it is a must. A good workplace experience increases productivity and engagement for all employees, including good ones. According to Fitoussi, happy employees are up to 20% more productive at work; however, 64% of employees feel that they do not have a strong work culture. She also says that unhappy employees take 15 more sick days per year than the average employee, and organizations with highly engaged workforces outperform their peers by 147% in earnings per share.

Organizations that invest in their culture, their employees' physical work environment, and the tools and technology that enable their employees' productivity enjoy much greater overall business success. As Fitoussi urges, "All companies should seek to build a culture around helping their employees succeed. For optimum performance, simple workplace experience management practices can be seamlessly integrated into company DNA."

The question for healthcare leaders is not *whether,* but *when* and *how* your organization can create what Meister calls "the workplace as an experience." To do that, you need to tap into the physical, emotional, intellectual, virtual, and aspirational facets of how an employee is engaged in your workplace.

WHAT IS WORKPLACE EXPERIENCE?

Workplace experience is in part just what it sounds like: a focus on the employee's experience of the physical workplace. It may include your employees' feelings about everything they experience at work such as your parking lot or the convenience of public transportation, the comfort of their chair, the technology and equipment they use, the temperature of the office, lighting, whether there are windows and what they can see from them, sounds, colors, décor, the coffee served in the staff break room, the restrooms they use, elevators, and hallways. Workplace experience also can include amenities such as employee cafeterias (and the quality and cost of the food they serve), gyms and locker rooms, break rooms, and childcare centers.

However, workplace experience also focuses on intangibles such as policies, overtime hours, pay and bonuses, opportunities for career advancement, levels of stress, employee development programs, and other benefits. It also can include the ways in which employees interact with one another and how they share space, resources, amenities, or services.

Likewise, it can include relationships with supervisors, mentors, human resources staff, and patients, and whether your healthcare organization is adequately staffed. And it can include employee services such as employee assistance programs, counseling services, professional development programs, healthcare benefits, tuition reimbursement, and enrichment and social activities.

Lane[4] suggests that we think of the workplace as an ecosystem. Each of these roles, resources, and experiences is significant by itself. However, Lane adds, "How these forces interact [with one another] is what manifests into 'experience.'"

WORKPLACE EXPERIENCE VERSUS EMPLOYEE ENGAGEMENT

Workplace experience as a concept has been building steam in recent years. But as Nolan Godfrey[5] suggests, it can be confusing to make sense of it after decades of emphasis on employee engagement.

What's the difference between workplace experience and employee engagement? Simply put, workplace experience includes employee engagement, but it is much more. Most importantly, the larger workplace experience concept or strategy is more effective than employee engagement alone. Godfrey explains, "Engagement reigned as the leading employee metric for several decades, and in many organizations, it is still a key metric. Yet, the promised results of focusing on employee engagement alone have never fully materialized."

In many organizations, engagement would increase right about the time of an engagement survey, and then it would return to the same level it was before, give or take a few points. Godfrey suggests, "Many organizations have been too focused on manipulating or increasing an engagement survey score — a noble, but somewhat myopic effort." Although employee engagement certainly matters, measuring engagement by itself isn't sufficient because such measurements typically drive short-term, tactical action plans that, at best, focus on a narrow set of employee needs, he says.

Workplace experience paints the employee's experience with a much broader paintbrush than employee engagement alone. It provides a big picture, strategic view of how well an organization is doing across the entire employee lifecycle, especially during what Godfrey refers to as "moments that matter."

For example, Godfrey says, workplace experience encompasses key moments such as when potential recruits become attracted to the organization or when an employee approaches HR to report a problem. It also includes the relationship an individual has with their supervisor, and how positively employees view their experiences with coworkers or community service efforts. "Viewed from this vantage," Godfrey says, "employee engagement is an outcome measure that looks at one piece of a larger puzzle." It is much more effective for organizations to focus on workplace experience than on employee engagement alone because workplace experience includes *everything* that contributes to an employee's overall experience.

Godfrey suggests, "With competition for top talent fiercer than ever before, it's critical to consider the entire full Employee Experience—from the moment a potential employee learns about your organization, through their full employment, and exit." Improving workplace experience can deliver strong employee outcomes such as engagement and retention, but also measurable business results, he says.

WHO IS RESPONSIBLE FOR YOUR EMPLOYEES' WORKPLACE EXPERIENCE?

Workplace experience falls under the domain of human resources. However, as Meister suggests, the HR shift to employee experience would not be complete without an actual role. Some organizations refer to this role as head of employee experience or workplace experience manager or workplace experience officer. Whatever the exact title, it is the role of an individual who focuses on creating a compelling employee experience. This new role is becoming what Meister calls the "new normal" for how human resource departments are transforming the workplace as an experience.

The role of workplace experience officer captures several shifts in the way people think about the workplace. First, Drew Suszko[6] suggests, it "embraces the movement away from business administration and towards workplace hospitality." Second, the role acknowledges that the focus on the experiences in the consumer space has forever altered the workforce's expectations of the workplace. Third, workplace experience officers recognize that digital and physical spaces are in the process of collapsing into one another. Finally, they eschew the notion of stepped career progressions along predefined paths. Specifically, Suszko says, workplace experience officers are responsible for crafting a workplace experience that:

- Authentically reflects the mission, vision, and values of the organization;
- Creates memorable, meaningful, and purposeful connections;
- Builds a team of service-minded stewards who work on behalf of the workforce;
- Delivers tools and technology that enable seamless workflow; and
- Instills enthusiasm, if not excitement, for the work at hand.

Suszko argues that the case for the workplace experience officer hinges on the notion that leading companies take ownership for the relationships that people have with their organization. He says that they are responsible for crafting memorable workplace experiences that connect, motivate, and inspire people. They wear many hats, he says, including the following:

- **Ethnographer.** Workplace experience officers are keen observers. They listen and leverage data to identify and understand what employees truly desire.
- **Promoter.** Workplace experience officers amplify purpose. They believe that employees want to do meaningful work and ensure that the "why" is relevant, authentic, and visible.
- **Matchmaker.** Workplace experience officers connect people. They deliver a workplace that supports employees' need to connect with one another in ways that are both productive and social. Suszko says that they develop a community "of and at work."
- **Designer.** Workplace experience officers reduce friction. They deliver a seamless workplace experience that embraces integrated design. They ensure that the parts (space, technology, process, and people) work in service of the greater whole.
- **Concierge.** Workplace experience officers surprise and delight employees. They create moments that matter and give employees license to be creative. As Suszko suggests, they give employees "something to talk about, stories to share, and memories to unite them."

Is a workplace experience officer necessary? In many organizations, physical layout, general ambiance, technology, communication, ease of interpersonal communications, and other components of the employee's work experience are managed by separate departments. One may think that with each variable designated to a separate team, each of these puzzle pieces would click together to create a harmonious environment. But this not always the case.

Katie Cavanaugh[7] warns, "Often times, each department has its own biases, priorities, and timelines that make it difficult to align harmoniously with one another. It's not enough to assume each of these departments will create a workplace best suited for the people who work in it." That is why the workplace experience officer is necessary to synthesize employees' experiences. Cavanaugh urges, "Every organization should pull up a seat at the c-suite table for a new CxO: the Chief Employee Experience Officer."

THE CHALLENGE OF IMPROVING WORKPLACE EXPERIENCE: WHERE TO BEGIN?

Your employees' workplace experience relies on countless moments every day. That's why improving workplace experience can be a formidable challenge. This experience is made up of *everything* your employees see, hear, smell, taste, and touch when they work for your healthcare organization. It's their experience with intangibles, too, such as their relationships with supervisors, coworkers, and patients. More importantly, it's their perceptions and possibly complex emotions caused by their workplace experiences. It's a tall order to improve so many components of your employees' experiences or even to know where to begin.

Further complicating the workplace experience improvement task is the fact that each employee may experience your workplace differently. Employees in each area of the healthcare organization may have radically different experiences. But even employees who experience the same things in the same physical locations may regard their experiences differently. What bothers or delights one employee may not bother or delight another.

In fact, if you ask 100 employees what they want you to do to improve their workplace experience, you may end up with 100 answers. Even so, those answers may not be reliable. Employees may not tell you what they really think, but what they think you want to hear.

So, where does that leave you? Hopefully, not giving up. You *can* improve your workplace experience and even enjoy the process. However, although you may have creative ideas and high aspirations, hold onto them, at least at first. The place to begin your workplace experience efforts is wherever you know that something is terribly wrong. It will do little good to focus your efforts on fun and splashy new workplace experience initiatives when there is an elephant stomping around your healthcare organization that is driving everyone crazy.

Fix what you know upsets your good employees before you devise new ways to please or delight them. Repair the broken copier or your heating and cooling system or the potholes in your parking lot that are making everyone miserable. Address tensions brewing between coworkers or between your employees and their managers. Fix your biggest and most upsetting problem(s) first.

TEN STRATEGIES FOR IMPROVING YOUR EMPLOYEES' WORKPLACE EXPERIENCE

After you've righted the most egregious wrongs in your workplace, focus your attention on everything else you can do to improve your employees' experience. Keep your eyes, ears, and mind open. You can't go wrong if you listen to your employees, empathize with them, and make changes that they will see, understand, and like. Following are 10 strategies to make most employees' workplace experiences better:

1. **Design a great onboarding experience.** Many organizations don't have a carefully crafted new employee orientation program, much less an employee onboarding experience, but this is critical to employee success. In fact, Diana Kaemingk[8] says, 33% of new hires look for a new job within their first six months on the job, and this can be largely attributed to their employee onboarding experience. Kaemingk suggests, "You should design a program that's measurable, tailored to specific audiences, and has clear objectives." Onboarding new employees well begins their workplace experience positively and sets them up for a smooth entry into your workplace. (See Chapter 17 for more information on creating an effective employee onboarding program.)
2. **Use employee journey mapping.** Employee journey mapping allows you to measure the employee experience at every stage of that employee's tenure at the healthcare organization. Think of journey mapping as a collection of dipstick measurements that you take at key moments in the employees' workplace experience, such as the first job interview, the first day of work, the first full performance review, the first-year

employment anniversary, the employee's birthday, and team events. According to Erik van Vulpen,[9] journey maps enable you to measure "the mood and frustration levels of employees at different times during the day and while working on different tasks." The data you collect can then be used to find points of improvement for the employee, but also for your staff overall.

3. **Focus on performance management.** Are your good employees motivated to be high performers? Communication platform First Up[10] warns, "Only 2 in 10 employees say their performance is managed in a way that motivates them to do their best work." An extremely effective way to focus on, motivate, and improve good employee performance is to foster active listening skills among your managers.
4. **Conduct "stay" interviews.** Stay interviews are conversations between the manager and employee that are designed to support retention. They provide an opportunity to learn what's important to your employees, what's bothering them, and what you can do to improve their workplace experience. Kaemingk explains, "By understanding what works and what doesn't, you can identify [employees'] motivation for staying with the organization and work towards goals that keep them interested." Stay interviews also enhance internal talent pipelines and provide insight into areas for improvement throughout the organization, Kaemingk says.
5. **Improve your technology.** Are your employees happy with their digital experiences in your healthcare organization? First Up cautions, "This doesn't necessarily mean convincing IT to run out and buy a bunch of new apps—it often just means getting more use out of the ones you already have." Work with your IT department to connect the systems your healthcare organization uses. First Up also suggests that you make sure that you don't frustrate your employees by making them toggle between tools all day long. In addition, be sure that your organization can communicate easily with your employees across channels.
6. **Invest in employee wellness.** Healthy employees incur lower healthcare costs and take fewer sick days. A workplace experience that includes gym memberships, healthy food choices, and other physical wellness programs is generally positive. However, employee wellness is more than just physical. Kaemingk suggests, "Programs that encourage mental, emotional, and spiritual wellness create employees who are rested and more attentive and productive at work."

7. **Act on employee feedback.** Many organizations implement employee engagement and feedback surveys, but not all act on that feedback. Kaemingk warns that this can backfire and cause "a loss of trust." Employees must feel comfortable telling you what is good and what can be improved in their workplace experience. They are more likely to share their opinions and engage with you if they believe that their feedback will make a difference. Unfortunately, your employees may stop giving you feedback and become jaded if they know that their opinions won't change anything. Be clear with your employees that you want and value their feedback, that you have heard them, and, most importantly, that you are making specific changes in response to their feedback.
8. **Improve your physical environment.** Abundant natural light, comfortable chairs, ergonomic workstations, and good air circulation can boost your employee workplace experience significantly. The staff at HRMorning[11] suggests, "The office should be a place where your employees can relax and feel part of a communal goal," not be distracted by their physical discomfort. Take steps to reduce noise pollution, both from outside and inside your workplace. Freshen up your decor. Make sure that you keep your workplace clean to a high standard, complete repairs promptly, and keep on top of general maintenance. Invest when you can in the little things that make a difference in the physical space, such as live plants, quality hand soap, and access to free tea and coffee.
9. **Share patient feedback with your employees.** Kaemingk suggests, "There's an undeniable link between employee experience and customer experience, and many employees feel joy from helping customers." However, when one of your patients gives your office a compliment, does your employee hear about it? Sharing your patients' positive feedback can boost your employees' morale and confidence and give them a sense of purpose in their job, thus improving their overall workplace experience. Kaemingk suggests, "Customer feedback should be broadcast throughout the entire organization, not only recognizing that the organization is succeeding, but the employee as well."
10. **Facilitate social interaction.** Employees who have good social interaction both inside and outside work tend to work better together, be happier, and collaborate more effectively. Organize employee events such as holiday parties and summer get-togethers. The face2faceHR

staff[12] suggests that you also encourage more regular low-key social events such as team lunches, running or cycling groups, cake sharing, or even a workplace choir. Also organize work-related programs and trainings where employees interact. It says, "Team-building days away from the office, regular informal meetings and other ideas which get employees away from their desks and talking to each other can build relationships which make the workplace a happier environment as well as leading to work benefits through better collaboration."

CHAPTER 3 BONUS FEATURE

FIVE WAYS TO ENSURE A POOR WORKPLACE EXPERIENCE

We can become so caught up in meeting our goals and delivering results that the employees' workplace experience becomes a secondary concern. This is often the case during stressful times, especially when we are receiving a lot of pressure from above.

Palmer[13] explains, "Having reviewed many 360-degree feedback reports, I can tell you that creating the 'sweet spot' between impressing the person above you while making sure the people below you want to respect and follow you can be tricky." We must take care not to stack the deck in favor of a terrible employee workplace experience, no matter how stressful the situation or how good our intentions.

Palmer identifies five tactics that eventually cripple your employees' workplace experience. Be sure not to resort to these tactics, even during challenging times. Ultimately, they will come back to bite you as your employees' workplace experience plummets.

1. **Over-glamorize the job description.** Healthcare leaders want to attract and be competitive for the best talent. However, the best way to set up your new employees for a bad workplace experience is to create the illusion of "the perfect job" during recruitment.

   Review the job descriptions you use when you are recruiting talent. Do your job descriptions sound too good to be true? If so, they probably are. For example, Palmer says, have you removed every potentially negative or boring detail? Have you described how exciting the job is when it is, for the most part, a dull job? Are you overly optimistic about what the person in the role can accomplish, or the breadth of their influence? Have you misrepresented or inflated the benefits, such as Free Lunch Every Friday without noting that the lunch provided is meeting leftovers in the break room fridge? Have you omitted the fact that 90% of the person's time will be spent on lower-order, repetitive tasks and only 10% on more creative ones? If so, you have over-glamorized the job and are setting up the new employee for huge disappointment.

2. **Put on the right "face."** Do you conceal things from your new employees once the contracts have been signed and they are in their new roles? For example, do you hide the true nature of your organization by suppressing or ignoring the bad parts of the culture to emphasize the good? Palmer explains that "you can do this by discouraging negative talk around the office." Or do you give new employees only creative and interesting assignments, only to dump the less desirable work on them once they've been there a few months?

   Overall, are you altering the new employees' workplace experience during the honeymoon phase of your relationship, only to let them see the reality of what they've gotten themselves into once you feel confident that they will stay? Once your new hire is somewhat invested in their role, do you "remove the bells and whistles?" You may be able to sustain the fantasy for your new hires for a while, Palmer says, but be warned: eventually, you won't be able to keep up the act, and reality will set in. When that happens, your new employees' workplace experience will take a nosedive and, worse, they will feel that they have been duped.

3. **Frequently adjust policies and procedures.** Do you frequently send your employees emails that request their compliance with new policies? Palmer says, "These emails can contain anything from making the dress code more formal to adding an additional weekly meeting to everyone's schedules." Frequent changes in policy, especially those effective immediately and without explanation, create a workplace experience that stresses and confuses employees.

4. **Implement negative changes to your pay and benefit structure.** Another great way to create a negative workplace experience is to renegotiate pay and benefits so employees end up with less. This strategy usually gets quick attention, and for good reason. Employees cannot

have a great workplace experience when you take money away from them. This is true even if you have beautiful office furniture or serve delicious food in your cafeteria or have the loveliest holiday party each year.

Palmer says, "Some common things you can do [to worsen employees' workplace experience] are to decrease bonuses, not grant additional PTO days for longer tenure, or give a promotion without a raise."

5. **Don't recognize your employees' good work.** Some employees value your recognition of them more than they value other aspects of their workplace experience, such as the money they earn, the quality of your physical workspace and technology, their relationships with coworkers, and their opportunities for advancement. They want to feel that they are making a difference because of what they do at work every day and that their leaders recognize and appreciate their contributions.

   For those employees, Palmer says, a workplace experience that doesn't include healthy doses of recognition and gratitude will never be enough. In fact, regular recognition for good work can compensate for shortcomings in other aspects of workplace experience. For example, Palmer suggests, your recognition and gratitude can compensate for the old furniture and equipment your employees must use or the fact that your technology could use an upgrade.

CHAPTER 4

Going Above and Beyond for Your Patients

Above-and-beyond customer service. That sounds great, doesn't it? We want and often expect employees to go above and beyond for patients, not to settle for doing an average, mediocre, satisfactory, or workmanlike job. In fact, the vast majority of healthcare leaders want their employees to exceed patients' expectations and hope that their employees will take the time and trouble to make the follow-up phone call, write the heartfelt thank-you note, and delight patients in countless other ways.

But why? What's wrong with average customer service? Why isn't good enough good enough? And exactly what do we mean when we say that we want above-and-beyond customer service from our employees? Is the sky really the limit in customer service, especially when we consider the time and potential costs involved in going above and beyond? Or is there a point at which your employees will have gone too far in their efforts to serve your patients?

If you want or require above-and-beyond customer service from your employees, help them understand the why's and how's behind that expectation. Don't assume, as many employers do, that healthcare employees, especially the good ones, already see the need for or reason to go above and beyond in customer service. Chances are, at least some of them will not. Additionally, don't expect your employees to define above and beyond precisely the way that you do. They may not know specifically what you want them to do, or how above and how beyond you truly want them to go.

It's essential that you get everyone on the same page about customer service if your employees are to become above-and-beyond thinkers and actors. Discussion and training can help. You can do several things to motivate your employees so they *want* to go above and beyond for your patients, not just to appease you or for your patients' sake, but for their sake as well. You can share with your staff more specifically what you mean by above-and-beyond customer service.

This chapter provides material you can use with your staff for these purposes. It will help you to explore with them the rationale for going above and beyond, and more precisely, what above-and-beyond customer service looks like in your healthcare organization.

WHY GO ABOVE AND BEYOND IN CUSTOMER SERVICE?

It takes dozens of moving parts to keep your healthcare organization running smoothly. However, your patients rarely see these moving parts, nor should they. Patients will see what they expect to see: the way you provide the services that they or their insurance carriers pay for. Most satisfied patients will believe that your healthcare organization fulfilled its end of the bargain if it provided the healthcare services they needed or wanted. That is good. However, doing what was expected is hardly something for most patients to get excited about or to talk positively about with others.

According to Christopher Kelly,[1] what wows patients usually isn't your wonderful clinical services. It isn't your convenient locations or your lovely reception area. And it isn't your attractive uniforms or the color scheme of your exam rooms. Patients will be most impressed by the above-and-beyond details that you provide for them: the mouthwash and lint rollers in the bathroom, the inexpensive rain poncho you give them when they get caught at your office during a storm without an umbrella, the coloring book and crayons you provide to amuse their waiting children, the thoughtful handwritten note, the extra time you spend with them, and most of all, the kindness provided by your above-and-beyond customer service-oriented staff.

"Surprise and delight" not only delivers that extra level of service, Kelly says, but also stands out to the patients who notice and talk about the small stuff. By promoting an above-and-beyond customer service strategy for your staff, Kelly says, you can turn your satisfied patients into your most vocal supporters and your strongest goodwill ambassadors.

However, the value of going above and beyond doesn't end with your patients — it also gives your good employees something tangible that they can be proud of. According to Kelly, "Human connections are a two-way street. Now, more than ever, employees are looking for purpose and context in their work, rather than just paychecks." Above-and-beyond customer service, Kelly suggests, creates experiences and stories that will mean more to your staff than simple numbers.

Most of all, patient loyalty and referrals are won by going above and beyond, not by meeting basic service needs. Kelly explains, "People expect to get good service — that's not where the accolades are won. The key is to give people service they will talk about." Above-and-beyond customer service will please, appease, and delight your patients every time, Kelly says, and help you to build a loyal, enthusiastic patient base. As well, a focus on above-and-beyond service can give your good employees an effective way to improve their already-good performance.

FIVE ESSENTIAL TRAITS FOR ABOVE AND BEYOND CUSTOMER SERVICE

At the core of every above-and-beyond customer service effort is a connection between the employee and the patient. In fact, no customer service script, no matter how eloquent or how beautifully delivered, can take the place of that connection. Therefore, above-and-beyond customer service relies first and foremost upon your employees' ability to connect with your patients. Michael Brown[2] identifies five essential traits that will help employees do this:

- **Personality.** Each employee has a unique personality. Brown suggests, "Knowing yourself and leveraging your personality temperament in naturally relating to clients and guests is a game changer." Encourage your good employees to know themselves and to let their personalities shine when they provide customer service for your patients. Do you have an employee who is extremely empathetic? Or who knows how to make things fun? Or who is a quiet observer? Or who is naturally curious? Each of these characteristics can be harnessed to provide above-and-beyond customer service. Help each team member to figure out precisely how.
- **A passion for people.** Ideally, you hire people who cultivate their passion for people, especially focusing on their well-being, pleasure, satisfaction, and joy. Find out what in customer service gets your good

employees most excited. What is it about helping people that they find especially rewarding?

- **Proficiencies.** Help your good employees identify personal proficiencies that they can use to provide above-and-beyond customer service. For instance, is the employee a good writer? An astute listener? A talented gift giver? How about a great memory? Explore with your employee how these and other proficiencies can be harnessed to serve and delight your patients.
- **Performance.** Are your employees enthusiastically engaged in customer service? If not, what do they, and you, think is getting in the way of their performance?
- **Presence.** Being fully present for patients is one of the most important things that you can do for them. However, being present sometimes means putting aside other things to give the patient your full attention. Is something interfering with your employees' ability to be fully present? If so, what can you do about it?

EQUIP EMPLOYEES TO GO ABOVE AND BEYOND

Although a good employee can do many things to provide above-and-beyond customer service, sometimes it helps to have some cash on hand to make the magic happen. Your employees may see an opportunity to buy something for your office that will enhance your patients' experiences, or to spend a little money to solve a problem for patients. When they see these opportunities, they will be empowered if they can act on them right away.

One way to equip your employees to provide above-and-beyond customer service is to establish an "above-and-beyond fund." You can manage the fund the same way you manage petty cash in your office. Your employees are able to access the funds up to an established dollar amount but must provide receipts and an explanation for how they spent the money. Accountability is key.

Another way to equip your employees to provide above-and-beyond customer service is to give each of them a monthly or quarterly personal budget for going above and beyond, again requiring them to keep track of and document how they spent the funds and why. Or, if you are not comfortable allowing your staff to have direct access to the funds, you or someone you designate can manage the funds and require that they submit their requests for funds for evaluation and approval prior to purchase.

However you do it, allowing your employees the discretion to use a small amount of money to provide above-and-beyond customer service will demonstrate your commitment to above-and-beyond customer service by putting money where your mouth is. And it will make them more enthusiastic and intentional about finding opportunities to provide exemplary service to your patients.

How can your employees use the funds? That is up to you and to them. However, here are some possible uses:

- Buy daffodils to give every patient on the first day of spring, or a big bushel of apples on a crisp fall day.
- Call and pay for a taxi or ride service for patients who find themselves stranded at your office or who uses public transportation but are not feeling well.
- Buy a condolence card for a patient who has lost someone special in their life. Have everyone in the office sign it and have your organization make a donation in memory of the deceased.
- Buy beautiful coffee table books for your reception area to supplement the magazines you provide.
- Send a relevant book to a patient who is going through a tough time.
- Fill a basket with travel-sized tubes of hand cream or hand sanitizer to keep by your reception desk, for patients to take with them.
- Send a small gift on behalf of your organization to a patient who has just gotten married, had a baby, retired, or celebrated another hallmark life event.
- Buy a subscription to a large-print magazine for your reception area.
- Buy and keep on hand individually packaged snacks for patients and their children.
- Buy and keep shawls in your office for patients who tell you they are cold.
- Buy and keep cards and small gifts in the office for patients who have appointments with you on their birthdays.
- Buy disposable plastic umbrella bags for patients' wet umbrellas.
- Send a gift basket with a sincere note of apology when you've really goofed.

CREATING AN ABOVE-AND-BEYOND EMPLOYEE CULTURE IN THREE STEPS

Getting employees to go above and beyond relies upon the culture you create in your healthcare organization. According to William Fleming,[3] going above and beyond goes far beyond simple permission to act with autonomy. It means that your employees, regardless of role, feel unfettered by red tape, doubt, or fear. Instead, Fleming says, they are empowered to "take the reins and do well by doing good — serving their customers the way they are naturally impassioned to do."

How can you create such a culture in your healthcare organization? Fleming suggests three steps:

1. **Encourage authenticity.** A foundational idea that Fleming suggests you share with your employees is "bringing your whole self to work." That means employees are comfortable in their own skin, as much in the workplace as in their personal lives. According to Fleming, "It goes beyond simply knowing that it's 'okay' to come to work with different backgrounds, experiences, and ideas, but being proud of it, believing that your employer and colleagues relish such diversity."

   It also means that employees realize that their employer values their health and well-being as a priority and wants employees to feel good about who they are and what they do. Fleming explains, "It's the first step, I think, in creating this safe environment where your employees can be authentic, feel appreciated, and start to feel free to work in their best capacity."
2. **Eliminate fear.** It's easy to establish so many rules, processes, and guidelines, especially in a highly regulated industry like healthcare that employees may worry about speaking up when they see a problem, have a suggestion, or want to step outside of bounds to do a better job, Fleming says. "Invest in efforts that show it's okay to 'test, fail, and scale.' Challenge the status quo. Or, as I often say, think like a rookie, asking the sometimes weird or uncomfortable questions," Fleming suggests. Employees will quickly get the message that real progress sometimes comes as the result of taking chances and abandoning fear.
3. **Champion the changers.** If you want a culture of employees who bring their authentic selves to work, don't operate in fear, and who feel free to serve patients at an above-and-beyond level, acknowledge and support the bold ones who stick out their necks. Recognize and reinforce employees who go above and beyond for your patients and celebrate their accomplishments publicly.

   Fleming adds that once you've followed these steps and have the right people doing the right jobs, you must get out of the way. Your employees will have the quickest and easiest route to providing above-and-beyond customer service for your patients only if you let them.

THE ABOVE-AND-BEYOND HEALTHCARE LEADER

Healthcare leaders who want and expect their employees to deliver above-and-beyond customer service for patients must talk the talk, but also walk the walk. Edward Matti[4] warns, "Leaders often ask their staff to go above and beyond the call of duty, but are not willing to do so themselves." Matti suggests that healthcare leaders share responsibility for customer service with employees and model above-and-beyond customer service for them whenever possible. That relies on healthcare leaders' understanding of what patients want and need, as well as their own commitment to taking action when opportunities arise.

In addition, healthcare leaders must be especially mindful to provide above-and-beyond service for their own customers: the employees they lead. When the boss goes above and beyond for the team, the team, in turn, is more likely to go above and beyond for one another and for patients. Unfortunately, the opposite is also true. As Matti warns, leaders who provide average or below-average customer service for their employees can expect the same kind of customer service from them.

HIRING ABOVE-AND-BEYOND EMPLOYEES

When you're hiring your next employee, look for someone who's not going to do just what's expected. Hire an employee who already has an above-and-beyond customer service mentality. According to JD Spinoza,[5] such job candidates have the following five traits:

1. **Ambition.** Everyone knows that it is challenging and often frustrating to manage employees who are not interested in where their careers go. But until you've worked with someone with true ambition and drive, you may not understand the difference it can make to your healthcare organization. Spinoza suggests, "Employees with ambition go above and beyond the call of duty every day, pushing their limits and making the entire team better."

   They are likely to go above and beyond for your patients without a lot of effort on your part. Therefore, when you're interviewing potential new employees, ask them how they would handle challenges at work where there's no clear leader. Spinoza says, "If they display an answer that shows they will step up and lead a team, you'll know whether you have an ambitious employee on your hands."

2. **Upbeat attitude.** Above-and-beyond employees usually are upbeat. When you're looking to add a new member to your team, make sure you're keeping an eye on applicants' overall outlook and attitude. Listen carefully to their tone, especially as they speak about former employers or frustrating situations in their past jobs. Spinoza suggests that you "ask specifics about how they dealt with other employees when they were frustrated, and you'll get a clearer picture of whether they're able to remain upbeat in the face of tough situations."
3. **Confidence.** Above-and-beyond customer service requires a fair amount of confidence, not only for employees to take action, but also to believe that their efforts are worthwhile and will make a positive difference. As you interview candidates, look for signs of confidence, both physical and verbal. If they can exude confidence in a job interview, chances are that they can bring that confidence into above-and-beyond customer service for your patients.
4. **Passion.** There is no substitute for passion. An employee who cares about the patients, their fellow employees, and the success of your healthcare organization will be a valuable member of your team. Ask job candidates why they want the job and, particularly, why they want to work in your healthcare organization. A lackluster response is a red flag. An employee who lacks passion is unlikely to go above and beyond for your patients, for you, or for anyone else.
5. **Empathy.** Spinoza suggests that empathy is an employee's most beneficial trait. Your employees deal with patients from diverse backgrounds every day. Each of those patients benefits from interacting with a caring person who truly understands and predicts how people feel, and who acts accordingly.

When you're interviewing prospective employees, Spinoza suggests, ask them for examples of how they interact with others who are diverse. Listen carefully to the way they talk about these experiences. This helps you understand how empathetic your future employees may be. (See Chapter 8 for more information on how to increase your employees' empathy once you've hired them.)

START AN ABOVE-AND-BEYOND PROGRAM IN YOUR HEALTHCARE ORGANIZATION

Your employees pay close attention to their behaviors that you recognize, reinforce, and reward. Therefore, one of the best ways to get your good employees to go above and beyond in customer service for your patients is to create and administer an Above-and-Beyond Employee Recognition Program. Here's how:

1. **Decide how you will recognize above-and-beyond staff performance.** For example, you can recognize one or more employees each month or quarter for going above and beyond in customer service. The recognition can be given at a staff meeting, in your marketing materials, in a framed poster in your reception area or hallway, in your patient newsletter, or on your bulletin board. Describe specifically what the employee did to go above and beyond in customer service. Ask for a round of applause during the staff meeting and offer your own appreciation and congratulations. Consider attaching a reward to the recognition such as a gift card, cash bonus, paid time off, certificate, or plaque.
2. **Publicize and explain your Above-and-Beyond Employee Recognition Program and invite participation.** Announce your program at a staff meeting. Tell your patients, visitors, employees, volunteers, and physicians about your program and ask them to nominate employees for recognition.
3. **Create a nomination form.** For example, the UPMC St. Margaret Above-and-Beyond Recognition Form[6] explains, "The employees, physicians, and volunteers of UPMC St. Margaret work together as a team to provide the best care and customer service possible. Frequently, our team members go an extra step in providing service that is above and beyond expectations. Please tell us about an exceptional member of our staff by completing and returning this Above-and-Beyond Recognition Form to [address] or by making a donation to the St. Margaret Foundation in honor of a special member of our staff."

   The UPMC St. Margaret form provides fields for the full name of the employee being nominated, the category of person making the nomination (employee, physician, volunteer, or department), details about the experience/reason for the nomination, date, and nominator's name and contact information. A simple form makes it easy to nominate employees and give you a quick and consistent way to receive the nominations.

4. **Collect and review nominations.** Make it easy for nominators to submit their completed forms to you online or when they visit your healthcare organization. Review each nomination and follow up by phone or email to get more details and to clarify anything that is unclear. Thank the nominator for making the nomination and reinforce your organization's commitment to above-and-beyond customer service.
5. **Recognize nominated employees.** Include in the employee's personnel file a copy of the nomination form and the recognition received.

CHAPTER 4 BONUS FEATURE

FIVE FEELINGS THAT MOTIVATE EMPLOYEES TO GO ABOVE AND BEYOND

Motivation to provide above-and-beyond service may vary by employee. For instance, they may strive to go above and beyond to improve their performance evaluations (if you make customer service part of what you evaluate). They may want the recognition and rewards that you have established, such as through an Above-and-Beyond Employee Recognition Program described above. Or they may be motivated just because they have big hearts and find it rewarding to do their best for your patients.

Every healthcare leader imagines having a "dream team" of employees — people who consistently go the extra mile at work. If your team is good but falling short of that dream team fantasy, it may be because they do not see what they will get personally out of pushing themselves harder. According to Lesonsky,[7] "It's all about the employee experience." Specifically, Lesonsky says, the following five positive feelings can make employees more likely to go above and beyond for your patients:

1. **Belonging.** Employees who join their co-workers in going above and beyond for your patients may feel that they are part of a first-rate team, department, or healthcare organization.
2. **Purpose.** Above-and-beyond employees understand and appreciate why their work matters.
3. **Achievement.** Going above and beyond gives employees a sense of accomplishment through the work that they do, especially when you recognize their achievements and reinforce the effort it takes.

4. **Happiness.** An above-and-beyond healthcare organization is a place where kindness is valued. It is a pleasant place to work.
5. **Vigor.** Going above and beyond increases energy, excitement, and enthusiasm at work.

Discussing these positive feelings with your employees can help them appreciate how their own work satisfaction depends on their going above and beyond for your patients. The key is to focus on the personal benefits they will enjoy by going above and beyond.

CHAPTER 5

How to Assess, Recognize, and Reward Teamwork

It is human nature to behave in ways that bring us positive recognition, praise, privileges, and riches. As Irvine[1] succinctly puts it, "You do things you get rewarded for." The rewards that motivate our behavior can be external and clearly stated to us, or they can be internal and no more than the good feeling we get from behaving in certain ways. But no matter the form or origin of our rewards, it is rewards that shape, propel, and reinforce a great deal of our behavior. This is true everywhere in life, including within the healthcare organization.

Therefore, good employees you manage will behave in the ways that bring them the most and the best rewards. A mistake leaders sometimes make is that they say that they want one particular behavior from their good employees yet they reward another. Specifically, they say that they want their employees to demonstrate teamwork, yet they reward only individual performance. Managing good employees in this inconsistent way encourages them to focus mostly or solely on their individual work and may even discourage them from making the needs and performance of the team a priority.

According to Michael Schrage,[2] "Organizations that truly want their people to work better together must stop publicly discriminating against teams in favor of individuals." He adds, "People need to feel that the benefits of being team players measurably *outweigh* the perceived and real costs of compromise and self-sacrifice."

The challenge healthcare leaders must face is how to reward teamwork without diminishing their good employees' desire to perform well individually. This is not always easy.

On the one hand, excessive focus on individual performance can ultimately backfire by undermining teamwork and by creating a tense, competitive, or cutthroat work environment. On the other hand, rewarding teams and not individuals can cause your star employees to become demoralized, especially if they feel that they are carrying the team or that there are some obvious slackers who are getting the same rewards that they are.

The trick is to recognize both team *and* individual performance, balancing the two while encouraging a cooperative culture. Fortunately, there are a number of strategies that can help.

FIVE GOALS FOR TEAM REWARDS PROGRAMS

Before creating and unveiling a team rewards program for your employees, know what you're trying to achieve. Shauna Geraghty[3] identifies five possible goals:

1. **Attract talented employees.** A team recognition and rewards program can entice talented employees to work for your healthcare organization. Therefore, you'll want to develop a team rewards program that you can publicize in job postings and throughout your recruitment efforts.
2. **Motivate employees to perform optimally.** The most effective team recognition and rewards programs focus on motivating desired behaviors. When you develop your program, be sure that recognition and rewards are tied to specific behaviors that you can observe, identify, and measure. At the end of the day, you want to motivate actions that achieve results, not simply effort and good intentions.
3. **Foster personal growth and development.** Team rewards can encourage and promote personal growth and professional development. Your team recognition and rewards program should be beneficial in the long run to each member of your team.
4. **Increase employee satisfaction.** Team recognition and rewards programs can promote employee engagement, resulting in increased workplace satisfaction. They can also motivate your employees to persist in the face of challenges and to come up with creative solutions to their problems. In brief, these programs can help employees derive more pleasure from their work. When you develop your team recognition and rewards program, focus on what you can do to help your employees increase their job satisfaction.
5. **Keep talented employees from leaving.** When employees love what they do and are recognized and rewarded for their performance, they

are less likely to seek employment elsewhere. Make sure that your good employees consider your team recognition and rewards program to be a plus. Help them to perceive and value it as a benefit of working in your healthcare organization.

ASSESSING AND REWARDING TEAMWORK: TEN TIPS

Establishing a team rewards program is similar to establishing an individual employee rewards program. Here are 10 tips to help you negotiate those similarities and a few important differences:

1. **Establish clear, observable, and measurable team objectives.** Team members must understand and agree upon what success looks like, just as they do for their individual performance goals. In addition, you need a common set of objectives or aspirations so that you have some way of assessing your team's performance.

   Amy Gallo[4] suggests bringing everyone together to discuss team goals and metrics. Establish goals that are specific, observable, and measurable. Ask your team: What would it take for us to give ourselves an A? Facilitating this dialogue can be highly motiving and can lay the groundwork for collaboration with a shared vision.
2. **Follow good employee recognition rules.** Many of the same rules apply whether you are recognizing an individual or a team. In both instances, you want to recognize significant accomplishments that are in line with your healthcare organization's goals and values. You want to be specific and timely about what you are rewarding.

   As well, you want to make sure that the recognition or award will be meaningful to the recipients. None of your employees is going to get excited about a reward that is not personally meaningful. In fact, the wrong recognition and rewards can make your good employees feel uncomfortable and unappreciated, and may be worse than no recognition at all.
3. **Reward both individual and team performance.** Do not reward teamwork at the exclusion of individual rewards. What is the ideal balance of the two types of rewards? According to Brooks Mitchell,[5] "There is substantial research that supports the greater importance of individual effort." Mitchell suggests that a well-balanced performance-reward

program consists of 75% emphasis on individual behavior and 25% emphasis on team behavior.

4. **Assess team progress regularly.** Gallo says that managers can pose questions that help the group assess its progress, such as, "How are we performing as a team?" and "What obstacles can we remove?" Gallo suggests asking these questions in a meeting or anonymously through a survey.
5. **Use both monetary and non-monetary team rewards.** There are many nonmonetary rewards at your disposal for both individual and team rewards, even if you cannot change how salaries and bonuses are handled in your healthcare organization. For example, send members of your team a handwritten note. Write a formal letter of appreciation for the excellent teamwork and place a copy in each employee's personnel file. Describe the team's successes during monthly meetings and thank your staff publicly. Or create and play a short photo or video montage that highlights your team's accomplishments.
6. **Organize a team awards event and reward teams by name.** Schrage suggests that the awards events should positively impact teamwork conversation and culture. For example, recognize and reward your staff's most dynamic duos and productive trios by name. Or, Schrage suggests, "Identify and celebrate the 'fab fours' and 'creative quintets' of innovation or efficiency."
7. **Encourage employees to recognize their peers.** Top-down recognition is not the only form of reward that matters or that motivates behavior. Also encourage your employees to recognize one another. For example, allow a few minutes at the beginning or end of staff meetings for your employees to recognize their fellow team members for their support and outstanding efforts.

   Ashley Bell[6] suggests buying a notebook and introducing it to your staff as your team "good" book. Keep it in a place that is accessible to your employees. Then, encourage them to write in your good book to recognize team members for their contributions and accomplishments, especially those that are work-related. Read the week's new good book entries aloud at your staff meetings. Bell explains, "Knights of old recorded good deeds in books for posterity."

   A good book empowers your employees to recognize one another in the same way and help you to foster a culture of recognition and gratitude, Bell suggests.

8. **Reward team-supporting efforts.** It is relatively easy to identify and reinforce the employee who is a standout for excellent performance. However, Joanna Krotz[7] warns that this strategy taken to the extreme can undermine teamwork. "Don't talk up teamwork and then empower the player who always goes to the hoop and never passes," she says.

   Also be sure to recognize and reward the "player" on your staff who supports their teammates by passing the ball, Krotz suggests. Furthermore, when you wish to recognize and reward an individual for exceptional performance, ask them to identify who on the team supported the effort and helped to make the success possible.
9. **Time your reward to the appropriate stage of work.** Geraghty suggests that rewards have a different impact on employees' motivation and subsequent performance during each stage of their work. Specifically, she suggests that rewards can motivate the employee to:
   - **Start a new task:** Rewards promote team "buy in" to start a new task and in fact increase employee motivation to start a new task by 15%, Geraghty says.
   - **Persist:** In this middle stage of a task, rewards serve as "motivational maintenance," Geraghty says. They help teams persevere in the face of distractions, challenges, and competing work tasks. Middle-stage rewards increase employees' motivation to persist on a task by 27%.
   - **Work smarter:** Rewards can also serve to increase the quality of the performance on the task when it is stagnant or lacking. They contribute to the team investing more effort, to thinking of creative approaches to solve problems, and to devising new strategies to be more effective and efficient. Rewards timed to when performance drops or stagnates can increase working smarter by 26%, Geraghty says.
10. **Keep it simple.** Ideally, a team rewards program has two to four key metrics, not 12 to 14. According to Ann Bares,[8] "Tying employees' compensation to a performance indicator they do not understand or do not believe they can achieve will only produce frustration." As Bares suggests, when it comes to team reward programs, "Less is more."

OVERCOMING THREE COMMON CONCERNS ABOUT REWARDING TEAMWORK

As you can see, rewarding team performance helps healthcare leaders achieve their organization's goals. However, Mitchell suggests that the strategy also raises three valid concerns:

1. **Reduced individual effort.** Team reward programs that reward only overall group performance can be counterproductive. They may encourage some employees to reduce their efforts because they don't think their contributions will be noticed or matter. This phenomenon, known as "social loafing," was first documented in a 1991 study by Williams and Karau.[9]

   What to do: The most effective way to prevent or counteract social loafing is to design performance reward strategies that reward individual team members as well as the team as a whole. Mitchell warns, "Despite enthusiasm for teams, the individual still wants to be recognized."
2. **Competition.** Another potential problem with team performance programs is competition between teams. According to Mitchell, "Constant competition between teams can deflect employee efforts away from achieving organizational goals and redirect them toward sabotaging other teams. This is not a healthy organizational environment."

   What to do: If you build competition into your team rewards program, do so only in controlled, short-term intervals, Mitchell suggests, warning that long-term competitive programs can be "dangerous."
3. **Underreporting.** Another potential problem with team performance programs is the possibility of hiding or underreporting accidents and errors. This occurs in programs that reward teams for going long periods of time without mishaps. On the surface, this seems like a good strategy. However, Mitchell warns that such programs may encourage teams to hide or underreport accidents and errors.

   What to do: Don't reward your team for avoiding errors and accidents. It is more effective to identify and reward non-accident and non-error *behaviors* such as education, safety checks, cross-checking, and meeting attendance, Mitchell says.

TYPES OF TEAM REWARDS

Team rewards programs can take various forms ranging from cash and public acknowledgment to prizes and group celebrations. The timing and frequency of rewards can also vary. But regardless of the strategy you choose, your team reward program should have three goals: to acknowledge the role of teams within your healthcare organization, to reward team performance, and to keep your employees motivated and committed to teamwork. The American Psychological Association Center for

Organizational Excellence[10] suggests three types of team reward programs that can accomplish these goals:

- **Financial incentives.** Performance-based bonuses and profit- or gain-sharing group incentives are traditionally based in large work units in large organizations. However, these strategies can be applied to smaller teams in the healthcare organization where members earn payouts for meeting team goals. This approach can boost cooperation and productivity and help teams stay focused on shared goals.
- **Recognition.** Both formal and informal recognition can reinforce the value of teamwork. Public recognition can occur at a formal event, be commemorated with a plaque or certificate, and/or posted on your healthcare organization's website and publications. It can also take the form of a more informal thank-you from your organization's leadership, or even, a well-timed, heartfelt email.
- **Teambuilding events.** Group teambuilding workshops and retreats can help set a tone of collaboration and trust, which reenergizes a team and boosts morale. Team celebrations such as a thank-you lunch or bowling party can mark smaller achievements. Offering prizes for team accomplishments or top contributors can also help maintain productivity and keep employees engaged. As well, training programs and expanded decision-making authority are additional ways to reward a team and increase its efficiency.

RECOGNIZE AND REWARD TEAMS SINCERELY, OR NOT AT ALL

The effectiveness of your team recognition and rewards program relies heavily on your own attitude about it. According to Joan Klubnik,[11] "The giver's attitude about the process is important because it influences the nonverbal messages that accompany the recognition." The best team recognition is given by a healthcare leader who considers the reward to be deserved and a win/win proposition for the employees and the organization. Both the giver and the receiver should benefit as a result of the process.

Without this mindset, team recognition and reward giving will probably be "less than successful," Klubnik warns. The giver will be frustrated because they don't feel right about giving the reward. And the receiver will become dissatisfied, she says, because of the nonverbal messages received during the giving process.

What should you do if you can't recognize and reward your team sincerely? First, own your feelings. You're entitled to feel as you do. Next, don't give recognition and rewards through clenched teeth. Hold off until you can feel more positive. Then figure out what's causing you to feel as you do. If the problem is that you're just not comfortable giving praise, work on that. "The good news is that the giving process is a learned skill," Klubnik says.

However, if the problem is with the rewards program itself, change it so it feels right to you. Whatever you do, don't give recognition and rewards that seem undeserved to you. It will come off as false and you'll be disappointed in the results, Klubnik warns.

CHOOSE THE BEST TEAM REWARD SCHEDULE

Timing your team rewards well ensures that your reward system has the largest possible impact on behavioral change. According to Geraghty, "The schedule of reinforcement can actually be more influential on behavioral change than the magnitude of the reinforcement." There are two types of reinforcement schedules, Geraghty says: continuous reinforcement and intermittent reinforcement.

Continuous reinforcement occurs when every target behavior is rewarded. An example of continuous reinforcement is paying a bonus every time an employee reaches a performance target. A continuous reinforcement schedule is effective in quickly shaping employee behavior, especially when they are starting an unfamiliar task, Geraghty suggests.

Intermittent reinforcement, as the name implies, does not administer a reward every time employees achieve their target behavior. It is most effective in maintaining the desired behavior *after* the behavior becomes a habit. Geraghty identifies four types of intermittent reinforcement schedules and describes how each can impact team behavior differently:

1. **Fixed ratio.** A fixed number of behavioral responses occur before the reward is given, such as a specific number of calls made or appointments scheduled. This type of reinforcement usually increases performance at first; however, the improved performance may plateau or stop when the thrill of the reward wears off.
2. **Variable ratio.** A random number of behavioral responses occur before the reward is given, such as giving gift cards randomly to employees

who have achieved goals. This type of reinforcement increases desired behavior and, unlike fixed ratio, it doesn't stop, Geraghty says.

3. **Fixed interval.** After a specific time period, the behavioral response is followed with a reward. For example, a bonus is paid quarterly, regardless of specific performance. Because this type of reinforcement produces an inconsistent performance pattern among employees, Geraghty does not recommend it.
4. **Variable interval.** The reward for behavior is bestowed after random periods of time have elapsed. For example, a healthcare leader randomly praises teams for their excellence. This type of reinforcement schedule increases desired behavior, Geraghty says.

As Geraghty suggests, continuous reinforcement quickly shapes employee behavior until it becomes a habit. Once the behavior has become a habit, variable ratio and variable interval schedules of reinforcement are the most effective in promoting the behavior. Using these schedules of reinforcement encourage the most significant positive behavior changes in your employees, Geraghty says.

CHAPTER 5 BONUS FEATURE

ASSESSING TEAMWORK: A RELIABLE FIVE-QUESTION SURVEY

How can you effectively assess your employees' teamwork? According to Lurie, Schultz, and Lamanna,[12] the following five-item questionnaire can be completed in three minutes or less and has proven to yield reliable estimates of your employees' views of team effectiveness.

Ideally, every member of the team would strongly agree with each of the five statements. If your survey results are less than ideal, probe deeper to learn from your employees what you can do to improve teamwork in your healthcare organization.

CONFIDENTIAL ASSESSMENT OF MY TEAM'S TEAMWORK

	Strongly disagree	Somewhat disagree	Neither agree nor disagree	Somewhat agree	Strongly agree
My team encourages everyone to share ideas.					
People on my team have the information that they need to do their jobs well.					
When people on my team experience a problem, they make a serious effort to figure out what's really going on.					
Leadership on my team creates an environment where things can be accomplished.					
Everyone on my team feels able to act on the team vision.					

Feel free to elaborate on your answers and share anything else you'd like to tell us.

____

____

____

____

____

CHAPTER 6

Increasing Employee Commitment: 25 Strategies

Commitment is at the center of many relationships, including your employees' relationship with you and your healthcare organization. If your good employees already have a high level of commitment, they will trust you and be loyal to you. They will look for and see the good in you and willingly provide their time, energy, hard work, and talent to help you and your organization succeed. With employee commitment, everything is possible.

Conversely, when employee commitment levels are low, even good employees are likely to become cynical and to stop caring, according to Eaton.[1] They may go through the motions every day, but they won't excel. Often, they will look for the flaws and faults in your healthcare organization and in your leadership, and most assuredly, they will find them. They will stop expending energy to help you and one another. Ultimately, they may become the dead wood in your healthcare organization or seek employment elsewhere.

The quality and depth of your good employees' commitment is, therefore, a critical factor in your success. Fortunately, you can use a number of tools to assess, foster, and increase your employees' commitment.

WHAT IS COMMITMENT?

Commitment is a willingness to persist in a course of action and a reluctance to change plans, often owing to a sense of obligation to stay the course. According to Robert Vance,[2] "Commitment manifests itself in distinct behavior. For example, people devote time and energy to fulfill their on-the-job responsibilities, as well as their family, personal, community, and spiritual obligations."

Commitment also has an emotional component, Vance says. People usually express positive feelings toward an individual, organization, or cause to whom or to which they have made a commitment. As well, commitment has a rational component. Vance explains, "Most people consciously decide to make commitments. Then they thoughtfully plan and carry out the actions required to fulfill them."

Commitments require an investment of time as well as mental and emotional energy. Therefore, most people make them with the expectation of reciprocation. They assume that in exchange for their commitment, they will get something of value, such as favors, affection, gifts, attention, goods, money, or property. In the healthcare organization, employees and employers traditionally have a tacit agreement: in exchange for the employee's commitment, the organization will provide forms of value for its employees such as skill training, secure jobs, fair compensation, bonuses, and opportunities for career advancement. Reciprocity affects the intensity of employee commitment. Vance suggests, "When an employer to whom an employee has made a commitment fails to come through with the expected exchange, the commitment erodes."

Commitments are likely to weaken quickly when employees feel that their organizations have let them down. This can be observed, for instance, when an organization goes through cutbacks and downsizing. Once-committed employees who believe that their employer has changed the deal often feel betrayed. They then put in less effort or look for employment elsewhere.

ASSESSING YOUR EMPLOYEES' COMMITMENT

It is relatively easy to get employees to comply but often difficult to get them to commit. Yet employee commitment is far more important to your healthcare organization's long-term performance. Michael Beck[3] suggests, "When someone is compliant, they simply obey — doing what is asked of them, but no more. Typically, they're doing just enough to keep their job." Conversely, Beck suggests, when an employee is committed, they will spend time and effort "outside of normal business hours thinking about work and solving problems, finding better ways to get the job done, seeking out new insights, and then acting on them."

Therefore, when assessing employee performance, it is not sufficient to look at their compliance with your organization's rules and management, but also at their commitment. That means that you need to consider not only what your employees say and do, but also what they *don't* say and *don't* do. The following questions will help you to assess employee commitment. Do your employees:

- Go above and beyond minimal job expectations?
- Demonstrate through actions a willingness to put others first?
- Volunteer to do more when your healthcare organization hits a rough spot?
- Show consistency between what they say and their body language?
- Suggest new and better ways to do things that will benefit others?
- Come to you with suggestions that they developed on their own time, outside of usual work hours?
- Speak positively about your healthcare organization when they think you're not listening?
- Maintain a high-quality work level when they think you're not observing?
- Genuinely and wholeheartedly celebrate the success of your healthcare organization and of other employees?
- Become excited by new opportunities that will improve your healthcare organization?

If you were able to answer *yes* to these questions, your employees are likely to have a high level of commitment. However, if you're not sure of an employee's level of commitment, or if you know that it is low, it's best to have a one-on-one conversation with that employee to learn more.

DISCUSSING COMMITMENT WITH YOUR EMPLOYEES

Below is a list of questions to ask an employee whose commitment level to your healthcare organization is low or unclear. It's best to carry on such conversations in private and in a helpful, nonthreatening way.

Encourage your low-commitment employees to answer honestly and to open up about their feelings. Through a free give-and-take, you may be able to uncover reasons for an employee's lack of commitment and to turn things around. When you speak with the employee, ask: "Do you feel that:

- You want to participate on our healthcare organization's (or your department's) team?

- You had/continue to have a choice about working here?
- You have input about our direction, goals, and choices?
- Our mission is important?
- You are part of something that is bigger than yourself?
- Your work is valuable?
- You make a difference through your work here?
- Our healthcare organization provides valuable and needed services to our patients?
- What you are doing now will help you with your long-term career?
- You are growing professionally because of this job?
- You would stay with our healthcare organization even if you were offered a comparable position and similar pay and benefits at another organization?
- You have a good and important use for your discretionary time at work?
- Our healthcare organization is the right place for you?
- You are proud of our healthcare organization and the work you do here?
- You would recommend our healthcare organization as a place to work?
- You are recognized for your achievements?
- Our healthcare organization and its leaders are committed to you?
- Our healthcare organization inspires you to do your best work?

INSPIRING COMMITMENT IN OTHERS THROUGH YOUR LEADERSHIP

Inspiring, creating, and nurturing employee commitment is possible when healthcare leaders practice and master a few key leadership activities. Jody Rogers[4] has developed a four-part "roadmap" to inspiring commitment through leadership:

1. **Care.** Employees who know that you care about them are likely to return the favor with greater commitment. On the other hand, if your employees don't believe you care about them, they probably won't be committed to you. Therefore, openly demonstrate your caring attitude toward your employees. Tell them that you care, but also demonstrate your commitment through your actions. Make sure your employees know that you're not just giving them lip service about your commitment to them, that you mean what you say.
2. **Create ownership.** You can enhance employee commitment if your employees believe that your vision is also *their* vision. Give your

employees a voice in how the work should be accomplished and explain how and why each team member's role is essential.

3. **Ensure security.** Your employees are more willing to commit to you and to your healthcare organization when they feel secure. For example, if your employees know that you won't punish them for taking prudent risks, they will more freely give the talent, time, and effort it takes to get the job done. On the other hand, if your employees believe you will punish them for making reasonable errors, they may not give you 100% of their effort and commitment.
4. **Practice accountability for everyone, including you.** Employee commitment and accountability are closely related. Make sure that each employee in your healthcare organization knows that they are held to a certain level of accountability. Rogers says that a culture of accountability encourages teamwork, reciprocity, and a willingness to cover for one another when needed.

FOUR DRIVERS OF EMPLOYEE COMMITMENT

Employees commit to your healthcare organization for different reasons. Observe and carefully listen to each employee to determine how to increase their commitment. According to Beck, there are four possible drivers of employee commitment:

- **Intrinsic motivation.** Committed employees are self-motivated or at the very least have the capacity for self-motivation, Beck suggests. Therefore, you may not be able to increase their commitment to your healthcare organization if they lack self-motivation or are overwhelmed by other commitments in their lives, which is something you cannot control. Assess whether each employee's commitment is within your control. If not, that employee may not be a good fit for your healthcare organization and may be better off elsewhere, Beck says.
- **Leadership.** Some employees find it easier to commit to individuals rather than to organizations and therefore are more likely to pledge their allegiance to a healthcare leader, manager, or boss they admire, like, and respect. Likewise, Beck suggests, motivated and committed employees quickly become unhappy (and their commitment deteriorates) if they believe that their healthcare leaders, managers, or bosses are untrustworthy, even if that is not true.

- **Organizational culture.** An organization that claims certain core values but acts in ways that clearly demonstrate that those values don't matter soon causes widespread disillusionment and disengagement, Beck warns. For example, an organization that says that it puts families first and values work/life balance but requires employees to work long hours of overtime is sending an inconsistent message. Similarly, an organization demonstrates a lack of integrity and consistency when it says that it values excellence but tolerates sub-par behavior and performance from its employees. Such inconsistencies lead to a loss of employee trust in, respect for, and commitment to the organization.
- **Initiatives.** An organization's new initiative undertaken without clear intent is simply a purposeless goal. Unfortunately, goals without purpose are "cold, unemotional targets, lacking any purpose other than to make the person who set the goals look good," Beck says. Employees become more committed when they believe in what they're doing and when they believe that they are making a difference through their work. Therefore, projects and goals require employee buy-in. Your employees must know the why, not just the what, Beck says.

25 STRATEGIES TO INCREASE EMPLOYEE COMMITMENT

Your good employees will be committed to your healthcare organization when you create a positive, nurturing work environment that is worthy of their commitment. Here are 25 strategies for making that happen:

1. **Study employee retention.** Employees who choose to leave to work in another healthcare organization or in another industry may be able to help you diagnose a management problem that weakens or interferes with employee commitment. Conduct exit surveys with your departing employees to learn what you did well and what you can do better.
2. **Clarify and communicate your mission.** Committed employees believe they are part of something larger and greater than themselves. Gary Dessler[5] suggests that you create a shared mission and ideology that lays out a basic way of thinking and doing things in your organization. He also suggests that you can create "charisma" for your healthcare organization by linking your mission to a higher calling.
3. **Use values-based hiring practices.** In many organizations, the process of linking employees to the organization's ideology begins before the

employee is hired. Values-based employers first clarify what their basic values are. Then they create and enforce procedures for screening new employees, requiring evidence from job applicants of their commitment to the organization's values. They reject applicants who do not demonstrate those shared values. Dessler explains, "Value-based hiring screens out those who might not fit."

4. **Stress values-based training.** Steeping new and current employees in your healthcare organization's values and culture through training fosters their commitment.
5. **Commit to people-first values.** Treating your employees as important and demonstrating that you respect them contributes to their commitment. Employee commitment also increases in healthcare organizations that put patients first.
6. **Build your traditions.** Tradition-building symbols, stories, rituals, and ceremonies can further enhance employee commitment. (See Chapter 13 for more information on creating rituals for your employees.)
7. **Promote organizational justice.** Organizational justice is simply the extent to which fair procedures and processes are perceived to be in place and followed. It includes the extent to which employees see their leaders as being fair and sincere and having logic or rationale for what they do. One obvious source of organizational justice is fair procedures embodied in formal grievance procedures. Involving employees in decisions that affect them is another.
8. **Create a sense of community.** A community creates commitment among its members, who typically develop a "we" attitude, as though they are part of a family or tribe. Frequent team meetings and contact can enhance your employees' sense of community.
9. **Clearly define responsibilities.** Each position in your healthcare organization should have a formal job description. Make sure that your employees know up front to whom they report, what kinds of decisions they are allowed to make, and what is expected of them each day. It will be hard for you to earn employee commitment without these essentials in place.
10. **Seek proper training.** Healthcare leaders should receive training in management techniques and in people skills. Employees often lack commitment to an organization because of a poor relationship with their boss, not because of the organization. Therefore, healthcare leaders need to be on top of their managerial game.

11. **Map out career plans.** Employees will be more likely to commit to a healthcare organization when they believe a career path is carved out for them. Make career planning a regular part of your performance review process.
12. **Conduct employee satisfaction surveys.** Ask your employees what they want more of in their positions and what they want less of. Then do what you can to show them that you are listening to them, even if you can't accommodate every request.
13. **Enrich and empower.** Increasing the breadth of responsibility and self-management in a job can appeal to your employees' higher-level needs. Empowering your employees fosters their commitment.
14. **Promote from within.** Your employees' commitment can soar when they believe that your healthcare organization provides opportunities for them to earn increasingly higher-level positions and pay.
15. **Encourage upward evaluations.** Healthcare leaders who want their employees to give them ideas for improving productivity must be open to their suggestions. They must ask their employees to tell them how they can do their jobs better and how they can make their employees' work lives more effective. When your employees see that you are willing to improve yourself, they get a sense that you respect them and that you value their ideas. This strategy enhances their commitment to you and to your healthcare organization.
16. **Provide fair and competitive salaries.** Below-market wages do not foster employee commitment. Rather, they encourage your employees to look elsewhere for employment. Stay up to date on what other healthcare organizations in your area are paying for similar work and be competitive.
17. **Create an effective employee onboarding program.** New employees feel a stronger commitment to your healthcare organization when you demonstrate your interest in their success from the start. Therefore, start strong. Once you get off on the wrong foot, it is difficult to turn things around. (See Chapter 17 for more information on creating an exceptional onboarding experience for your new employees.)
18. **Be forthright with news.** Keep your employees informed of any changes you must make and why. Let them hear good and bad news from you first.
19. **Create learning opportunities.** Developmental activities such as workshops and conferences enhance employees' opportunities for

promotion from within, appeal to their desire to grow and learn, provide opportunities for lateral moves, and give them a chance to grow personally and professionally. Employees interested in advancement want to learn new skills and knowledge so they can create value in their position. Provide those opportunities with internal or external education sponsored by your healthcare organization. Make professional development a part of your employee review process.

20. **Offer competitive benefits.** Your employees will be more committed to your healthcare organization if they believe you are taking good care of them and their families.
21. **Provide tools.** Employees need equipment and supplies to do their jobs well. Employers who get behind on technology and best practices or that provide insufficient resources often thwart employee commitment.
22. **Listen.** Your employees want to know that their voices and opinions are heard. Healthcare leaders who listen actively are often rewarded with employee commitment.
23. **Ask employees to verbalize their commitment.** Words can be very powerful. Ask your employees to speak their commitment to your mission and vision, to their colleagues, and to providing the best healthcare possible for every patient.
24. **Get employees involved in something they enjoy.** Look for projects that engage your employees and that have wider implications and benefits for your healthcare organization. Provide opportunities for your employees to be creative and to exercise their talents.
25. **Reinforce employee commitment.** For example, hold ceremonies to recognize outstanding employee commitment. Give your employees years-of-service certificates or pins, especially for milestone employment anniversaries. Or put the number of years your employees have worked in your organization on their nametags for all to see. Even small numeric stickers to indicate years of service applied to name tags can increase commitment, especially when distributed to employees inside personalized and signed cards on their annual employment anniversaries.

CHAPTER 6 BONUS FEATURE

THE FIVE COMMITMENTS OF LEADERSHIP

Employees know that there is a huge distinction between what leaders *say* about commitment and what they actually *do*. As Mark Leheney[6] suggests, the concept of a commitment means that it shows up in leaders' actions, not just in their words. This can be the difference between the "talk" and the "walk," he suggests, citing five commitments every leader must make:

1. **Self.** Leaders need to learn about and know themselves first. With self-knowledge, commitment can follow. For example, self-committed leaders do not dictate strategy; rather, they explain their thought process and request feedback. Self-learning can happen this way because blind spots, oversights, and faulty assumptions can surface. Additionally, leaders who ask for feedback demonstrate that they do not think they always have all of the answers. Self-committed leaders check their egos at the door and are interested in other opinions. They are committed to their own development and are humble enough to learn from others.
2. **People.** When employees see leaders focusing only on a task, output, or goal, they may feel as though they are no more respected than machines in a factory. However, employees want to know that their contributions are valued. No one ever thanks a machine, Leheney says. Therefore, committed leaders respond by saying *thank you* to their employees and by doing more. For example, you can help your employees learn new skills to further careers. You can recognize your employees' willingness to help and acknowledge how they have made a difference. As well, a genuine display of empathy, gratitude, and praise can be most welcome to those looking for signs that their leader respects their work.
3. **Organization.** A committed leader finds meaning, value, and purpose in the organization and then shares that commitment with others. Anything less than a total commitment to your healthcare organization and its mission is likely to be picked up by sensitive "employee antennae," Leheney warns. This, in turn, can easily hamper or weaken a leader's effectiveness.
4. **Truth.** Commitment to the truth is perhaps the most difficult of all commitments because it requires up-front honesty. Any attempt to sanitize reality through spin or less-than-forthright assessments could

permanently damage your credibility and erode any possibility of trust. That is why Leheney suggests, "Anything less than the truth from leadership is unsustainable."

5. **Leadership.** Committed leaders are committed to leading, more so than to themselves. They may be incredibly ambitious, but their ambition is directed first and foremost to their organization and its mission, not to themselves. In fact, leadership-committed leaders often display surprising humility and don't let their egos get in the way of their effectiveness, Leheney says.

CHAPTER 7

Using Morning Huddles to Build Your Team

The morning huddle meeting for the healthcare staff is a highly regarded management strategy that can get everyone on the same page. Huddles are quick daily meetings that provide a reliable time and space for the manager and the rest of the team to plan for changes in the day's workflow and to anticipate, prevent, and manage crises before they arise. They can give employees an opportunity to make adjustments that will improve patients' experiences and their own quality of life at work. They can also give the team a chance to make sure that no one drops the ball before a busy day gets the better of everyone.

These practical benefits of morning huddles will help you improve your efficiency and productivity. However, morning huddles can help you achieve much more. In fact, Alina Vrabie[1] suggests that the morning huddle is probably the "single most effective meeting that you can have with your team." That's because morning huddles build teams and foster teamwork.

Elizabeth Stewart and Barbara Johnson[2] suggest, "Huddles work because they demand rapid team formation." The act of getting your staff together quickly and consistently each day, if only for a few minutes, can make each employee feel connected to the rest of the team. It can counteract any feelings of isolation that employees may have.

In addition, Mary Fisher-Day[3] suggests that huddles can foster teamwork when employees identify who will need help throughout the day and make sure that someone is available and ready to jump in. Employees will feel that they are truly part of a team and that they won't have to fend for themselves when the going gets tough. The huddle reassures your employees that someone always has their back.

Healthcare leaders can also use morning huddles to build team morale. For example, you can lift everyone up by closing morning huddles consistently on a positive note, Fisher-Day suggests. Thanking everyone for their participation and wishing everyone a great day can go a long way toward building morale. Morning huddles can also provide an opportunity for the staff to participate in a daily team building ritual. For example, you and your employees can recite particular words at the start or end of your huddle, pass an object from person to person, or even sing a song to strengthen team bonds.

Huddles don't cost anything other than a few minutes of time. They don't require lots of down time or planning and they can benefit healthcare organizations of any size. Stewart and Johnson suggest that large organizations can have a representatives from each group or department attend the huddle and take important information back to their teams. In smaller organizations, huddles can prevent problems that can arise when one person assumes that everyone else in the office knows what's going on.

How can you use morning huddles to increase effectiveness and build your teams? How can you use morning huddles to help your good employees improve their performance? The keys are to understand the benefits of huddles, establish goals for them, get employee buy-in for them, streamline them, and use them consistently.

THE BENEFITS OF MORNING HUDDLES

Committing to morning huddles can help you to improve and grow your healthcare organization. DuCharme[4] suggests that huddles offer eight benefits:

1. Better organization by planning the day instead of just letting it happen.
2. Peace of mind that comes from knowing that supplies and room set-ups are correct for the patients you're going to see that day.
3. Increased productivity by having the entire team aware of patients who are coming in that day who have not yet scheduled needed follow-up treatment and procedures. Staff members armed with that knowledge can gently encourage those patients to make the needed appointments.
4. Improved profitability by identifying gaps in the schedule while there's still time to fill them, especially if those gaps occur later in the day.
5. Improved employee morale by deciding who needs help throughout the day and assigning a team member to assist.

6. Effective handling of patients who are particularly challenging. The clinical team will be involved in selecting the best way to handle them.
7. Keeping employees informed of and working toward daily goals.
8. Reinforcement that it is a whole-team effort to meet those goals.

The Fluence management group[5] suggests a less-obvious benefit of morning huddles: "The doctor and the team are reminded to put on their 'game face.'" How comforting would it be for patients if staff members greeted them yawning, complaining how they didn't sleep well? Or how would it be for patients to witness your employees arguing about petty things? The group explains, "During patient time, the doctor and team need to leave their baggage at the door." The morning huddle is the perfect opportunity for everyone to do this, the Fluence Group says, adding, "No one leaps out of bed with the same amount of energy each and every day. That is why the morning huddle is so important."

FOUR GOALS FOR MORNING HUDDLES

Healthcare leaders can use morning huddles to help them accomplish four important goals. According to Paige,[6] these goals are to:

1. **Motivate your employees.** A morning huddle can help you send your employees back to their work areas each day with a sense of shared commitment to their tasks, to one another, and to your healthcare organization's mission and goals. You can motivate higher performance by acknowledging and reinforcing staff contributions. As well, you can encourage and applaud your employees' excellent communication with team members and with you. Healthcare leaders can then end the morning huddle by sharing a motivating thought for the day.
2. **Teach and reinforce team values and culture.** Morning huddles can help you and your employees promote your healthcare organization's culture and values, such as commitment to excellent patient care and to one another. On occasion, use huddle time to bring up issues that are not directly work-related but that relate to your organization's values and that may impact employee performance. For example, use your huddle to solve an employee's temporary transportation problem by arranging a ride to and from work with a coworker. Or if a team member is out sick, use huddle time to pass around a card for everyone to sign.

3. **Review your day's schedule.** Make sure that your employees leave the huddle knowing how their daily tasks fit in with their coworkers' goals for the day.
4. **Review upcoming practical concerns.** Remind your staff about employees who are taking time off so that everyone knows who will be performing in what roles on any given day.

HOW TO GET EMPLOYEE BUY-IN FOR MORNING HUDDLES

You may encounter some resistance when you introduce the morning huddle to your healthcare organization. After all, few employees are looking for a new mandatory meeting, especially one that occurs every day bright and early. Even your best employees may not feel that they need them. If this is a new strategy in your healthcare organization, use these three strategies to reduce resistance to your morning huddles:

1. **Get top-down support.** The top management in your healthcare organization must be behind the huddle from the start. Their commitment to the short daily meeting will show everyone that the meeting is important and that, at least in the organization leaders' opinion, it is a worthwhile use of time.
2. **Don't call it a huddle.** Some employees may resist a meeting that is called a huddle. Steven Anderson[7] says, "Yes, teams huddle on the field, but it's a brief meeting where one person calls the play and everyone yells 'break.'" He explains that your staff may reason that a healthcare organization is not like football team and suggests that you may have more success with the huddle concept if you call the meeting by another name. "The most effective teams we have worked with don't have a morning huddle at all," he says. "They have transformed the 'get together and call the play of the day' morning huddle into something we have coined the 'Morning Opportunity Meeting,' or M.O.M. for short." The primary quality of the M.O.M. is its middle name: opportunity, Anderson says, a concept that sits especially well with employees.
3. **Explain why you're huddling.** Share the benefits of the morning huddle with your employees so they will be more likely to support the idea. Otherwise, they may think you're using the huddle time just to check up on them or to put pressure on them.

12 TIPS FOR CREATING AND USING MORNING HUDDLES

These 12 tips will help you get the most from your morning huddles, whether the idea is brand new in your healthcare organization or one that you've been using for a long time:

1. **Meet someplace in your office where your employees can gather easily.** Lois Banta[8] suggests that it is helpful to meet in a place where the day's schedule can be displayed. "Typically, the huddle takes place in the break room with a flat-screen TV displaying the schedule for easy viewing," Banta says. If this is not possible, each team member should have a hard copy of the current day's schedule, plus the previous day's schedule handy for review.
2. **Make attendance and punctuality mandatory.** Don't remind your staff of the meeting each day or ask them to join you before the huddle. Make it their responsibility to show up on time without your reminders. Then start on time. Don't delay for stragglers. If employees consistently come late or don't show up, address the matter with them privately. For huddles to work best, no one can be routinely exempt from them, any more than they can be routinely exempt from being part of the team. If possible, start your huddle at an odd time, such as 8:43 am. The odd time can get your staff to think in minute increments and subtly influences the pace of the meeting. Interestingly, an odd start time makes people more likely to show up on time.
3. **Huddle for 15 minutes maximum.** Vrabie suggests, "The shorter your team huddle, the better." If huddles go on too long, you'll start to get a lot of glazed over looks from staff members who don't need to be part of the discussion, Vrabie warns. As well, your employees may come to dread long-winded huddles. Keep your morning huddles short, sweet, and to the point.
4. **Leave a sign at your front desk.** If you will be unlocking your front door before your morning huddle, be sure that patients who arrive early to your reception area know what's going on. Laura Jamison[9] suggests that you create and display a sign at your front desk that says something like this: "In order to be better prepared for your visit, we are in a brief team meeting. We will be with you promptly at 8:00."
5. **Lead by example.** Arrive at your office at least 15 minutes before your morning huddle begins. Ask each team member to make the

same commitment. Teach your staff to come prepared for the morning huddle, as you do, not simply to show up. Ask your employees to review the day's schedule, to anticipate potential snags and bottlenecks, and to come to the huddle ready to discuss these issues and to work out helping strategies collaboratively.

6. **Include physicians in the daily huddle.** Mayer Levitt[10] suggests, "Ideally I would like to see the doctor arrive first and pass out coffee to the staff members as they arrive! But I will settle for the doctor at least being there on time and ready to participate." Including physicians in the morning huddle clearly demonstrates that they are part of the team.
7. **Rotate huddle leaders.** Levitt suggests that you rotate leaders of the huddle daily or weekly. Doing so gives members of your team an opportunity to practice and refine their meeting facilitation skills and to present material from their own perspective.
8. **Stand.** Ask everyone on your team who is able-bodied to stand during your morning huddle. Standing meetings are typically shorter and more to the point than those in which everyone is seated. As Jamison aptly puts it, a morning huddle "is not a coffee break." Standing will keep the meeting short.
9. **Keep your huddle agenda simple and consistent.** All of your huddles should follow the same basic format. Create an agenda checklist. For example, you can designate two important purposes for your huddle. The first can be to provide a quick snapshot of how your organization or department did the day before. Sharing key figures will help everyone see how well you're progressing toward your goals and what adjustments the team may need to make. A quick review of any snags you experienced in the previous day's schedule can help you to identify and solve ongoing problems. Time to reflect on what you did particularly well can also be helpful.

   The second purpose of the huddle can be to provide valuable information about the patients who are coming in that day and to highlight challenges and changes to the day's schedule. These two agenda items, coupled with some brief spirit-building comments or activities, can make for an effective morning huddle agenda.
10. **Have everyone speak, if only briefly.** Provide an opportunity for each person to share something quickly at each huddle about what they are working on. As Vrabie suggests, "Vocalizing individual status updates in front of the whole team will lead to greater commitment and task

accountability from each team member." If your team is too large to allow everyone to speak each morning, be sure each member of your team speaks at least once each week.

11. **Save bigger problems and discussions for longer meetings.** Problem-solving may require debate, discussion, a thorough review of options, research, and time. When problems threaten to derail your morning huddle, schedule separate meetings to work on them with only those team members who are concerned.
12. **End on time.** Use a cell phone alarm or another device to ensure that you end your meeting when you should. End with a ritual such as a special words you say together that speak to your team values. Make sure you end early enough that everyone has at least five minutes before you begin seeing patients.. That will give your team time to make any changes that were discussed at the huddle and to shift gears.

CHAPTER 7 BONUS FEATURE

EIGHT FUN IDEAS FOR MORNING HUDDLES

If you've been using morning huddles in your healthcare organization for some time, you may be looking for new ways to spice things up. Here are eight fresh and fun ideas for you to try:

1. **Announce a contest.** For example, create and announce a competition with prizes for top performers. Or simply announce that if your team meets a certain goal you'll treat them all to lunch. Another idea: Hold a tongue twister competition. Divide your staff into at least two groups and assign them tongue twisters to memorize. Have one employee recite the assigned tongue twister at each huddle, and time them. The group that takes the least amount of time in total wins the competition.
2. **Teach your employees a new skill that will help them.** This can be a quick lesson that can be completed in under five minutes, such as: How and why to answer the phone with a smile. How to shake hands. How and when to use the patient's name more often in conversation.
3. **Feature one staff member at each huddle.** Give that employee three minutes to share something about themselves that others probably don't know. In time, you'll learn a lot more about one another.

4. **Pair them up.** Ask paired employees to perform a task, such as: Find three new things you have in common. Share one interesting thing that the other person doesn't know about you. Come up with one new and different idea for our staff holiday party.
5. **Tell a lame joke.** You can bring the joke if you like. Or assign your employees the task of preparing and sharing a corny or lame joke with the team. Just be sure that you set some guidelines about what an appropriate joke is.
6. **Sing a song.** It may take a little doing to get your staff to sing with you, but group singing can be a fantastic morale builder. Patriotic songs, favorites like "Take Me Out to the Ballgame," and other easy songs generally encourage singing. Or bring in a karaoke machine and see what happens.
7. **Hold a show-and-tell.** Have one employee per day bring an item to share with the rest of the team. Give them one or two minutes to introduce and talk about the item.
8. **Play a "minute to win it" game.** Ask your employees to compete while performing some simple task for one minute. For example, empty one or more bags of miniature marshmallows or small candies onto a table. Ask everyone to stand around the table, each team member equipped with a pair of chopsticks and a small container. Give your team one minute to see how many marshmallows or candies they can put in their containers, moving only one piece at a time with the chopsticks. The employee with the most items in the container at the end of the minute wins a prize.

CHAPTER 8

Developing Your Staff's Empathy

At first glance, empathy may seem to be a topic that is more suitable for a book about personal, outside-of-work relationships rather than one about healthcare employee development. However, empathy is an extremely important topic for you and your employees because it is connected so closely to the quality of the work you do every day. In fact, it is essential. According to Jessica Stillman,[1] "Having empathy . . . improves your leadership, teaches you to ask the right questions, boosts teamwork, [and] allows you to understand your customers. . . ."

In your healthcare organization, an empathetic staff will get along well with you and with one another and will be in the best position to provide excellent customer service to your patients. In fact, it is hard to imagine working with healthcare employees who are devoid of empathy. Most of us would not want to be employees — let alone patients — of healthcare organizations that hire unempathetic people.

This is all well and good, but it begs several questions: Do we have any control over the empathy we feel? Is empathy a soft skill we simply have or don't have? Is our ability to empathize with others something that we establish in childhood and that is unlikely to change? Can we learn to empathize?

According to Roman Krznaric,[2] an empathy advisor, research suggests that empathy is a habit that we can and should cultivate to improve the quality of our lives, both inside and outside of work. Krznaric says, "Empathy doesn't stop developing in childhood. We can nurture its growth throughout our lives . . . Research in sociology, psychology, history—and my own studies of empathetic personalities over the past 10 years—reveals how we can make empathy an attitude and a part of our daily lives, and thus improve the lives of everyone around us."

Most definitely, your employees can develop their empathy. In this chapter, we will explore precisely how you can help them do it.

WHAT IS EMPATHY?

Empathy is our ability to imagine ourselves in another person's shoes. As Carter McNamara[3] suggests, it is our capacity to understand another's situation, perceptions, and feelings from *their* point of view, not ours, and be able to communicate that understanding back to the person. It is also our ability to use that understanding to guide our own actions.

Empathy is different from sympathy in an important way. Similar to empathy, with sympathy, we recognize and understand another person's perceptions, opinions, and feelings. However, when we sympathize, we find ourselves taking on those same emotions and points of view. For instance, if people we know are sad and we sympathize with them, we become sad too. Their grief becomes our grief, their outrage our outrage, their anger our anger, and so on.

When we are empathetic, however, we are able to understand what others may feel, but we do not ourselves feel those same things. If they grieve, for instance, we understand but we do not ourselves grieve.

Interestingly, empathy is the more useful, desirable, and preferred response in the healthcare organization, both for you and for your employees. McNamara suggests, "If an employee is frustrated and sad, the sympathetic leader would experience the same emotions, resulting in the leader many times struggling with the same issues as the employee. Thus, sympathy can actually get in the way of effective leading."

Likewise, employees who sympathize closely with a frustrated or sad patient or colleague may become so frustrated or sad that they become paralyzed and ineffective. Their emotions may overwhelm them and cloud both their judgment and their ability to act in the moment. Empathy, the preferred response, enables your employees to be understanding, yet allows them to remain much more subjective and effective. Therefore, you want to develop your staff members' empathy, not their sympathy.

One important distinction about empathy is that it is 100% about understanding the other person. It is not necessarily acting as we would wish others to act if we were in the same situation. Krznaric explains, "Don't confuse [empathy] with the Golden Rule, 'Do unto others as you would have them do unto you.' As George Bernard Shaw pointed out, 'Do not do unto others as you would have them do unto you. Their tastes may not be the same.'" Empathy, therefore, is about discovering those tastes, not our own, and acting on them accordingly.

Think of empathy as skilled gift-giving. The goal in giving a thoughtful gift is to give recipients what they want, not what we would want for ourselves. Likewise, when we empathize, we must consider what will be most effective with or wanted by the other person, not what we would want or what would be effective for us.

TEN CHARACTERISTICS OF HIGHLY EMPATHETIC PEOPLE

Nearly all of us are capable of being empathetic. Thankfully, only a small number of people display extremely little empathy or no empathy at all. As Krznaric explains, among these are psychopaths, who have a cognitive ability to enter your mind but form no emotional bond with you. (Think Hannibal Lecter.) As well, Krznaric says, some people with autism spectrum disorders such as Asperger's syndrome have a harder time understanding the emotions and experiences of others.

On the flip side of the coin, there are also relatively few people who can be described as *highly empathetic*. Nonetheless, we can learn a lot from them. Those who have a high level of empathy tend to share the following 10 characteristics. Highly empathetic people:

1. **Accurately identify their own feelings.** We do not always understand ourselves, McNamara suggests. "Many of us are so 'processed' and 'sophisticated' about feelings that we cannot readily identify them in ourselves, much less in others." However, highly empathetic people are in touch with themselves. They can unpack their emotions and understand how they and others are being affected by them.

   McNamara suggests that it will be difficult if not impossible to empathize with others when we are unable to understand what's going on within ourselves. Therefore, self-knowledge is a good place to begin developing the habit of empathy.
2. **Ask.** Highly empathetic people do not assume that they know how others think and feel; they ask. Then they silently compare what

they hear to what they may have thought the responses would be. McNamara suggests that this approach sharpens empathy, but also provides more concrete information about others. This can eliminate a lot of misconceptions.

Beirne[4] adds that a great question to ask others is, "How do you feel about that?" Beirne explains, "Ask genuinely, with good eye contact and strong vocal production." Then pay close attention to the response. That's what highly empathetic people do.

3. **Cultivate curiosity.** Highly empathetic people have an insatiable curiosity about strangers. Krznaric explains, "They will talk to the person sitting next to them on the bus, having retained that natural inquisitiveness we all had as children, but which society is so good at beating out of us."

   Cultivating curiosity requires more than having a brief chat about the weather. It drives us to understand the world inside the head of another person. Chad Fowler[5] adds, "Put down your cell phone. Instead of checking Twitter or reading articles while you wait for the train or are stuck in a traffic jam, look at the people around you and imagine who they might be, what they might be thinking and feeling, and where they are trying to go right now." That's what highly empathetic people do.

4. **Listen and be vulnerable.** Increasing empathy is not simply an intellectual exercise. It comes from interacting with others. That's why highly empathetic people engage in deep and revealing conversations, both by listening and by making themselves vulnerable. Krznaric says, "Highly empathetic people listen hard to others and do all they can to grasp their emotional state and needs, whether it is a friend who has just been diagnosed with cancer or a spouse who is upset at them for working late yet again."

   However, listening alone is not enough. Highly empathetic people are also vulnerable. Krznaric explains, "Removing our masks and revealing our feelings to someone is vital for creating a strong empathetic bond. Empathy is a two-way street."

5. **Expand their circle of empathy.** Highly empathetic people empathize with people they may not even like. For example, they empathize with people whose beliefs they don't share, people they find unappealing, and even those who are their political, social, and religious adversaries.

To do this, Krznaric says, they embrace what he calls *experiential empathy*; they "try on" another person's life. For instance, they may spend their vacations volunteering in a village in a developing country. Or they may attend religious services outside their own faith or political meetings outside their own party. Krznaric suggests that first-hand experience enables highly empathetic people to come to a better place of understanding, which leads them to greater empathy.

McNamara adds that empathy tends to run high in people who have traveled or worked in multicultural environments. Such experiences can lead to significant revelations. As McNamara suggests, until people experience the differences between themselves and others firsthand, their skills in empathy will probably remain "quite limited."

6. **Consume empathy-enhancing media.** Although experiential empathy is important to the development of highly empathetic people, so, too, is what Krznaric[6] calls "travel in your armchair." We are able to transport ourselves into other people's minds with the help of visual art, literature, film, and online social networks, Krznaric says. In fact, we often teach empathy to young children through stories and fables, and even through cartoons, especially when we discuss with them how the characters may have felt, and why. Highly empathetic adults continue to develop their empathy by consuming media that enables them to see the inner workings of another person's mind, Krznaric suggests.
7. **Are often introverted or have introverted tendencies.** Highly empathetic people focus a great deal on others. Judith Orloff[7] suggests that they tend to be introverted and prefer one-to-one contact or small groups. Orloff explains, "Even if empaths are more extroverted, they may prefer to limit how much time they spend in a crowd or at a party."

   Orloff adds that as super-responders, highly empathetic people find that being around people can be draining. Therefore, they periodically need time alone to recharge. Even a brief escape prevents highly empathetic people from experiencing emotional overload, Orloff says.
8. **Focus on feelings, not facts.** Highly empathetic people do not necessarily believe the particulars about what others tell them. They focus more on how the person feels, not on whether what the person says is accurate, just, sensible, or even logical. For example, Fowler explains, "We all have friends and loved ones who complain to us about how they have been treated by other people. It's human nature to complain and it's the duty of a loved one to listen." Highly empathetic people

do not dwell on whether the complainer is justified. They focus on the complainer's feelings, even when he/she/they are in the wrong.

9. **Are sensitive.** Highly empathetic people have highly tuned senses. Their nerves can get frayed by a lot of noise, strong smells, or excessive talking. Orloff says, "Empaths become overwhelmed in crowds, which can amplify their empathy."
10. **Pay attention to what they say.** Empathetic people understand that words are a weapon that can hurt people. Because of this, they are very careful about what they say. When they speak, they do so without judging, demanding, or pointing things out. Okairy Zuniga[8] suggests, "This even means that they'll ask if they can give some advice before sharing it."

WHY YOUR EMPLOYEES MAY NOT BE EMPATHETIC

Empathy takes a significant amount of dedicated work and patience. It is a lot easier and faster for busy employees to focus on themselves rather than on others. Furthermore, empathy can lead your good employees into uncomfortable situations and difficult decisions. Once they know and understand how another person feels, they will be changed in ways that can sometimes be challenging. It will be harder for them to ignore problems.

Empathy also can lead them to take action that they find difficult, unpleasant, or even distasteful. They may find it a lot easier *not* to know how someone feels so they can avoid those challenges.

To make matters worse, some employers discourage their employees' empathy, even though they don't intend to do so. DeLores Pressley[9] warns, "Many organizations are focused on achieving goals no matter what the cost to the employees." As you consider what you can do to encourage and foster empathy in your employees, take an objective look at your own employee assessment practices and the metrics you use to measure employee performance. If employee rewards are linked only to numbers and the bottom line, employees may not value or develop their empathy skills. Why should they? If empathy leads them to difficult challenges and not to raises and promotions, they probably won't.

Remember that employees most often focus their attention on whatever you measure and reward. Although you cannot measure empathy as well as, say, patient retention or collection rates, you can encourage empathy if you link some of your rewards to soft skills. Chief among these soft skills should be your employees' empathy.

HOW BEING EMPATHETIC BENEFITS YOUR EMPLOYEES

Empathetic employees are clearly beneficial to your healthcare organization. In addition, Fowler offers many reasons that your employees should want to develop their empathy for their own benefit. Consider sharing this list with them and discuss it before you introduce new empathy-building activities and discussions.

Specifically, Fowler suggests that empathetic employees:

- Better understand the needs of people around them.
- Treat the people they care about the way they want to be treated.
- More clearly understand how others perceive their words and actions.
- Better understand the unspoken parts of their communication with others.
- Have less interpersonal conflict, both at home and at work.
- Predict more accurately the actions and reactions of people they interact with.
- Learn how to persuade and motivate the people around them.
- More effectively convince others of their points of view.
- Experience the world in higher resolution as they see it through other eyes.
- Find it easier to understand and deal with the negativity of others.
- Are able to be better leaders, better followers, and, most important, better friends.

CHAPTER 8 BONUS FEATURE

THREE EXERCISES TO TEACH EMPATHY YOUR STAFF

Empathy may come easily and naturally to some employees in your healthcare organization, but with much more difficulty and effort for others. Either way, you can help. Jennifer Winter[10] offers three hands-on exercises that you can use with your employees to help them develop their empathy.

These require no costs, little prep work, and can be facilitated in conjunction with your regular staff meetings:

1. **Curious George or Georgina.** We're not all alike, so the more we know about others, the better able we will be to help them.

   How to do this exercise: Assign each employee the task of finding out three specific pieces of information from a complete stranger. Establish a deadline. The precise information can change each time you do the exercise, or it can remain the same. However, the answers must come from conversation. Simply having your employees pepper strangers with questions won't achieve the intended effect.

   They must engage and interact with someone they don't know and figure out how to elicit the responses required within the natural flow of conversation. For example, your employees may have to find out where a person grew up, their favorite food or restaurant, or where they would go on vacation if the sky was the limit. Your employees can come up with the information they must gather or you can give them the assignment.

   Once you reach the deadline, gather your employees together to share what everyone learned and how the conversations impacted them. This exercise can be fun for some but challenging for others. Consider making this a monthly or quarterly exercise.
2. **Weekly highs and lows.** A surprising way to develop our empathy is to allow others to be empathetic toward us.

   How to do this exercise: Gather your employees for a quick stand-up meeting at the end of each week. Ask each employee to share one personal high and one personal low point of their week. You can also share your own highs and lows. Allow a minute or two for discussion following each high and low; however, keep the remarks brief and balanced.

   This exercise is a fast, easy way that any small- to medium-sized team can develop empathy. Divide larger teams into more manageable groups so the exercise can be completed in 10 to 15 minutes.
3. **Active listening/polite eavesdropping.** This exercise requires employees to listen to but not participate in conversations they overhear, creating time for them to listen actively and to practice empathy. However, before sending your employees out to eavesdrop on unsuspecting people, it's important first to express the intent of this exercise.

Remind your employees that the goal is not to invade anyone's privacy, but rather, to pick up on bits of conversations we'd hear in our normal daily lives. They don't need to look for conversations to listen to. Ask them to listen actively to what people are saying within earshot.

How to do this exercise: Ask your employees to pay close attention to conversations they overhear as they go through their usual work and their lives. As they listen, they should identify what they believe the speakers are feeling and how they came to those conclusions. Typically, one week is sufficient time to allow employees to listen actively to at least one conversation. Follow up with a meeting to share observations and insights. Since this exercise requires work outside the office, you may want to try it semi-annually or annually.

CHAPTER 9

Helping Your Employees Become Better Actors

Every good employee who has ever worked successfully in a healthcare organization has had to fake it at times. For example, your employees probably have had to act as though they were interested in what a patient or coworker was telling them, even when they were not. Or they made it seem as though everything was well-in-hand when it wasn't. Or they remained calm and unruffled when they were feeling frustrated, angry, frazzled, or fed up. Or they acted as though they were fully engaged in and enthusiastic about their work when they were tired, sick, or bored and would rather have gone home.

To succeed in any workplace, we must *all* squelch our impulses at times and rely on our acting skills. Gregory Ciotti[1] suggests that employees rely on basic acting skills to maintain their usual "cheery persona," even when they must deal with grumpy, angry, boring, and otherwise challenging people and situations. However, while acting a part can be useful to us, it has a potentially ugly underbelly. We want employees to act professionally; we don't want to encourage them to lie.

Therefore, it's important for us to regard acting in the healthcare organization as a set of skills that can help employees align their outward behavior with their inner truth. For example, we can encourage employees to act calm, centered, interested, and cheerful, and then to find those characteristics within themselves and bring them to the surface. In fact, acting can be a great way to help employees find those parts of themselves that are buried deep inside them. Simply acting a part can help employees become it. The key is to encourage acting that draws on a greater truth than the employee may feel in a moment of anger, frustration, boredom, hurt, or despair.

HELPING YOUR EMPLOYEES FIND THEIR INNER TRUTH

There is an inner actor inside of every healthcare employee. Doug Stevenson[2] explains, "He or she shows up multiple times every day. You play roles. You assume different personas. You will yourself into different states of being in order to accomplish your goals." Your employees can use acting as a tool to call upon different aspects of their personality using different levels of energy and different emotional states at specific times and places for specific purposes. In all of those situations, Stevenson says, "You didn't turn into a phony, you merely dug deep inside and found an inner reserve of talent and skill."

For example, when your employees act as though they are confident when they are not, they can find that kernel of confidence within themselves, nurture it, and help it to flourish. Focusing on the physical manifestations of confidence can help. Specifically, if your employees assume a confident posture, they will start to believe that they are confident.

There is a physiological basis for this transformation. Jane Maria Robbins[3] explains, "Studies from the Dana Alliance for Brain Initiatives show that your physical behavior influences your brain chemistry just as your brain can influence your physical behavior. In other words, the more you stand as if you are self-confident, the more your brain will be convinced that you are."

An employee who stands straight with their shoulders back and down and their chin up will look confident. Employees who sit, stand, and walk with confidence and speak with confident voices encourage their brains to tell them that they are confident. But for this to work, the confidence must have been buried somewhere deep inside them. Acting will help them find that truth and bring it out of them.

10 ACTING TECHNIQUES AND EXERCISES FOR YOUR EMPLOYEES

There are several ways that you can help your good employees to develop their acting skills so they can use them in your healthcare organization. Here are 10 techniques and exercises for you to try with them.

1. **Method acting.** Actors like Robert DeNiro, Hilary Swank, Christian Bale, Kate Winslet, and Leonardo DiCaprio are proponents of method acting. Method actors prepare for roles by involving themselves fully in the characters they play. They use techniques such as sense and memory to achieve realism. Method actors use their own emotions based on past experiences to bring new depth to a part.

   Some of your employees are front-line customer service representatives of your healthcare organization. In that role, they can learn about common patient concerns and problems, empathize with patients, and prepare to help them. But as an Open Mind[4] blog suggests, by applying method acting, they can draw upon their own experiences with customer service representatives from other organizations.

   Exercise: Ask your staff to talk about specific customer service representatives with whom they've interacted on the phone, in writing, and in person. Encourage them to explore the range of emotions those representatives likely felt, including those representatives' concerns about their customers, how they must have felt when things went well and when they didn't, and how good and bad customer service representatives may feel about their jobs. Also help them connect those emotions and physical responses with times when they may have felt and responded in the same or similar ways, whether in the workplace or elsewhere. That work can inform what your employees do when they are face-front with your patients.

2. **Improvisation.** Many seasoned actors use improvisation as a tool to help them prepare for roles. Improv performers don't know what will happen onstage until they're up there. The performers start with a prompt from the audience, making up the story, dialogue, and movements as they go along. Rawley[5] suggests that improvisation can help actors prepare for their roles and develop "a connected flow" with their fellow performers.

   Some actors have the freedom to improvise within their performances and rely upon improvisation to deliver the best performance possible. For example, Richard Gere improvised the famous scene in the film *Pretty Woman* in which he closes the jewelry box he is offering to Julia Roberts, and she laughs exuberantly.

   In your healthcare organization, nearly everything your employees say will be improvised, not scripted for them. You can help them become better at improvisation by leading them through improvisation exercises.

Exercise: Create or ask your staff to create prompts for an improvised scene likely to take place in your healthcare organization. Ask employees to assume the various roles. End the improvisation when you believe the scene has been sufficiently played. Then, have a debriefing session by asking employees what they observed — what went well, what didn't, how they felt at each point in the improvisation, and what they took away from the experience. Participating in regular improvisation exercises will help your employees develop trust in one another. The shared experience also can help them bond as a team.

3. **Stay in character.** Many actors use tricks to help them stay in character. For example, some stay in character as long as they are wearing their stage makeup. Once the makeup is removed, they become their usual selves. Sam Waterston famously parted his hair differently whenever he assumed the role of attorney Jack McCoy on the television series *Law and Order*. According to the website These Are Their Stories,[6] Waterston explains, "I part my hair in real life the way I do in my commercials — on the right . . . When I took the role, I decided to part it on the left side as one step in the process of creating the McCoy character."

   Exercise: Encourage your employees to develop and rely upon a trick, preferably of their own choosing, to help them to stay in character as an employee of your healthcare organization. For example, they can teach themselves to stay in character whenever they are wearing their name tags. That way, the act of putting on and taking off the name tag cues them that they are going into or getting out of "character."

4. **Stay in the moment.** It's so easy when we interact with others to focus on what we want to say and to let our minds wander. Actors do many things to help them stay completely in the moment. As Jesse Scinto[7] explains, actors need to pay attention to everything that is going on around them. Scinto explains, "Everything's moving so fast, you may have missed the most interesting thing. The audience may have heard it, and if you missed it you haven't really driven the scene forward, you don't know what to react to."

   It can be challenging for your employees to stay in the moment in your healthcare organization. They may be juggling many balls and have a lot on their minds. Exercises that can help them practice staying in the moment may help them during crunch time in your organization and when they are distracted with personal problems.

Exercise: Put your employees in pairs and have them face one another. Ask one member of each pair to be the leader, the other the follower. Instruct the leaders to move their bodies slowly and deliberately, continuing to face their partners, while the partners mirror their movements. After sufficient time, ask the pairs to switch roles. Debrief your employees to give them a chance to explore what it felt like to be fully in the moment, and how they can be more in the moment when they perform their roles in your healthcare organization.

5. **Active listening.** Active listening is a direct upshot of staying in the moment, though it focuses more on words than actions. It is a vital tool actors use to rehearse, to perform, and in their auditions. Craig Wallace[8] explains:

   "I've been in casting rooms over the years where the decision as to who will get the job is in a seemingly unbreakable stalemate based on the reading. Half the room is convinced Actor A is the best choice and the other half feels as strongly about Actor B. One way I've seen the tie broken is to watch the tape of the two people again and turn the sound down to see who had the more connected listening and brighter reactions. It never failed to be a unanimous decision after that."

   More than half an actor's job is listening and reacting, Wallace says. The same is true of your employees. More than half of their jobs is listening to your patients, coworkers, managers, and doctors, and reacting appropriately.

   Exercise: A good first exercise in active listening can be one in which you model active and distracted listening. Lindsay Price[9] uses the following exercise to get her acting students to work with one another within a drama class context.

   To begin, ask one employee to come to the front of your meeting space and instruct them to start a conversation with you on a topic. It may be helpful to give the employee a topic, such as, "What is your favorite type of music and why?" As the employee talks, model the difference between a distracted listener and an active listener, using nonverbal and verbal cues. Afterward, ask the observers on your staff to describe the specific behaviors they saw for both the distracted and active listening, as well as any observations they have about how the listening seemed to affect the speaker. Then ask the employee who took part in the conversation with you to compare what it was like to try to talk to someone who was distracted versus someone who was listening actively. Ask your employees when and how they can use active listening techniques in their jobs.

6. **Personal experience.** Actors who are preparing for a role sometimes design experiences for themselves in which they come as close to the character as possible. For instance, entertainment business website WhatCulture[10] reports that Marlon Brando prepared to play a wounded World War II veteran in the film *The Men* by spending almost a month confined to a ward in an army hospital. During that time, Brando used a wheelchair as his only means of getting around. Likewise, WhatCulture reports that Daniel Day Lewis prepared for his role in *The Last of the Mohicans* by spending months living alone in the wilderness. Day Lewis survived by hunting for all of his meals and he even taught himself to build a canoe.

   Of course, these are extreme examples that required unusual physical fortitude, stick-to-itiveness, and a significant investment of time. Nonetheless, healthcare employees can craft smaller-scale experiences for themselves that will prepare them for the roles they play in your organization.

   Exercise: Ask your employees to design experiences for themselves that will put them as close as possible to the experiences of your patients. For example, they may call a business or another healthcare organization, ask questions, and see how they are treated. They may spend time sitting in your reception area imagining that they are waiting for an appointment with nothing to do but to read your magazines and watch the clock. Or they may interact with a customer service representative in person at a store to resolve a problem and imagine how a patient in your healthcare organization would feel when trying, similarly, to resolve a problem.

   Ask your employees to share their experiences at your staff meetings. Guide each employee to describe not only the experience, but also their feelings about what happened. Help your employees connect their experiences with those of your patients. Explore what they can do to create the best experiences possible for them.

7. **Character research.** Actors often undertake extensive research to prepare for their roles, especially if the characters they are going to play are based on real people or if they are set in another time in history. For instance, Forest Whitaker underwent an extremely thorough research process to prepare to play the role of Ugandan dictator Idi

Amin in *The Last King of Scotland*, WhatCulture reports. Whitaker moved to Uganda to breathe in the atmosphere and politics of the nation in which the film is set. There, Whitaker met with many of Amin's relatives, former generals, friends, and victims in an attempt to build up a broad and unbiased portrait of Amin.

Whitaker also was reported to have read dozens of books about Amin, WhatCulture says. Your employees are not going to move to another country to prepare for their role in your healthcare organization. However, you can guide them to conduct their own research.

Exercise: Task your employees with undertaking at least one research project to help them to prepare for and better understand their roles in your healthcare organization. For example, they might identify a colleague in your organization or in another one who they believe does an excellent job and interview that person to learn more about they do and why. Or they might read a book or books, listen to audio programs, or watch videos to help them learn more about what it takes to do their jobs well. You may even select a book for your entire staff to read or videos for them to watch, choosing titles that support their work in your healthcare organization.

Help your staff to connect their research to their jobs. Ask them to identify how they felt about what they learned and how that will influence them as they move through their day-to-day tasks.

8. **Shadowing.** Actors sometimes prepare for their roles by spending time shadowing people who resemble the characters they will play. For example, Elizabeth[11] reports that Jack Nicholson prepared for his role in *One Flew Over the Cuckoo's Nest* by being paired with mental patients in a hospital so he could shadow their day-to-day lives. Likewise, Emily Zemler[12] reports, Day Lewis prepared to play Christy Brown in *My Left Foot* by shadowing disabled patients at Sanymount School Clinic.

   Of course, actors don't hold the monopoly on shadowing; many workplaces use job shadowing. However, shadowing typically is done with new employees or when employees are training for new roles. This is unfortunate because employees can benefit from a shadowing exercise at any point in their careers.

   Exercise: Encourage each employee in your healthcare organization to design a unique job shadowing experience. Ideally, ask the employee to spend one full day — or at least a half-day — shadowing another person. It's important that your employees have sufficient time to shadow the individual to observe how they face and handle a variety of challenges. The individual to be shadowed could be within your healthcare organization or could be in another one. Or, have your employees shadow customer service professionals in other industries.

Prepare your employees for the shadowing exercise by instructing them to brainstorm questions to ask. Suggest that they take a notebook and pen with them so they can take notes about what they observe throughout the exercise. After the shadowing, bring your staff together to share their experiences with one another. Ask each employee to give an oral report of their observations and to discuss best and worst practices observed.

Help your employees link their shadowing exercise to what they do in your healthcare organization every day. Encourage them to focus on takeaways and lessons learned from the shadowing experience.

9. **Voice work.** Most actors take vocal training to help them use their voices effectively for the parts they will play. They learn to speak clearly, expressively, and pleasingly, and in ways that engage their audiences. For example, *Backstage*[13] reports that Kunal Nayyar, well known for his role in *The Big Bang Theory,* studied the Fitzmaurice Voicework Technique®,[14] which combines adaptations of classical voice training with modifications of yoga, shiatsu, bioenergetics, energy work, and many other disciplines. And according to Ajay Kingman,[15] Lauren Bacall, who was known for her deep and resonant voice, wasn't born that way. Wingman says, "She was born with a shrill and unpleasant voice, but took up the challenge and undertook extra effort to transform it."

   Your employees use their voices in your healthcare organization every day. It would be beneficial for them to develop their voices for the work they do, just as actors do.

   Exercise: There are many vocal exercises that you can use with your staff. Here's one that Kingman recommends that can help them deepen their voices.

   Lead your staff in singing a song. After they've sung it once, ask them to sing it a second time, this time a little louder but without lifting their faces up to sing louder. Rather, ask them to sing at a higher volume, but with their faces intentionally tilted down and their voices at the lowest part of their natural registers. That will train them to speak at a lower pitch, Kingman says. This exercise requires regular practice.

Therefore, sing together with your staff often, perhaps at the start or end of each of your staff meetings. A bonus is that communal singing is an excellent way to build goodwill and increase morale.

10. **Body work.** Actors pay a great deal of attention to the way they use their bodies. Many study movement techniques to help them hone their craft. KC Wright[16] explains, "Great actor training focuses on the whole instrument: voice, mind, heart, and body."

    Wright recommends a number of movement-based methods that all actors should study. One method Wright recommends, the Suzuki method, teaches that acting "begins and ends with the feet" and includes controlled forms of stomping and squatting. Wright also recommends the Williamson technique, which draws upon the five senses, and the Jacques LeCoq method, which uses a mix of mime, mask work, and other movement techniques to develop creativity and freedom of expression.

    Of course, you are working with healthcare employees, not actors, and you are probably not in a position to teach these and other movement techniques. Nonetheless, you may be able to use body work exercises with your employees to help them be more effective in their roles with patients.

    Exercise: Your employees already know that body language is a powerful communication tool. Draw upon this foundation of knowledge. At a staff meeting, ask two employees to participate in a role play, one playing the part of a patient who has a problem or complaint, the other as an employee in your healthcare organization. After a first attempt at the scene, ask them to sit or stand closer to one another and repeat the scene, this time focusing on ways to express physically what they are saying.

    Debrief the two employees by asking them to explore how the change in distance and body language affected them. Then ask participants to share their observations about both scenes. Discuss how they can apply lessons learned through this exercise in your healthcare organization every day.

WHAT ROLES DO YOUR EMPLOYEES PLAY?

Each of us chooses to play different roles in different situations. According to Linda Sherwin,[17] "Some [roles] are conscious choices at the time, and some are simply an unconscious but learned reaction to the moment." Actors work hard in the initial steps of role preparation to figure out how to become the character in the moment, Sherwin says. Likewise, your employees need to identify their various roles and when they need to play each one, so they will be prepared to play them when needed.

Sherwin suggests as an exercise that employees brainstorm all of the roles that they play throughout a day, week, and month in your healthcare organization. Sherwin says, "To identify as many as possible, you need to take the time as you go about your day to mark down the roles you are playing."

For example, an employee in your healthcare organization may answer the phone, process insurance paperwork, check inventory, or prepare an examination room. But they also may focus on the personal and not task-oriented roles played throughout the day such as supporter, listener, team player, leader, problem solver, role model, friend, advocate, authority, teacher, coach, or consultant. This list-making takes a little time, Sherwin warns, but it is beneficial. Sherwin explains, "Often, people are surprised when they realize the various roles that they play." They may be surprised, too, at how vital each of these roles is to their success.

Help your employees identify the roles they play in one situation that would be transferable to and useful in another, Sherwin says. An employee who is a good listener with your patients, for instance, may see that they can be a good listener at your staff meetings, too.

CHAPTER 9 BONUS FEATURE

ACTING SKILLS FOR HEALTHCARE LEADERS

Like their employees, healthcare leaders can benefit from having well-developed acting skills. Stephson[18] suggests, "Managers need to always be aware of how they present themselves and the impact of their behaviors on their subordinates." She suggests three common and challenging managerial scenarios to illustrate this point (see the table below). Healthcare leaders can identify the roles they may play in each scenario and then carefully select the one that will yield the best results with their employees.

Challenge	Details	Your Best Role
An employee has repeatedly performed or behaved poorly, despite your many discussions with them about the problem.	You're frustrated and angry. However, you don't want to show it to the employee. You want to stay on an even keel no matter what.	Calm, firm, and clear setter of expectations.
You're having a really bad day.	You don't want to be cranky, angry, whiny, icy, or curt with your employees. And you don't want your employees to think that you are an unpredictable roller coaster leader who has lots of ups and downs.	The consistent grown-up.
You click with some of your employees, but not with others.	Your tendency would be to favor those you prefer and who are easy to get along with, and to steer clear of the others. However, you know that playing favorites is not the best strategy for a healthcare leader.	The parent who cares about all of their children equally.

CHAPTER 10

Teaching Your Staff to Reframe Negatives into Positives

"What's wrong?" "Are you dissatisfied?" "What's the problem?" "Are you confused?" "I'm sorry, I don't understand you." "You're not being reasonable." "There's no need for you to be rude to me." "We can't do that for you." "*No.* The answer is *no*."

Do you cringe when you hear your staff use negative phrases such as these in your healthcare organization? If you don't, you may want to rethink that. According to Andrew Newburg and Mark Waldman,[1] negative words are the most dangerous words in the world. That's because they worsen the way people feel and function emotionally and physically.

Newburg and Waldman explain, "If I were to put you into an fMRI scanner...and flash the word 'NO' for less than one second, you'd see a sudden release of dozens of stress-producing hormones and neurotransmitters. These chemicals immediately interrupt the normal functioning of your brain, impairing logic, reason, language processing, and communication." In fact, just seeing a list of negative words for a few seconds will make a highly anxious or depressed person feel worse.

The more a depressed person ruminates on negative words, the more damage will be done to key structures that regulate memory, feelings, and emotions, Newburg and Waldman warn. Negative words can ultimately disrupt sleep, appetite, and even a person's ability to experience long-term happiness and satisfaction. On top of that, negative words lead to negative thinking, which is self-perpetuating. "The more you engage in negative dialogue — at home or at work — the more difficult it becomes to stop," Newburg and Waldman say.

Clearly, then, negative language brings with it a host of physical and emotional problems. It will undermine good customer service in your healthcare organization, too. But it can also make your organization an unhappy, stressful, and miserable place to work. So how can you get your employees to stop speaking negatively, even when your patients speak negatively to them? How can you encourage the use of more positive language without forcing your staff to sound like they're reading from an overly upbeat and insincere customer service script?

The answer is: First, get your good employees to want to reframe their communication, then teach them how to do it. According to Carter McNamara,[2] "Reframing is seeing the current situation from a different perspective, which can be tremendously helpful in problem solving, decision making, and learning." The key is for your employees to believe that that's true and to regard reframing as a truthful and empowering new way to look at things.

When the healthcare organization's employees learn to reframe negative ways of communicating into sincere positive ways, they do not change the basic situation or problem; they change the way that they and others look at it. Brenda Hooper[3] explains, "The purpose of reframing is...to shift the person's feeling about the issue/problem."

Reframing makes the most of positive language (and congruent body language) to reinforce positive yet accurate messages. It can help your good employees shift your patients, the other members of your staff, and even themselves away from anger, frustration, and blame, and move gently and steadily toward openness, satisfaction, and gratitude. Fortunately, as you'll see in this chapter, reframing can be taught, practiced, and learned.

FIVE WAYS THAT REFRAMING CAN IMPROVE YOUR HEALTHCARE ORGANIZATION

Although negative language has all of the disadvantages just described, reframing to more positive language offers equally powerful benefits. According to Conversational Receptionists,[4] "Not only do positive words encourage and motivate others more effectively than negative words, but they also help forge meaningful connections between the speaker and receiver." Reframing language from negative to positive leads to:

1. **Less patient conflict.** The wrong words can put a tense patient on the defensive and make a bad situation worse. "When you start every

interaction with positive language, you'll experience less conflict overall," according to Conversational Receptionists.

2. **Better relationships with your patients.** With fewer instances of conflict, better relationships and connections can be formed. Reframing paves the way for building the connections with your patients that are necessary for creating and fostering their loyalty.
3. **Faster resolution times.** Miscommunication, patients' perceptions of negative language, and allowing an angry patient to take control may result in longer resolution times. However, as Conversational Receptionists suggests, "Using positive communication from the start... can keep the conversation focused on the issue at hand and resolve it faster."
4. **Improved reputation.** Less conflict will create better relationships and faster resolution times. Therefore, patients will be more satisfied in general with your healthcare organization. Satisfied patients are more likely to remain loyal to your organization and to recommend you to their friends, colleagues, and family. That ultimately leads to improved patient retention and a better reputation for your healthcare organization.
5. **Stronger culture for your healthcare organization.** The changes that occur as a result of reframing negative language can create a stronger organizational culture that is unified toward a common goal. When your employees can see for themselves the positive changes that occur with positive language, they will be more invested in what you do. That, in turn, creates a stronger loyalty to your culture with more faith in your organization and its inner workings, Conversational Receptionists suggests.

HELP YOUR STAFF SEE THE VALUE IN REFRAMING

Despite these advantages, it will do little good for you to give your staff a list or chart of reframing words and phrases and require them to start using them. If you do that, you may be able to get them to say the right words; however, you cannot get them to mean them. Unfortunately, insincere positive language is easy to detect. A phony, overly positive style of communicating can sound like the speaker is out of touch with reality. It can easily come off as uncaring and condescending and backfire by fanning the flames of anger and hostility.

Therefore, the first step in introducing reframing to your staff will be for you to share how negative and positive communication affects others. Help your staff recognize that communicating negatively almost always works against what they are trying to accomplish. Explain that using positive words and phrases can enhance patient engagement, increase satisfaction, and reduce patient ambivalence. Also help them to see how reframing their negative language can be beneficial and how it can make your healthcare organization a happier place for everyone. In other words, bring your staff along with you on this journey.

TEACH YOUR STAFF TO REFRAME

As a next step, introduce reframing as both a concept and a tool your employees can use with your patients. Share with your staff a quote that supports reframing, such as this one from Justyna Polacyzak[5]: "The most important rule of verbal communication is to forget 'no, 'can't' and 'don't,' as these are the worst words that can be said [to a patient]." Discuss with your staff whether they agree and why.

Make sure that your employees understand that reframing does not require them to lie or to do something that feels false. Rather, reframing encourages them to look for and discover true, accurate, and positive new ways to look at things. Then offer them some examples. For instance, ask them to suggest truthful, positive ways to reframe typical negative communication such as:

- "No. We have no openings next Tuesday."
- "No. We can't do that."
- "I don't know the answer."
- "Well, I'm not the one who told you that/established this policy/made that mistake."
- "You don't have things right."

Explore with your staff how they feel about the negative and the more positive reframe of each phrase. Be open to what they say. Remember that they must feel comfortable with the concept of reframing before they can use it effectively in your healthcare organization.

An excellent way to reinforce the value of reframing with your employees is to use role playing to demonstrate the power of both negative and positive language. A good place to begin is to ask an employee to participate in a role play with you in which you play the part of an employee and the employee plays the part of an angry patient. Suggest one or more scenarios or ask your employees for suggestions. Encourage the employee playing the part of the patient to be forceful but realistic.

In the first role play, respond negatively to the "patient." Focus your language on what you can't do, what the patient can't do, problems, what the patient is doing wrong, how unreasonable the patient is being, and how bad the situation is. Then, do a quick debrief. Ask the staff to give you examples of your negative responses. Ask the employee who played the part of the patient to describe their feelings about the negative communication.

Then, do a second role play, asking the same employee to behave the same way. This time, respond with more positive and constructive language. Again, debrief your employees. Ask the staff to give you examples of your positive responses. Ask the employee who played the part of the patient to describe their feelings about the more positive communication. Describe the truth in your positive reframes. Draw from your staff the lessons they learned through this role play. Offer to do a second or third set of role plays as need, interest, and time permit.

Going forward, share examples of positive language for reframes and give your employees opportunities to practice using them through additional role plays. You may need several sessions with your staff to allow the lessons to sink in and to provide ample practice time. While your employees are learning to reframe, ask them to pay closer attention to their day-to-day interactions, especially with patients or colleagues who are confused, displeased, or angry.

With practice, your staff will begin to identify opportunities for reframing in their daily activities. They will become increasingly more comfortable reframing their communication and will eventually master the technique.

TEACH YOUR STAFF TO FOCUS ON WHAT THEY *CAN* DO

As your employees become more comfortable with and adept at reframing, they will be able to express themselves more frequently with positive language. However, there will be times when they just can't give your patients what they would like. In such instances, they may be tempted to focus on words like *unfortunately, but*, and *I'm sorry.* However, as Gao[6] suggests, such words still express a negative thought. They focus your patient's attention on what can't happen.

Of course, a sincere, well-deserved apology is always a good idea. In addition, Gao suggests that you teach your staff not to leave the communication on a sour note if there is a legitimate way to end things more positively. Teach your employees to focus their communication whenever possible on what they *can* do, Gao says, not to leave things stuck on what they *can't*.

For example, if a caller can't be fit into the schedule that day, the employee should provide the soonest appointment and offer to put the patient on a short notice call list in case of a cancellation. Or, if the patient objects to paying for services the day of the appointment, the employee can require that day's payment but offer to work out a payment plan for future appointments, if your policy allows for that.

Or, if you are behind schedule and the patient complains about the wait, the employee can offer to reschedule the appointment or suggest that the patient leave your office and return in 45 minutes or an hour. Never let patients leave before they know all of their options. They may not get their first choice, Gao says, but they may end up feeling much better about things if they believe your office is doing something for them or giving them a choice.

GIVE STAFF REINFORCEMENT FOR REFRAMING AND USING POSITIVE LANGUAGE

Becoming expert in reframing negatives into positives takes time. Along the way, be sure to offer additional training and support as employees expand and hone their skills. Highlight and praise the good examples of reframing that you observe. Continue to design role plays and encourage your staff to analyze their daily interactions with patients and with one another. When you catch your good employees slipping back into negative language, consider these to be teachable moments. Ask your employees to revisit those interactions and explore more positive phrasing.

Of course, an effective way for you to stress the importance of reframing negatives into positives in your healthcare organization is to include it in employees' performance appraisals. Employees will take notice of what you measure and what you reward. Be mindful, however, that you will not be privy to every conversation your employees have with your patients. It will be hard for you to quantify improvement. One possible strategy is to ask employees to establish reframing goals and to self-assess their progress. That, along with your own observations and positive reinforcement, can help employees become masterful reframers.

Finally, good employees who have excellent reframing skills may find that they can reframe their thinking as well as their language. They can learn to reframe their own perceived weaknesses, job stress, and other potentially negative challenges as positives. For example, if employees were to stop calling themselves *impulsive* and instead referred to themselves as *spontaneous,* they would be reframing a weakness as a potential strength.

Recruitment firm Pinnacle[7] suggests, "It wouldn't be surprising if reframing employee weaknesses made for a stronger and more productive workforce." In addition to making employees potentially more productive, reframing also can be an effective stress manager. According to Pinnacle, "Reframing aids employees in not only seeing themselves in the best light, but also situations." With reframing practice, employees may come to see that *problem* and *opportunity* are two sides of the same coin.

As Elizabeth Scott[8] aptly put it, "Reframing is a way of changing the way you look at something and, thus, changing your experience of it. It can turn a stressful event into either a major trauma or a challenge to be bravely overcome. Or it can depict a really bad day as a mildly low point in an overall wonderful life. Or it can see a negative event as a learning experience."

Clearly, reframing offers potential benefits in customer service within your healthcare organization and for your employee personally.

THE TOP 25 REFRAMING WORDS FOR CUSTOMER SERVICE

One way you can help your good employees reframe their negative communication is by providing them with positive words to use. The website Call Centre Helper[9] has devised the following list of the top 25 reframing words for your employees, suggesting "These little words should win medals, as adding any one of them to a conversation has the potential to transform [negative or] average customer service into great customer service." Here's the list:

Word	Example
Definitely	I definitely will make sure that....
Absolutely	I absolutely agree with you.
Certainly	I can certainly help you.
Exactly	That is exactly right.
Completely	I completely agree with you.
Quickly	I will quickly run through this with you.
Fantastic	That is a fantastic alternative.
Great	Great news!
Marvelous	That's a marvelous choice.
Excellent	That is an excellent suggestion.
Enjoy	I hope you enjoy your....
Splendid	Splendid! All that is left to do now....
Essential	Yes, it is essential that you....
Generous	You have been very generous with your time....
Recommend	I can highly recommend....
Friendly	Thank you. We aim to provide friendly service to our patients.
Impressive	That's certainly impressive, Ms. Anderson.
Interesting	That is an interesting idea.
Brilliant	Brilliant! I'm glad we're on the same page.
Exciting	Yes. It is an exciting prospect.
Terrific	I think that it's a terrific option.
Fascinating	That is absolutely fascinating.
Expert	You are certainly an expert on this.
Favorite	That is personally my favorite option.
Ideal	It would be ideal, considering your situation.

Call Centre Helper suggests that using these reframing words in conversations can make your employees sound upbeat and highly energetic. But is there such a thing as reframing language that's too upbeat? "You'll never hear a customer complain about how the employee was too positive or upbeat," Call Centre Helper says.

CHAPTER 10 BONUS FEATURE

10 POSITIVE PHRASES FOR YOUR EMPLOYEES TO USE

How else can your employees turn sour interactions with patients into positive ones? The Conversational website[10] offers 10 positive phrases your employees can use to "spread a little kindness." As Conversational suggests, your employees can write down their favorites from this list and put them somewhere in the office where they (and not patients) will see them. Posting their favorites from the list below will remind them to put their new positive words and phrases into frequent use.

Phrase	Why It is Important
It's my pleasure.	Offering great service means "taking a servant position." This phrase suggests that your employees are happy to serve your patients. It means the most when employees say this with a genuine smile.
I'd be happy to recommend....	This phrase establishes the employee's expertise and leaves patients impressed with your service.
Thanks for choosing us.	Your patients may have had a choice and chose you. This phrase acknowledges this and allows your employees to express their gratitude on your behalf.
I'll find a solution.	We all want to know that we will be taken care of. This phrase reassures patients that the employee will personally take care of them, even if the solution is not yet evident.
What is most convenient for you?	In some instances, patients may feel that what they want doesn't matter. This phrase demonstrates that your patients' convenience matters to you and that it is a priority.
You made my day.	Who doesn't love to hear this? This phrase will brighten your patient's day. It succinctly expresses how much your employee appreciates his/her/their cooperation, positive attitude, or compliment.
How can we make this right?	This phrase gives the patient a chance to participate in the solution.
I completely agree with you.	We all want to be heard and acknowledged. This phrase can quickly calm a patient who is upset or angry.
I'm on it!	An enthusiastic phrase such as this one demonstrates to your patients that the employee is not only ready to assist them, but excited about doing so.
We will figure this out.	Patients want to be reassured. This phrase buys time and encourages patience when it will take time for your employee to come up with a solution to a complex problem.

CHAPTER 11

Fostering a Culture of Gratitude in Your Healthcare Organization

Quite a bit of scholarly and popular literature suggests that being grateful is good for us. For instance, *Psychology Today*[1] reports that over time, feeling grateful boosts our happiness and fosters our physical and psychological health, and that "Studies show that practicing gratitude curbs the use of words expressing negative emotions and shifts inner attention away from negative emotions such as resentment and envy."

Likewise, Harvard Health Publishing[2] cites several research studies that suggest that gratitude is strongly and consistently associated with greater happiness. A *Harvard Health Publishing* blog concludes, "Gratitude helps people feel more positive emotions, relish good experiences, improve their health, deal with adversity, and build strong relationships." In addition, Jamie Ducharme[3] suggests numerous benefits that come with practicing gratitude including better impulse control, better decision making, and more patience.

Finally, Susan Pierce Thompson,[4] a cognitive scientist who specializes in the psychology of eating, suggests that gratitude can reduce our overeating. In turn, Thompson says, "People who are more grateful get sick less often, they exercise more, they get better sleep for longer on average, they're 25% happier, they're 20% more generous with their time and with their money, they have better relationships, [and] they're more forgiving." In short, if there were a drug that offered those benefits, Thompson says, whoever patented that drug would be very, very rich.

Is it any wonder, then, that we have seen a proliferation of gratitude-themed publications, calendars, keychains, t-shirts, coffee mugs, magnets, podcasts, memes, and apps? Go into any card or gift shop or shop online these days, and you're likely to see a plethora of gratitude-themed products for sale. Do an online search and you will find coaches, psychologists, and authors galore teaching us why and how to practice gratitude.

Clearly, as our world becomes increasingly more complex and as our stress rises, we are attracted to the simple idea that gratitude can make us happier and healthier. But can gratitude promise equally powerful benefits to a healthcare organization? And, if it can, how can healthcare leaders develop and foster a culture of gratitude among their good employees without it feeling contrived, insincere, and maybe more than a little saccharine?

THE BENEFITS OF GRATITUDE IN YOUR HEALTHCARE ORGANIZATION

Practicing gratitude has benefits that extend beyond the individual's personal health and wellbeing. Grateful employees experience boosts in dopamine resulting in fewer sick days, greater optimism, increased self-esteem, and increased energy at work. They also demonstrate better stress management, more resilience, better decision-making, reduced aggression, and better relationships with their coworkers. Grateful employees also self-regulate their behaviors and are likely to remain honest and true, even when there is opportunity to stray.

They also tend to be good team players. Peter Economy[5] says, "Gratitude encourages social and moral behavior while discouraging disruptive behavior." Simply put, he suggests, grateful employees are "better corporate citizens."

The power of gratitude increases significantly in organizations that demonstrate sincere gratitude for their employees. A grateful leader or manager can increase productivity, employee retention, wellness, and engagement. Christine Riordan[6] explains, "When employees feel valued, they have high job satisfaction, are willing to work longer hours, engage in productive relationships with coworkers and supervisors, are motivated to do their best, and work towards achieving the company's goals."

In fact, employees who feel that their employers are grateful for their contributions are more likely to develop a glass-half-full attitude about their work, even when faced with adversity. As Kelly Siegel[7] suggests, employees who experience gratitude will focus their attention on what they already have, rather than on what they want.

Fortunately, gratitude is an employee development tool that does not cost a lot of money and does need not to take a great deal of time. And once you establish a culture of gratitude in your healthcare organization, it can be easy to maintain. Siegel suggests, "Gratitude is viral, so once people see appreciation catching, they are likely to jump in and keep it going." Feeling grateful in your healthcare organization is something that every employee — and every patient —can do.

Cultivating gratitude may be accelerated when the healthcare leader demonstrates and models gratitude personally and on behalf of the organization. Jeremy Adam Smith[8] suggests, "Employees need to hear 'thank you' from the boss first. That's because expressing gratitude can make some people feel unsafe, particularly in a workplace with a history of ingratitude." It's up to the person or people with power in your healthcare organization to say "thank you" clearly, authentically, and consistently, Smith says, and in both public and private settings.

10 WAYS TO ESTABLISH A CULTURE OF GRATITUDE

When a healthcare leader takes the time to recognize the modest acts that can so easily go unnoticed, they encourage others to do the same. Don't wait for the big opportunities to present themselves. Karl Sun[9] suggests, "People might feel uncomfortable calling out the sometimes seemingly insignificant things people do. But it's a snowball effect — the more you express gratitude, the more natural and almost subconscious it becomes." Of course, a manager who says "thank you" is off to a good start in expressing gratitude. However, a culture of gratitude relies on much more than that.

Following are 10 guidelines for effectively expressing gratitude to your good employees:

1. **Make it specific.** Of course you can issue blanket statements such as, "Thanks so much for all you do." However, your expressions of gratitude will be much more meaningful and effective if you focus your remarks on particular acts. For example, don't just thank your employees after an especially hard day when you're understaffed or

when your schedule is strained by emergencies. Rather, thank them specifically for working through lunch, for staying late, for working so well as a team, for keeping their thoughts positive, and for keeping all the balls in the air despite the tremendous challenges of the day. Your employees will appreciate those thanks much more because they will see that you cared enough and paid close enough attention to them to know what they had to do to make the day work. As Sun suggests, "Calling out the specifics means so much more."

2. **Be creative.** Traditional expressions of gratitude to employees such as retirement parties and employee appreciation programs can be effective, but dig deeper to find your own ways to express gratitude. The Academy of Management[10] suggests, "More creative and pervasive efforts can work better." For example, why not start each staff meeting by expressing your gratitude for some quality about each person in the room? Or ask for volunteers to express gratitude for someone else at the meeting. These can be powerful ways to foster gratitude because they allow employees to participate.
3. **Do it daily.** If you stand up in a staff meeting once a quarter and rattle off a scripted thank you, your employees will see right through that half-hearted attempt. Your thanks won't mean much. Instead, make gratitude a daily habit. Sun suggests, "Set a goal to thank someone for something specific each day." When you take the time to go out of your way to do so, he says, people will know you are genuine, and you'll see significant improvements in staff morale.
4. **Make your gratitude inclusive, not competitive.** Of course, some employees will perform better than others, and some will be more likeable than others. You will no doubt have your favorites. However, the Academy of Management warns, employee gratitude works best when it focuses on effort and perseverance rather than on a competitive metric or favoritism. Reward excellent performance with bonuses and raises and with opportunities for promotion. But be grateful for and express that gratitude to everyone on your staff who works hard and who tries. As the Academy succinctly puts it, "Avoid envy among workers by applying your gratitude programs to everyone."
5. **Be grateful for the big and small.** It's easy to take note of big efforts and big successes. It can be much harder to pick out the employee who quietly took on extra work for a sick coworker or an employee who spent their weekend hand-cutting Halloween decorations to put up in

your office on Monday morning. Be grateful for all of the above. For larger staffs, you may need to enlist the help of others to know who has done what behind the scenes. Sun suggests, "Be aware that gratitude for the smaller actions often needs to be encouraged at the team level."

6. **Don't just recognize — thank.** Don't just recognize employees for what they accomplished and ask for a round of applause. "Actually express gratitude for all the work they put into it," Sun suggests. Again, be as specific as you can. Use words like *thankful* and *grateful.*
7. **Be grateful for individual effort, but also for teamwork.** The Academy of Management suggests, "Avoid fostering too much pride or a sense of entitlement. Emphasize appreciation for teamwork and the need to give as well as receive gratitude." Excessive pride can hinder collaboration.
8. **Teach your staff how to accept gratitude.** Some members of your staff may naturally dismiss the gratitude they receive. They may say that what they did was not that important or point to others who they say did more. It can be difficult for some of us to receive expressions of gratitude. Try this exercise if you find this is the case: Pair up your employees and ask them take turns saying something complimentary to each other. Instruct the one who is receiving the praise, compliment, or gratitude to say, "thank you" and nothing else. Ask the pair to maintain eye contact throughout the exchange. With practice, your employees will learn how to accept compliments and gratitude more comfortably. More importantly, they will learn to believe in and absorb the gratitude being given to them.
9. **Make it easy to express gratitude.** Perhaps you can reserve a few minutes at your staff meetings for expressing gratitude. Or why not establish a way for your employees to recognize and appreciate the contributions of a coworker in writing? Sun reports that office managers in his organization keep thank-you cards available at the front desk for anyone to use. Sun suggests, "A handwritten note means worlds more than an email." Whatever you do, make it easy for your employees to express their gratitude to one another, especially if they are shy about doing so face to face.
10. **Don't assume.** Our gratitude may be so obvious to us that we assume that it must be obvious to the other person as well. David Ludden[11] refers to this as the "curse of knowledge." He explains, "If you know something, it's hard to imagine that other people don't know it as well." "It's obvious," we say. However, nothing is ever obvious. Your employees

can't read your mind or know what is in your heart. As a corollary to this, Ludden warns, people often think that they can read your mind and make inferences about what you're thinking and feeling, but they are mistaken. Therefore, don't assume that your employees know that you are grateful for their contributions. Express your gratitude and you will clarify a lot of misunderstanding.

MAKING YOUR GRATITUDE FEEL GENUINE, NOT CONTRIVED OR SACCHARINE

If you haven't been generous with your gratitude in the past, your staff may be surprised and suspicious when you suddenly change. Therefore, be careful when you begin to dole out the compliments and thanks. Otherwise, your gratitude may sound false, overly sweet, and forced.

Tread lightly with new, formal gratitude initiatives. The Academy of Management warns, "Employees might regard a 'gratitude initiative' launched by management with cynicism, seeing it as a way to improve the bottom line and draw more work out of employees." There's no need to announce an effort to begin practicing more gratitude in your healthcare organization. Instead, try expressing your gratitude slowly and naturally at first. Once your staff becomes accustomed to that, you may be able to talk with them more broadly about gratitude in your healthcare organization. For now, just begin.

Also be mindful that forcing gratitude may not lead to genuine gratitude. Therefore, avoid strategies that force public expressions of gratitude or that require employees to fabricate gratitude on demand. Begin your efforts by simply being more mindful about expressing your own gratitude in natural situations. Then, as Smith suggests, "Create times and spaces that foster the voluntary, spontaneous expression of gratitude."

Likewise, be careful not to overdo it. Too frequent expressions of gratitude will come across as contrived and insincere, even if you truly mean what you say. Smith suggests, "Studies consistently show that there is such a thing as too much gratitude." In fact, trying to be grateful too much induces "gratitude fatigue," Smith warns. Your staff will probably discount a profusion of gratitude and compliments, and your efforts may end up doing more harm than good.

Moreover, Smith suggests that you go out of your way to thank the people in and around your organization who never get thanked. For instance, every organization has someone who empties the trash, mops the floors, and does other thankless tasks to keep the office functioning. Your healthcare organization is no exception. Smith says, "Thanking those who do thankless work is crucial because it sets the bar and establishes the tone [of gratitude]."

Seize opportunities to express personal and public appreciation for the unsung contributors to your healthcare organization. That will bolster their morale and shine a light on their contributions. It also can broaden everyone's understanding of how your organization functions and who the behind-the-scenes players are. Thanking those who never get thanked ultimately will improve morale and increase trust for everyone, Smith says.

Finally, don't inflate or exaggerate the importance of an employee's contributions. Your good employees are too savvy for that. Describe each person's contributions realistically and don't gush. Simply look into your employees' eyes, focus your attention, and thank them sincerely but not profusely for what they have done. In other words, when it comes to expressing gratitude to your staff, don't overdo it. Just keep your gratitude real so your employees can accept and absorb what you have to say to them.

TWELVE THANK-YOU MESSAGES TO EXPRESS GRATITUDE TO YOUR EMPLOYEES

A heartfelt thank-you to your good employees can do a world of good in your healthcare organization. But how can you express those thanks without using the same words again and again? Brandon Gaille[12] suggests developing specific thank-you messages for employees that you can use verbally or in writing. Below are 12 of those messages that would be most appropriate for healthcare employees.

Be sure to cite specifically what the employee did to deserve your gratitude. Then, say *thank you*.

1. Thank you for bringing your positive attitude to work every day. Projects become easier to execute, changes become easier to implement, and problems become easier to solve, thanks to you.
2. Employees like you are the epitome of professionalism. Thank you for bringing your best to work every single day.

3. Thanks for being that employee who assumes leadership when the boss is not around and ensures compliance when she is.
4. Our office would be weakened without your presence. Thank you for helping us stand strong.
5. Thank you for realizing that by taking ownership of every project, you have taken ownership of your own success.
6. Thank you for all your efforts and dedication. Your sincere service deserves our encouragement and appreciation.
7. I see how hard you worked on this task and I appreciate all that you are doing for us. Thank you.
8. How can I ever forget your committed service as an employee here? It is something very valuable to all of us. Thank you.
9. I hold you in high regard because you have set the bar high for all of us. Thank you so much.
10. My words can never be enough to praise your actions. Your work always meets or exceeds my expectations. Thank you.
11. Thank you for shouldering responsibility and for putting our patients' interests ahead of your own time and time again.
12. Your professionalism embodies our philosophy and your hard work is a prime example of how employees can make a difference. Thank you.

CHAPTER 11 BONUS FEATURE

WHEN TO EXPRESS GRATITUDE TO YOUR EMPLOYEES: SEVEN OPPORTUNITIES

Of course, there are spontaneous moments in every day when you may see opportunities to express your gratitude to your good employees. While these moments can be very effective, so, too, can those moments that are planned. Chris Murchison[13] identifies seven opportunities for you to express your gratitude to your employees. By seizing these moments, he says, your employees will feel that they matter to you, and you can create a culture of gratitude.

1. **One-on-one meetings.** Murchison suggests that front-line managers regard their one-on-one employee meetings as opportunities to support

employees and help them thrive individually and as a team. "For me," Murchison says, "there's an amazing opportunity in one-on-one meetings to be present with our employees, to spend time with them, to see them, and to support their flourishing as human beings." Murchison suggests that performance reviews be reframed as "conversations" and that they include sincere and specific expressions of your gratitude.

2. **Rituals.** Rituals are opportunities to celebrate and be grateful for your employees. Birthdays, employment milestones, weddings, and other moments can be cause for ritualistic gathering and celebrating. These are perfect moments to express gratitude, Murchison says.
3. **Debriefs and lessons-learned reflections.** The end of projects or the achievement of milestones provides opportunities for you to express gratitude to your employees. Particularly focus on the ways that your team worked together to accomplish its goals, Murchison suggests.
4. **Whenever an employee comes to mind.** Front-line managers and their superiors can send notecards to employees whenever they think positively about them. Most people will feel honored that you thought of them, especially if you did so when you were out and about in your community, not at work. Perhaps you'll see or hear something that reminds you of that particular employee. If so, let them know. Doing so will help your employees feel "seen" by you, Murchison says, and that they matter to you.
5. **Staff meetings.** Create opportunities at meetings to talk about the work you're doing together, and to appreciate one another.
6. **Beginnings.** Murchison contends that you have a great opportunity to express gratitude every time you bring a new staff member on board. Appreciate the applicants who prepared and submitted their materials to you, and who gave their time and energy to participating in your interviews, Murchison says. Welcome and onboard your new employees in ways that express your gratitude for their taking the job and joining your team. Also express your gratitude to the applicants you did not hire.
7. **Endings.** Similarly, healthcare leaders can express their gratitude to employees who leave the organization. Murchison says, "Some endings are chosen. Some are not chosen. But I think both are opportunities to appreciate that person as they're getting ready to transition out of your organization."

CHAPTER 12

How to Develop Your Employees' Patience

Many challenges arise in the healthcare organization that can test even a good employees' patience — and we needn't look too far to find them. Just reflect on your typical workday, and you will identify many times when it would be easy for your employees to lose their patience.

Of course, your employees' patience is essential to your ability to provide quality care to your patients. George Root[1] suggests, "Patience is not only a virtue in customer service, it is a necessary skill in order to deliver excellent service." Certainly, impatience can make pretty much any bad situation worse. It rarely — if ever — leads to the most desirable outcomes. Impatience can make employees irritable and turn them into people who are not very nice for your patients to be around. It can make them unpleasant for you and your staff to work with. And it can make them unhappy, as nothing will ever seem to go their way.

Jane Bolton[2] says, "What's the purpose of building patience abilities? In a word, *happiness*. Better relationships, more success." Developing employee patience, therefore, goes far beyond the benefits to your healthcare organization. As a blog post from Operation-Meditation[3] succinctly puts it, "You'll find that once you become a more patient person that you will enjoy life much, much more."

You may manage employees who claim to lack patience, as though the condition is a foregone conclusion or a characteristic beyond their control. However, nothing could be further from the truth. Bolton says, "An important idea here is that developing patience is just that. Developing a skill. We aren't born with it." This is true even for employees who have a long track record of impatience and for those who claim to have been impatient all their lives. If they want to change, they can. Operation-Meditation suggests,

"Even if you consider yourself to be an impatient person, having patience is something that can be learned. It doesn't matter how old you are, either. You can learn how to be patient regardless of your age."

That's good news both for your employees and for you. But this brings up several questions: What conditions support or negatively affect patience? If impatience feels so bad, why are people impatient? How do people develop patience? And how can you help your employees develop their patience? We will explore the answers to these questions below.

HEALTHY LIFESTYLE HABITS THAT SUPPORT PATIENCE

The condition of the physical body affects an employee's ability to be patient. Employees who feel lousy are more likely to be impatient. That means they are more likely to be impatient when they are tired, dehydrated, hungry, overstressed, sick, or otherwise in poor physical condition. Of course, you can't control the lifestyle choices your employees make. However, you can encourage, support, and reinforce good habits and model them for your employees.

The following are healthy lifestyle habits that support patience and ways you can encourage them in your employees:

- **Eat a nutritious breakfast.** Skipping breakfast starts the day poorly and sets employees up for feeling tired and irritable as the day progresses. To encourage employees to eat a good breakfast, stock the staff refrigerator with healthy breakfast choices if you have the budget to do so. Encourage employees who skip breakfast at home to get together early to eat breakfast in the office to start the day right.
- **Eat nutritious foods throughout the day.** It will be difficult for your employees to exercise patience if they hit an afternoon slump. Be sure they have sufficient time to eat a nutritious lunch. When you provide food for a staff meeting or a staff celebration, offer and encourage healthy options, not junk food or overly rich food. Corleone[4] suggests that the consumption of aspartame, a sugar substitute found in many food products, has been linked to an increase in irritability and depression. When you cater staff events, limit or avoid food and drink choices that contain aspartame.

- **Stay hydrated.** Even mild dehydration may decrease patience and increase irritability. Unfortunately, dehydration is more common than many people realize. Jennifer Stone[5] recommends drinking half of one's body weight (as measured in pounds) in ounces every day. Share this information with your employees and encourage them to drink water regularly throughout the day. Suggest that they track their water consumption daily to be sure they stay well hydrated.
- **Get enough sleep.** According to Remez Sasson,[6] "Having enough sleep at night affects your degree of patience during the day." Of course, you can't enforce how much sleep your employees get each night, but you can encourage them to have more and better-quality sleep. You also can try to eliminate work-related stress that may be keeping them up at night. Review your typical workday and look for ways that you can make it less stressful. Heather Huhman[7] also suggests that you put a cap on the number of hours employees work and make sure they take their vacations and all other paid time off. Huhman explains, "Consider the benefits paid time off has on the sleep habits of your employees."
- **Exercise.** Exercise is another good way to increase one's patience. Operation-Meditation explains, "Getting a good workout or going on a long walk helps to release built up tension." It isn't possible to control how much exercise your employees get, any more than you can control their sleeping or eating habits, but you can encourage them to exercise. Melinda Gaines[8] suggests, "An easy way to nudge employees to exercise is to partner with a local gym or fitness center, ideally one close to your workplace." Gaines also suggests that you encourage exercise groups, hold friendly contests to encourage your employees to exercise, and encourage short bursts of exercise during the day.
- **Address illness.** Employees who push themselves to work when they are not up to it are more likely to be impatient and more likely to make mistakes. It is also possible that their illness is contagious. If an employee is under the weather, do not allow them to come to the office or continue to work.

If you notice a sudden uptick in an employee's impatience, meet with that employee individually, in private, to find out what's going on. Tell them what you have noticed and see what they say. If the employee doesn't know what the problem is, you may suggest that they consider a change in lifestyle habits. Also consider the possibility that the employee is dealing with addiction, depression, or another condition that requires treatment. Suggest that the employee have a physical examination and refer them to any sources of help that you deem appropriate.

UNDERSTANDING IMPATIENCE

Impatience makes us feel so bad and leads to so many other problems that it seems illogical that we would allow ourselves to become impatient. However, impatience isn't always a bad thing. Jim Stone[9] explains, "Impatience can actually serve us well at times." For example, impatience can motivate us to understand our options better, to explore new options so we can meet a deadline, to find a shortcut, or to switch to a better or more viable goal. If we're driving a car and become impatient with traffic, most of us will look for another route and take it if we can. That's the upside of impatience.

Human beings may be impatient because our biology is at play. It is quite likely that impatience was a primitive self-protection and survival skill. Stone explains, "On the ancestral savannah, we had to decide whether or not to persist in a hunt. When it took longer than expected to find game, it was time to consider alternative strategies for obtaining food. Impatience often was good. If it took more than two days to reach a goal, perhaps it was time to switch strategies or switch goals."

Today, Stone says, we have goals that require much more persistence. If we get impatient too quickly, we may never finish a project or do work that adds up to anything. Nevertheless, our primitive impatience is still with us and may bubble to the surface even when it doesn't offer us any actual benefit.

While our primitive ancestors may explain where our impatience originated, that isn't the whole story. Impatience is still taught and learned, and the workplace today can most certainly foster and fuel our impatience. In fact, impatience is probably much more common today than it was for our primitive ancestors, and even for our parents. According to Stone, "Fifty years ago companies had five-year plans. Now five-year plans are mostly a joke. CEOs and entrepreneurs today must pay much more attention to the new, and they must be willing to consider changing course much more frequently than they used to." Add to this that workplace technology today changes at a dizzying pace. We've learned that our patience pays off less and less, Stone suggests. That's what happens, for example, when we overcome our impatience to learn a new technology only to have that technology replaced the moment we have mastered it.

In addition, job switching is much more commonplace today than it was for our parents. Many employees have learned that if they become impatient in one job or with their progress up the career ladder, they can quit and move easily to another job. In fact, for some employees, job switching is much more than a possibility; it is an expectation.

When we take a helicopter view of our modern world outside the workplace, we see that it is exponentially more complicated than our ancestors' world. There simply are more things to become impatient about today. Our social lives are more complicated. Our personal schedules are more complicated. Our gender roles are more complicated. The barrage of news we receive is more complicated. And, inevitably, the more complicated things become, the more the various parts of our lives collide with one another.

We answer our work email and phone calls at night and on weekends. Working parents deal with their children's and their aging parents' needs and concerns while they are at work. Many of us remain accessible to our employers and our employees even during our vacations and when we are out sick. Stone warns, "Many of those collisions will bring unexpected costs. And those unexpected costs will lead to impatience."

There is one more factor at play that challenges our patience today more so than it did for our ancestors: increased reinforcement from others. In fact, Bolton suggests that today, impatience can be reinforced so strongly that it becomes "absolutely addictive." Within the healthcare organization, employees may become "addicted" to impatience if their leader, manager, and coworkers reinforce their impatient behaviors, even if that reinforcement is not intended.

Consider this: A young boy who is denied a cookie may throw a temper tantrum. If his behavior leads to him getting the desired cookie, he learns that his impatience pays off. That same boy, now grown up, behaves impatiently in the healthcare organization and enjoys kid glove treatment from his manager and may get himself out of doing unpleasant work tasks. He quickly learns that his impatience in the workplace pays off, just as it did when he was a little boy. He will most likely become impatient whenever he is denied a "cookie."

HOW TO DEVELOP YOUR EMPLOYEES' PATIENCE: TEN STRATEGIES

Even though nature and nurture have conspired to make us impatient, the situation is not hopeless. There are many ways that healthcare leaders can develop their employees' patience. The following 10 strategies have been shown to be effective:

1. **Model patience.** It is not reasonable to ask your employees to be patient if you show them through your words and behaviors that you are not. Become a role model of patience by handling challenges in your healthcare organization thoughtfully and calmly. If you have trouble doing this, seek help to improve your own patience.
2. **Exploit teachable moments.** If employees demonstrate a lack of patience, wait until the moment is over and revisit what happened. Help your employees explore what went wrong, what could be done better next time, and lessons learned. Most importantly, help them own their impatience and commit to improving.
3. **Reinforce patience, not impatience.** As suggested above, healthcare leaders reinforce impatience when they give impatient employees what they want. Don't give in to appease an impatient employee. As well, don't avoid an impatient employee or assign tasks unfairly to the rest of your staff simply so you don't upset them. Instead, reinforce the behaviors you want to see from your employees — those that are thoughtful, calm, and patient. Talk about patient and impatient behaviors at your staff meetings and performance reviews. Praise and reward your employees for their patience. Above all, don't soothe or placate an employee who is behaving poorly. That's too much of a reward and reinforcement.
4. **Upgrade your employees' attitudes toward discomfort and pain.** You may have employees who believe that being comfortable is the only state they can tolerate. They become impatient the moment something is challenging or doesn't come easily to them. However, working in your healthcare organization can put employees in uncomfortable situations every day. They have to deal with difficult patients, new technologies, coworkers who are out sick, equipment that malfunctions, and much more. You can help your employees become more tolerant of their discomfort. Talk about impatience at a staff meeting

or workshop. Describe the impatient behaviors you've observed. Teach your staff that although they may not always be able to control the circumstances, they can control their reactions to them. Help them see that their impatience is a choice. As Bolton says, "The solution to pain is an inside job."

5. **Create and use positive affirmations to increase your employees' patience.** Positive affirmations, first popularized in the 1920s, are sentences that we repeat to ourselves. Kathryn Lively[10] explains, "Affirmations are used to reprogram the subconscious mind, to encourage us to believe certain things about ourselves or about the world and our place within it." Encourage your employees to think about patience at the beginning of each day and to recite positive affirmations such as "I am a patient person," "I am in control of how I react," "I can tolerate discomfort." Ask your employees to recite positive affirmations aloud with you at the start of each workday. In time, they may increase their patience. Lively suggests, "What we believe about ourselves at a subconscious level can have a significant impact on the outcome of events."
6. **Reduce your employees' exposure to impatience triggers.** We can't always anticipate the challenges that will trigger our impatience. Often, however, we can see the problem coming. Help your staff identify the challenges that are most likely to trigger their impatience, then do something about them. Does the phone ring off the hook every Monday morning? Does Mrs. Grimsley always need a little extra time and attention during her appointments? Does Denise need to take a 10-minute break every afternoon to check on her latchkey daughter when she gets home from school? And do those things trigger your employees' impatience? If so, anticipate the trigger and amend your schedule accordingly. Likewise, physically fix what you can fix in your office. For example, improve the speed of your Internet service, replace the slow coffee pot in the staff break room, and improve your inventory control system if those nuisances trigger impatience.
7. **Squash employees' impatient talk and self-talk.** Ranting about the source of one's impatience, whether aloud, online, or internally, only reinforces the bad feelings. Do not allow impatient talk inside your healthcare organization. Ask employees not to vent their frustrations on social media. Encourage them to examine their impatient self-talk. Bolton suggests, "The main thing here is to just stop the story."

8. **Build your team.** Employees may be more likely to be impatient with one another if they don't know each other. Sasson suggests, "Employees who get along well will have fewer reasons to become impatient with one another." Develop a culture in which employees greet one another every day, even coworkers they may not know well. Establish and teach patience-related values such as being kind and helpful to one another. Insist that employees are inclusive and treat everyone with respect.
9. **Help your employees practice patience.** Sasson suggests, "Now and then, put yourself on purpose in situations that make you impatient, and try to keep calm and patient. This is a powerful exercise that will increase your patience skills." Create patience-building activities for your staff. For example, put a jigsaw puzzle or brain teaser puzzles in your staff break room for your employees to work on. Plant seeds in pots and wait for them to grow. Or invite your staff to string popcorn together for your office Christmas tree. Give your employees opportunities to delay gratification so they can practice their patience. For example, plan a fun staff outing or party that is many months away. Continue to build excitement for it. Make being patient part of the fun.
10. **Link patience to raises, promotions, and job security.** You cannot control what your employees think or how they feel, but you do have a say about what they do. Explain that impatient behavior will not be rewarded with raises and promotions in your healthcare organization and that it can jeopardize employment. If an employee behaves impatiently with you, coworkers, or your patients, specify precisely what they must do to change their behavior and by when. Exercise your right to fire an employee whose impatient behavior interferes with the smooth running of or the goodwill of your healthcare organization. Just be sure to document the behaviors you observe as well as the appropriate verbal and written warnings that you have issued. Make special note of witnesses to the impatient behaviors and any other evidence that supports your observations.

EQUIP YOUR EMPLOYEES WITH SELF-CALMING IMPATIENCE REMEDIES

Regardless how much self-care your good employees do and how much you encourage them to be patient, there will be times when they become impatient anyway. Here are eight remedies to share with them that can help them lessen and stop their impatience.

1. **Notice the signs of your impatience and act right away.** Encourage your employees to pay more attention to how they feel in their bodies when their impatience begins. For example, do they feel tension in their muscles? Do they notice that their heartbeat and breathing start to accelerate? Noticing these symptoms and taking action right away is important. Once the impatience escalates, it can be a lot harder for them to get control of themselves.
2. **Practice presence.** Employees who become impatient may be so carried away by their negative feelings that they get mired in them. When this happens, the 7 Mindsets blog[11] suggests that impatient employees bring their attention back to the task at hand by repeating this phrase: "Be here right now and do what needs to be done." That will interrupt the impatient feelings and calm them.
3. **Remind yourself that impatience is self-sabotaging.** In many instances, the action we take that is driven by impatience is ineffective, and it may be self-destructive. Encourage your employees to revisit the bad choices and mistakes they made in the past when they were impatient. With practice, they can learn to recall these unfortunate moments as soon as they feel themselves becoming impatient again.
4. **Find the soft place in your heart.** Employees can shift their focus away from their impatience when they learn how to empathize with others. Help them to remember that everyone has a story. Remind them of the bigger goals of their jobs.
5. **Take five deep breaths.** Employees who are impatient should remove themselves from the situation as soon as they are able to do so. Once alone, they can close their eyes and inhale deeply into their belly, hold the breath for a second, and let the air out slowly. Your employees should feel their bodies calm down. Encourage them to let that physical relaxation flow into their minds, soothing their impatient thoughts.
6. **Understand what you can and can't change.** Employees can learn to accept those things that are outside of their control if they stop trying to change them. This is a hard lesson. However, employees who are impatient can stop themselves and evaluate whether they can do anything productive to change the situation. If not, understanding that

they cannot do anything may help them let go of their impatience and come to a place of acceptance.

7. **Be kind to yourself about your shortcomings.** Employees can become impatient with themselves when they believe they should be perfect. If they are having trouble mastering a new skill, for instance, they may become frustrated and impatient if their progress is slow. Encourage them to accept and love themselves. Teach them that they need to be as kind to themselves as they are to others.
8. **Practice gratitude.** Employees may be able to regain their patience if they stop to innumerate the things for which they are grateful. This is a great way to shift their emotions from negative to positive. (See Chapter 11 for more ideas on developing your employees' gratitude.)

DEALING WITH IMPATIENT COWORKERS AND PATIENTS: TEACH YOUR EMPLOYEES THESE FIVE STRATEGIES

Your good employees may believe they have their own patience under control but find themselves confronted with the impatience of a coworker or patient. M.T. Wroblewski[12] suggests that you can suggest that your employees try the following.

1. **Remove yourself from the impatience when you can.** At some point, an impatient person's conversation may stop being productive. When that happens, Brenner suggests that employees politely excuse themselves by telling the impatient person that they have to get back to their work.
2. **Reveal how you feel.** For example, if a coworker loses patience with you, Brenner suggests that you say something like this: "I was frustrated today when you complained about such and such. I understand your feelings, but we need to find a way to work together to complete this project. How can we make this a better experience for both of us?"
3. **Don't become impatient.** Make the decision that your attitude and work performance are more important than someone else's impatience. Don't rush beyond the level of performance that you know is right just to please someone else. Brenner suggests, "Don't let them control your attitude, productivity, or quality of work."
4. **Be polite but firm and direct.** For example, Brenner suggests that if impatient coworkers or patients interrupt your conversations with

others, let them know that you will address their concerns as soon as you are done. Or, if they find a way to insert themselves into your private conversations, tell them that you appreciate the input but that you need to speak to the person you're talking with privately.

5. **Take a stand.** Don't let an impatient coworker or patient run all over you. Brenner suggests, "Stand up for yourself and be assertive."

CHAPTER 12 BONUS FEATURE

FIVE WAYS LEADERS PRACTICE PATIENCE

Leaders who are unable to practice patience will find their careers short-lived. So says Glenn Llopis,[13] who suggests, "The marketplace demands patience and employees will see patience as a sign that their leaders are more compassionate, open-minded, and willing and able to manage any circumstance." Llopis suggests five powerful ways that leaders can practice patience in the workplace:

1. **See through the lens of others.** Impatient leaders sometimes lose their objectivity. According to Llopis, "As a leader, you must be objective enough to step back and remove yourself from personal opinions and begin to see the situation at hand through the other person's lens."
2. **Evaluate tension points in an unbiased way.** Patience requires a leader to evaluate tension points carefully. Remain unbiased and don't choose sides.
3. **Listen and ask questions with a positive attitude.** Llopis warns, "Don't be in a hurry. Respect and embrace the process."
4. **Seek perspective from a trusted resource.** Don't pretend to know all of the answers. Learn how to choose your battles. More importantly, know when it's time to seek further counsel.
5. **Be responsible to yourself.** The next time you encounter a situation that tests your patience, conduct the proper due-diligence and be prepared to learn that you are the one who is at fault. As well, Llopis suggests, "The next time your patience is tested, use it as an opportunity to evaluate your purpose, vulnerability, and maturity as a leader."

CHAPTER 13

Using Rituals to Strengthen Your Team

Reciting or reading learned words, performing symbolic actions, or participating in a ceremony — we've all experienced these sorts of rituals. Every culture in the world builds community through rituals. In fact, rituals are arguably a universal part of human social existence. Just as we cannot imagine a society without language, we would be equally hard-pressed to imagine a society without rituals.

A group's rituals are, in part, what makes it different from every other group. For example, Americans recite the Pledge of Allegiance, sing "The Star Spangled Banner," and say "I do" when they marry; Boy and Girl Scouts make their promise and make the scouting sign; and religious groups follow dietary laws, chant, light candles, kneel, stand up, sing songs, eat symbolic foods, fast, and make sacrifices, all following carefully specified rules.

Individuals sometimes develop idiosyncratic personal rituals to help them prepare for or overcome great challenges. According to Francesca Gino and Michael Norton:[1]

> Basketball superstar Michael Jordan wore his North Carolina shorts underneath his Chicago Bulls shorts in every game; Curtis Martin of the New York Jets reads Psalm 91 before every game. And Wade Boggs, former third baseman for the Boston Red Sox, woke up at the same time each day, ate chicken before each game, took exactly 117 ground balls in practice, took batting practice at 5:17, and ran sprints at 7:17. Boggs also wrote the Hebrew word *chai* ["life"] in the dirt before each at bat, even though Boggs was not Jewish.

Do rituals like these actually improve performance? As it turns out, the superstitious rituals Gino and Norton describe enhanced the athletes' confidence in their abilities, motivated greater effort, and, indeed, improved subsequent performance. These findings are consistent with research in sports psychology demonstrating the benefits of pre-performance routines, from improving attention and execution to increasing emotional stability and confidence.

The healthcare team, like every other group, can create and teach its members unique rituals. These workplace rituals need not be costly, time-consuming, or difficult to execute. Yet, they can be worthwhile. According to Lee Colan,[2] rituals are the "fabric of our culture," and they are critical for defining connections within a team. He suggests, "Once we establish deeply engrained team rituals, we view them as *the way we do things around here*."

WHAT IS A RITUAL?

Serge Kahili King[3] defines a ritual as a well-defined sequence of words and/or actions designed to focus attention, establish significance, and achieve beneficial results. The word *ritual* commonly brings to mind exotic images of primitive others engaged in mystical activities. However, Kevin Carrico[4] says, we can find rituals, both sacred and secular, throughout modern society. For example, we continue to use rituals to mark the beginning of significant events (e.g., baby showers, grand openings, ship launchings, coronations, taking the oath of office); the end of life or periods of life (e.g., funerals, bachelor parties, happy hours); the completion of important tasks or performances (e.g., graduation ceremonies, curtain calls, awards ceremonies); the transition of one state or time period to another (e.g., birthday parties, anniversary celebrations, baptisms, Bar and Bat Mitzvahs, confirmations) and commitments (e.g., marriage ceremonies, ordinations).

There is a marked difference between a ritual and a custom or tradition. According to Linda Neale,[5] a custom is any frequent or common repetition of a social convention. For example, you may have a custom of singing a certain song in the shower. Customs become traditions when they are passed on to others, particularly to succeeding generations. Your custom of singing your song in the shower won't become a tradition unless you teach it to your children and they sing it in their showers, too.

Rituals go a bit deeper. The word *ritual* is related to *rites*, which are formal acts of observance or procedures in accordance with prescribed rules.

Rituals, Neale says, are performed in the same way, at the same time, and without fail, and they are taught to and performed by others. As well, rituals often have symbolic components and they are always meaningful. So, singing your song in the shower may not have much meaning; however, the ritual of singing our national anthem at public gatherings most definitely does have meaning.

SIX BENEFITS OF CREATING AND USING TEAM RITUALS

Healthcare leaders are in the ideal position to use rituals to build and strengthen their teams. Here are six benefits of using rituals in your organization:

- **Rituals can create and cement your team's unique identity.** Organization-specific rituals will be unique to your team and bring a cohesiveness to it. Rituals will help every employee feel connected to every other employee, present and past.
- **Rituals can save your team time.** By ritualizing certain actions, you can get started without having to invest much strategic planning into them. For example, if you ritualize the way you celebrate staff birthdays, everything you do to celebrate birthdays will become automatic. You will know which cake and beverages to serve, which plates and cups to use, which balloons to buy, how to set up the area for the celebration, who will say what, and who will lead the singing of "Happy Birthday."
- **Rituals can act as your team's social glue.** Rote repetition of team ritual tasks creates a feeling of togetherness. Often you see teams invent their own, sometimes secret rituals to bind the group more closely. Executing well-known procedures together synchronizes people and strengthens the common ground on which to build trust.
- **Rituals can pace your team's workday/work week/work year.** Rituals create a rhythm that is unique to your organization. For example, your team will get used to having a morning huddle at the start of every day if you make it a ritual. They will know that staff meetings are always on the same day and at the same time. Adapting to changing schedules depletes energy; rituals become second nature to everyone and create an environment where work can flow without friction. (See Chapter 7 for more information on morning huddles.)

- **Rituals require team discipline.** It may be tempting to skip a ritual or to abbreviate it, especially when time is short. However, keeping faithful to a ritual will help your team learn not to cut corners, even when they may be tempted to do so.
- **Rituals help us connect to specific mental states or emotions.** For example, practicing a ritual that is designed to help your employees relax or have fun helps them connect their emotions to other times when the same ritual helped them relax or have fun.

THE HALLMARKS OF EFFECTIVE TEAM RITUALS

If you'd like to design a ritual for your team, make sure that whatever you come up with actually works. First, establish your goal. What would you like your ritual to do? Do you want to make everyone on your team feel that they belong? Clear the decks for a new project? Mourn a failure so you can move on? Mark an important milestone? The more specific your goal, the more likely it will be effective.

Beyond setting the goal, make sure your ritual has staying power. Researchers Christine Legare and Andre Souza[6] of the University of Austin, Texas, studied ritual efficacy and found that rituals were likely to be more effective if they had three elements:

- **Several steps.** Strive to create a ritual that has at least three distinct steps or parts. For example, light a candle, say certain words, and pass a certain object to each member of the group. Or hold hands, sing a song, and have everyone repeat after you.
- **Procedures that are repeated.** For example, you may repeat certain words two or three times during the ritual. Or you may have each member of your team take turns performing the same act.
- **A specified time or occasion to which it is linked.** For example, you may tie your ritual to an anniversary, a specified day in a specified month, the beginning of a season or quarter, the end or beginning of the year, or the day a new employee joins your team.

SIX KINDS OF ORGANIZATIONAL RITUALS

Hahn[7] identifies six kinds of rituals that are used in organizations:

- **Rites of passage** rituals mark a change in an employee's status, such as the beginning of employment or a shift to another department.

- **Rites of degradation** sometimes accompany the removal of high-status individuals.
- **Rites of enhancement** heighten the status and social identities of individuals, such as a ritual that acknowledges a promotion.
- **Rites of renewal** strengthen existing social structures and thus improve their functioning, such as a ritual to mark performance evaluations.
- **Rites of conflict reduction** resolve conflicts, such as those connected to arbitration or mediation.
- **Rites of integration** increase the interaction of potentially divergent subdivisions. Participating in the ritual revives shared feelings of unification and commitment to a larger system.

20 OPPORTUNITIES FOR TEAM RITUALS

Linking your team rituals to specific occasions makes them more meaningful. Here are 20 opportunities for you to create and practice rituals with your employees:

- Start or end of the year.
- Start or end of the work week.
- Weekdays (Fun Dance Mondays, Tacky Tie Tuesdays, High Five Wednesdays, Thirsty Thursdays, and Fun Food Fridays.)
- Start or end of the workday.
- Start of each month, quarter, or season.
- End of the organization's fiscal year.
- A new staff member's first day.
- Start or end of every staff meeting.
- Employees' birthdays or work anniversaries.
- The anniversary of the founding date of your healthcare organization.
- When you achieve milestones such as a specified production figure or a specified number or patients.
- Offbeat holidays such as International Talk Like a Pirate Day or National Pickle Day.
- When team members have performed exceptionally well.
- When you experience failures and setbacks.
- When an employee comes up with a cost- or time-saving idea that you implement.
- When an employee earns a new credential.
- When an employee retires.

CHAPTER 13 BONUS FEATURE

SEVEN INTERESTING WORKPLACE RITUALS

Are you ready to create a new ritual for your healthcare employees? You may be able to draw inspiration from corporate rituals. Here are seven interesting ones:

1. **Cheer ritual.** Yum! Brand is a huge restaurant corporation that includes Taco Bell, KFC, Pizza Hut, Long John Silver's, A & W, and others. According to Lee Colan,[2] employees at Yum! Brand start each staff meeting with the Yum! cheer, and it's an honor to be asked to lead it. Colan explains, "Everyone participates, every time, with everything they have! Trust me, I've been a guest during the meeting and done the cheer myself. Sound corny? Not at all. It's an energizing and fun way to connect a team and start a meeting . . . a powerful ritual."
2. **Gratitude ritual.** Colan also reports that employees at the Maritz Performance Improvement Company conduct a ritual called the Thanks a Bunch award. It begins with one employee who brings in a bunch of flowers and a thank-you card to give to a hardworking employee. That employee keeps one flower and the card, but passes on the remaining bunch and their own thank you card to another employee who, in turn, repeats the process. At the end of the day, after all the flowers and cards have been distributed, the team members gather together to collect all the cards and draw for prizes.
3. **Event ritual.** John Warrillow[8] reports that Gentle Giant, a moving company based in Somerville, Massachusetts, hosts an annual Stadium Run up and down the stairs at Harvard stadium. The ritual has become a rite of passage for new movers and is deeply engrained in the corporate culture, which celebrates hard work, he says.
4. **Innovation ritual.** Warrillow also reports that at Australian-based Atlassian, engineers receive one day off each quarter to tinker with a pet project. The only stipulation is that the engineers must present the results of their day in the lab to the rest of the company the next morning.
5. **Joy ritual.** According to Judi Neal,[9] Ben & Jerry's has a ritual known as the joy squad. Each month a different group of employees is selected to be members of the joy squad. For that month, the full-time job of these

employees is to bring joy to other employees. They dress in costume, do skits, pass out ice cream, bring in balloons, and do whatever else they can think of that will make Ben & Jerry's a more joyful place to be.

6. **Failure ritual.** Neal also reports that at Pfizer Research and Development Labs, a celebration is held every time a particular compound fails to meet scientific and financial standards. Employees gather together for a lunch or cake as a way of marking the end of the failed project they had been working on, and to acknowledge that it is better to let go of something that will not be successful.
7. **Halloween ritual.** The Matrix Group[10] reports that it holds a Halloween pumpkin carving contest for its staff every year. Each Matrix team carves and submits an entry. Clients, friends, and fans are then asked to vote for their favorite carved pumpkins, which are awarded prizes.

CHAPTER 14

Staff Coaching: Using Active Listening and Powerful Questions to Unleash Your Staff's Potential

Let's begin by stating the obvious: A healthcare leader, by definition, is an individual who leads or manages a healthcare organization. Does it make sense, then, that a healthcare leader is concerned with the organization's day-to-day operations? Of course. That is as it should be. When it comes to scheduling, inventory control, equipment, facilities, finances, contracts, insurance, patient records, and so forth, managing daily operations is exactly what healthcare leaders need to do.

However, healthcare leaders also need to think strategically. And, the more human aspects of the healthcare organization sometimes call for a different approach. Managing alone will not always foster, nurture, and draw out the very best from healthcare employees.

Sometimes, employees will benefit much more if the healthcare leader functions less as a manager and more as a coach. As Holly Green[1] puts it, "We have to be both coaches *and* managers. To lead effectively, we need to know when to wear which hat." Coaching can be helpful to healthcare leaders who are trying to improve the performance of their good employees because they can customize their approach to the people in their organization who may be the most receptive to the strategy.

MANAGING VERSUS COACHING

When we manage others, we generally tell them what to do to get a job done. Usually, managers act from more experience, knowledge, and/or training than those they manage. In some cases, the manager has done the very job of those they manage and manages from the strength of that experience. Nonetheless, managers manage from above and their primary tools are command and control. Managers get things done by directing and monitoring staff performance. They set the bar for their employees. They share their expectations and requirements through tasking, directives, and initiatives, and by measuring outcomes.

Certainly, it makes sense to manage in situations where immediate needs are paramount and when we need to achieve specific outcomes efficiently and quickly. Laura Stack[2] suggests, "Your team members look to you for answers, and rightly so in critical circumstances." Managing can also be a useful approach when employees have never undertaken a task before and whenever they need a leader to tell them what to do and how to do it. Stack adds, "Sometimes a team just needs someone to coordinate while everyone else does their piece of the project."

Coaching, on the other hand, is the more effective approach when we are trying to develop the best in others. A coach does not direct others. In fact, a coach doesn't set an agenda for the coaching; the person being coached does. Green explains, "Coaching involves exploring, facilitating, partnership, long-term improvement, and many possible outcomes."

The coaches' position is beside their employees; their primary tools are active listening and powerful questions. Coaches get things done by guiding staff performance, by anticipating and clearing obstacles from their paths, and by supporting their employees' immediate and long-term career goals. Stack explains that when you coach, "You teach your people the ropes as necessary, acting as a mentor rather than autocrat, and otherwise make suggestions in real time concerning what they can do to tweak their behavior toward an optimum."

When employees don't quite reach a standard or goal, coaches may praise what they did well, but they also shine a light on where employees showed weakness. They focus attention on what employees can improve, but they won't tell them how to do it. Whenever possible, they draw next steps from the employees themselves rather than telling them what to do.

Healthcare leaders who use a coaching approach with their employees develop more effective teams in the long run. That's because they develop better people. Coaches change people's lives, often in profound ways. Clifton Harski[3] explains, "Good coaches show team members their potential, help them find confidence in their work, point out the value of what they do, and inspire them to be the best versions of themselves." They help employees to feel that someone is in their corner and that with that needed support, they can improve and grow. Harski adds, "Every time we coach an individual, we as leaders have that opportunity to have an impact on him or her."

There's another slightly less obvious benefit of coaching employees: Coaching can help healthcare leaders engage their employees, foster employee loyalty, and improve employee retention. Most employees want to work in a place where they believe they can achieve their career goals and where they feel supported in their own development. A healthcare leader who coaches employees can help them to feel that way about the healthcare organization. According to Stack, "Coaches create the kind of engaged, empowered employees needed for survival today." In the end, employees are more likely to stay with an employer who they feel brings out the best in them.

WHEN TO MANAGE, WHEN TO COACH

Knowing when to manage and when to coach your employees is critical to your effectiveness. Stack suggests that management is needed when:

- A crisis requires quick, positive results.
- You are handling new, inexperienced employees, especially those tackling a task for the first time.
- Your team needs to complete (and may be resisting) low-level or unpopular tasks.
- You are meeting difficult deadlines when every minute counts.

Coaching is needed when you wish to:

- Support your employees while guiding them in their career goals.
- Work with your employees to define and facilitate the best strategies for them and for your healthcare organization.
- Share your mission, vision, and goals with your employees in a transparent way and invite them to join you in your quest for success.
- Facilitate everyone's progress toward the goals you've mutually set, as well as toward organizational goals.

ACTIVE LISTENING IN COACHING

Active listening is an essential skill in coaching. Yet, listening is probably the most overlooked, misunderstood, and undervalued communication skill. Laura Hills[4] suggests, "Most of us take listening for granted and don't think much about our listening skills." Unfortunately, we can fall into passive, uncritical, distracted listening all too easily. When that happens, our listening becomes short and shallow.

On the surface, active listening seems to be a simple skill. We listen all the time, so how hard can it be to listen actively? However, we listen actively only when we're paying very close attention. That means that our minds can't wander, even for a little while. We can't drift into our own memories. We can't start generating solutions for the issue at hand. And we can't mentally argue with the speaker. When we listen actively, we fully concentrate to absorb all of what the speaker is saying, even if the speaker is dull or illogical or all over the place. We pay careful attention to the speaker's body language and how the speaker uses the space they occupy. We also consider what the speaker is *not* saying.

Active listening is challenging for a couple of reasons. First, many of us assume that we listen well enough and therefore don't try to improve our listening skills. Second, most of us have had little or no training in active listening. Hills suggests, "Listening is rarely taught or intentionally practiced and it is almost always assumed."

Another reason active listening can be difficult is that listening is the easiest communication skill for us to fake. Hills explains, "Some of us have become masterful at pretending that we're listening when we aren't." For these reasons, many people find it difficult to stay engaged in active listening even when they want to. Old habits do indeed die hard. For most of us, listening actively requires new habits, care, and consistent effort.

Although active listening is challenging, it is essential whenever a healthcare leader steps into the role of coach. In fact, Elena Aguilar[5] argues, "Active listening is the *highest* priority skill for a coach to master and it must be mastered prior to success using any other strategy." This is so, Aguilar says, because the core of active listening is empathy. "It's not so much about the exact words that you use as the listener, it's about the feeling behind them. It's about *who you are being* when you use them — are you being a caring, compassionate coach? Or are you being someone who is trying to be right . . . ?"

Active listening is an essential foundation for building trust and connection between you and your employee. Coaches who use active listening effectively can guide their employees into personally challenging coaching explorations, even into "the scary realm," Aguilar says. From there, employees may be able to experience deep insights and make big changes that ultimately will lead to their personal growth.

THE EIGHT CHARACTERISTICS OF ACTIVE LISTENING IN COACHING

The International Coaching Federation (ICF)[6] defines active listening in coaching as the ability to focus completely on what the client is saying and is not saying, to understand the meaning of what is said in the context of the client's desires, and to support client self-expression. Of course, as a healthcare leader, your coaching "client" will be your employee. Nonetheless, the ICF offers good advice that healthcare leaders can use when they coach their employees. Specifically, the ICF says that any coach who listens actively does the following:

- Attends to the client and the client's agenda and not to the coach's agenda for the client.
- Hears the client's concerns, goals, values, and beliefs about what is and is not possible.
- Distinguishes between the client's words, tone of voice, and body language.
- Summarizes, paraphrases, reiterates, and mirrors back what the client has said to ensure clarity and understanding.
- Encourages, accepts, explores, and reinforces the client's expression of feelings, perceptions, concerns, beliefs, suggestions, etc.
- Integrates and builds on the client's ideas and suggestions.
- "Bottom-lines" or understands the essence of the client's communication and helps the client get there rather than engaging in long, descriptive stories.
- Allows the client to vent or "clear" the situation without judgment or attachment in order to move on to the next steps.

According to Lee,[7] two conditions must be present for a coach to listen actively. The first is *calmness*. Lee suggests, "A calm mind will free you from the anxiety and need to try to be helpful." When your mind is calm and at rest, all thoughts are silenced so you can focus on the one thing that matters: listening. The second condition that Lee suggests will help you to listen actively is *curiosity*. "A healthy level of curiosity will heighten your interest in the person you're speaking to," Lee says. If you are curious, you will naturally pay close attention and ask the right questions to make the coaching conversation productive.

TEN TIPS FOR LISTENING ACTIVELY

When it comes to active listening, as with most skills, there is no substitute for practice. You've got to close your mouth, focus your mind, and listen purely for comprehension, and you've got to do this repeatedly to hone your active listening skills. To help, Hills suggests the following 10 strategies:

1. **Eat well and get plenty of rest.** It's challenging to listen actively when your stomach is grumbling or you're exhausted.
2. **Commit to being fully present.** Consciously decide to put aside the task you're working on or whatever is on your mind. Don't attempt to multitask. Give the speaker your full attention.
3. **Put aside biases.** You may have a history with some employees or topics that bias you for or against them. Let go of prejudgments and keep an open mind.
4. **Choose a venue with good ventilation and a comfortable temperature.** If you can control the listening venue, make sure that the room is neither too warm nor cool and that the air circulates. Poor air quality can impede your ability to pay attention.
5. **Turn off electronic distractions.** Make sure that you won't see or hear anything to derail your active listening.
6. **Don't interrupt.** Let the speaker complete the thought. Allow time for silence when the speaker stops. Pause and reflect before you respond. This is a difficult habit for many of us, but essential for processing the messages we're receiving.
7. **Focus on meaning, not words.** Don't let a speaker's occasional malaprop, mispronunciation, or grammatical error derail you from the message. Don't be distracted by words with an emotional charge. Recognize your hot buttons and defuse them.

8. **Stay with it.** Listening in spurts and then taking breaks may cause you to miss important information or cues. Recognize when your mind is wandering and intentionally pull it back to the listening task.
9. **Listen between the lines.** Search for meaning that isn't necessarily put into the speaker's spoken words. Pay attention to nonverbal communication (e.g., facial expressions, gestures, and speed, volume, and tone of voice) to see if you can tease out meaning.
10. **Paraphrase to check for comprehension.** Ask the speaker to elaborate on any point that isn't clear to you.

ASKING POWERFUL QUESTIONS IN COACHING

As the title of this chapter suggests, there are two tools healthcare leaders can use to unleash their staffs' potential through coaching: active listening and powerful questions. At first glance, it may seem that powerful questions are simply questions that have the potential to make a profound impact. While this is true, it is helpful for us to explore more specifically what powerful questions are and what they can do. Let's look at this in three ways.

First, Eric Vogt[8] suggests that powerful questions are distinguished from ordinary questions by nine characteristics. According to Vogt, powerful questions are those that:

1. Stimulate reflective thinking.
2. Challenge assumptions.
3. Are thought-provoking.
4. Generate energy to explore.
5. Channel inquiry.
6. Promise insight.
7. Are broad and enduring.
8. Touch a deeper meaning, and
9. Evoke more questions.

Following Vogt's advice, a coach would focus on the depth and quality of response the questions elicit. Powerful questions would be those you ask to dig deeper and to expand your employee's thinking. They are also questions that are likely to propel the coaching conversation forward.

Second, the ICF suggests that coaches who have the ability to ask powerful questions do so to reveal the information needed for maximum benefit to the coaching relationship and the client. According to the ICF, a coach using powerful questions asks questions that:

1. Reflect active listening and an understanding of the client's perspective.
2. Evoke discovery, insight, commitment, or action (e.g., those that challenge the client's assumptions).
3. Are open-ended and create greater clarity, possibility, or new learning.
4. Move clients toward what they (the clients) desire.

The ICF suggests that powerful questions are not those that ask clients to justify or to look backward. Powerful questions are designed first and foremost to be beneficial to the client, not to serve some other purpose.

Finally, Merci Miglino[9] suggests three characteristics of powerful questions. They are:

1. **Open-ended.** They're not *yes* or *no* questions and they often begin with the word *What*. Example: What opportunity is here?
2. **Challenging.** Powerful questions may cause a little discomfort.
3. **Free of judgment.** They are curious questions with no agenda behind them.

Miglino's focus on discomfort is important. Personal and professional growth sometimes requires us to go places that we'd rather not go. Be mindful, however, that a coach is not a therapist. If you uncover concerning issues through your powerful questions, discontinue the coaching session and refer the employee to a qualified mental health professional for appropriate help. Do not overreach your capabilities.

As we consider the use of powerful questions in coaching, it becomes clear that powerful questions cannot be answered easily or quickly. Powerful questions require a thoughtful response that has the potential to lead the employee to new and better insights. Clearly, the healthcare leader who asks powerful questions must have the employee's trust. Otherwise, the employee is unlikely to open up to the coaching experience.

The coach also must be very careful in tone, demeanor, and words not to come across as accusatory. There are many ways to ask an employee, "Why did you hesitate just now?" or "What do you think was behind your behavior?" Asking powerful questions well is a skill that can be learned and honed. Practice asking powerful questions with someone you trust and who can provide you with feedback.

FIVE TOOLS TO KEEP THE COACHING CONVERSATION GOING

When you coach a good employee, there may be lulls, stalls, and even dead ends in your conversations. The Coaching Tools Company[10] recommends having a plan in place for those challenging moments. When coaches get stuck, the trick is to take a deep breath and ask a question to get the employee to show you the next step. The company recommends that you trust the coaching process and trust your employees to know what is best for them. Specifically, develop a bag of coaching tricks that includes the following five tools to help you propel the coaching conversation forward.

1. **Catch-all questions for when you don't know what to ask.** Examples: What would be the best question I could ask you now? If you were coaching yourself, what would you ask yourself now? I don't know where to go with this; where would you go?
2. **Softeners for tough questions.** Examples: I'm curious... Just for a moment...Let's suppose...I was wondering... Would it be OK for us to play with this idea?
3. **Phrases for dealing with talkative employees.** Examples: I'm going to interrupt you here. So, tell me what finally happened. In a nutshell, what is the issue? If we were to take a helicopter view, what would you need me to know? If you could sum up the situation in one word or phrase, what would it be?
4. **Responses to "I don't know."** Examples: Just feel into the question for a moment. Just let me know when you've thought of something. What's it like for you not to know right now?
5. **Wrap-up phrases to end a coaching session.** Examples: What do you feel was the most beneficial part of today's session? What was your biggest win of today's session? What specifically that you've learned here today can you use/will help you most as you move forward?

TAKING YOUR COACHING SKILLS TO THE NEXT LEVEL

Coaching is attractive to healthcare leaders who are looking for new ways to develop their employees and also to those who wish to grow professionally and personally. In fact, coaching can add an exciting new dimension to your career. Currently, coaching is not regulated by any country or state.

You do not need to be credentialed to coach and you may begin coaching your employees, or for that matter anyone, any time you believe you are ready to do so. However, you may want to learn more about coaching and improve your coaching skills. If so, there are many ways to do this.

For example, many books, articles, and videos are available that will help you to broaden your understanding of coaching. If coaching is new to you, this may be a good place for you to begin. You may find it particularly helpful to watch videos of actual or mock coaching sessions so you can get a feel for how coaching typically looks and sounds.

Another good strategy is to engage a coach personally so you can experience the power of coaching first-hand. You also may find it helpful to practice coaching one or more people you know and whom you can trust to give you useful feedback. That will give you some valuable experience before you take your coaching live with your employees.

If coaching becomes important to you, you may want to pursue coach-specific training face-to-face or online. Look for a reputable program. You also might work one-on-one with a coach-mentor who can help you improve your coaching.

Ultimately, you may decide to join a professional coaching organization such as the International Coaching Federation and pursue coach credentialing. Truly, with coaching, there is no limit to what you can learn and how much you can help others.

CHAPTER 14 BONUS FEATURE

50 POWERFUL QUESTIONS YOU CAN USE TO COACH YOUR GOOD EMPLOYEES

The most powerful questions grow organically from the coaching conversations you have with your employees. Still, the list below of 50 powerful coaching questions can help you learn what powerful questions sound and feel like. Identify those that you believe will be most useful with your employees. Practice them aloud so you can ask them comfortably during your coaching sessions.

1. What's missing from this picture so far? What is it we're not seeing?
2. What do we need more clarity about?

3. What's most important to you about it and why do you care?
4. What assumptions do we need to test or challenge here in thinking about it?
5. What opportunities can you see in this?
6. What would it take to create change on this issue?
7. What would be the biggest impact if you achieve your goal?
8. What's emerging for you? What new connections are you making?
9. What's been your major learning, insight, or discovery so far?
10. If there was one thing that hasn't yet been said in order to reach a deeper level of understanding/clarity, what would that be?
11. If our success was completely guaranteed, what bold steps might you choose?
12. On a scale of 1 to 10, how excited do you feel about taking these actions? What would make it a 10?
13. What's your favorite way of sabotaging yourself and your goals? If you were going to sabotage yourself on this project, how would you do it?
14. What are you trying to prove to yourself?
15. What small steps can you take to get you closer to your vision?
16. What do you think the moral of that story is?
17. What are you waiting for?
18. What part of what you've just said could be an assumption?
19. If I were in your shoes and asked for advice, what would be the first thing you'd tell me?
20. What mistakes have you made today?
21. Where do you have unrealistic expectations of yourself?
22. What parts of yourself are you keeping bottled up but are dying to let out?
23. What's keeping you from taking action?
24. How can you get the skills/knowledge/information you need?
25. What should I say to you if I spot you doing this?
26. What do you want more of/less of in your job?
27. What are you tolerating/putting up with?
28. Can you imagine your desired outcome? Describe it to me.
29. Where are you not respecting yourself right now?
30. How could you bring more creativity, fun, and joy into your work?

31. If the same obstacle came up again, what would you do? What can you learn from this?
32. What other areas of your work/life may be affected by this change?
33. What do you not want me to ask you?
34. What's the problem in a nutshell? In one sentence? In a word?
35. What are you avoiding? How does this impact you in your work? In your life?
36. Where could you be more forgiving and understanding of others? Of yourself?
37. What might need to change?
38. Let's take your concern to its logical conclusion. What's the worst thing that can happen?
39. If you secretly didn't want to achieve your goal, what would you do?
40. How would you like to be held accountable?
41. What would happen if you raised your expectations?
42. What are you not saying?
43. What do you consider to be your role in our healthcare organization? In your life?
44. What do you need to stop saying *yes* to?'
45. What part of you is not being acknowledged?
46. What would you be willing to give up to achieve this?
47. How do you feel in your body when you say that?
48. How are you going to maintain momentum?
49. What would you like to express in your work more?
50. If you dared say it aloud, what would you make happier in your career? In your life?

CHAPTER 15

Working Well with the Informal Leaders in Your Organization

The informal leaders among your employees can be exceedingly valuable to your organization. They can influence their teammates to perform at higher levels and to work toward your organization's goals. They can rally the troops on your behalf, increase morale, and make your job much easier.

Conversely, informal leaders can be a barrier to your success. They may not support you or see eye-to-eye with you about your agenda and vision for your organization. They may sabotage you or tank your initiatives if they wield enough power. Therefore, identifying the informal leaders in your healthcare organization and working well with them is extremely important.

WHAT IS AN INFORMAL LEADER?

Informal leadership is the ability of a person to influence the behavior of others, Shawn Grimsley[1] says, by means other than formal authority conferred by the organization through its job descriptions, rules, and procedures. Robert Bacal[2] suggests that an informal leader is someone within an organization or work unit who, by virtue of how they are perceived by peers (or others in the organization) is seen as worthy of paying attention to or following. The major attribute that distinguishes an informal leader from a formal one is that the informal leader does *not* hold a position of power or formal authority over those who choose to follow them, Bacal says.

The ability of informal leaders to influence or lead others rests on their ability to evoke respect, confidence, and trust in others. Informal leaders may or may not be intentionally trying to lead. Despite a lack of leadership authority, informal leaders nonetheless influence members of their organizations and can be even more effective than formal leaders in certain circumstances, Grimsley suggests.

Grimsley further states that informal leaders typically have three bases of power. First, they are able to use *referent* power. That means they lead by example, influencing others to think and act more as they do. Second, an informal leader can use *expert* power. In such cases, others seek them out for knowledge and skills that no one else in the organization possesses. Finally, they can use *reward* power, Grimsley says, where they may praise and recognize members of the organization for a job well done.

An informal leader cannot use coercive power. Such power typically is wielded by someone who holds a position of authority and who has the authority to carry out the rewards or punishments sanctioned by the organization. One exception to this general rule may be the ability of an informal leader to apply peer pressure to a misbehaving group member to conform to group norms by the threat of ostracism. Otherwise, the informal leader's strength generally comes from influence, not from control.

SEVEN CHARACTERISTICS OF INFORMAL LEADERS

While the traits of informal leaders vary greatly, they share seven characteristics:

1. **They have influence, whether or not they seek to have it.** Some informal leaders purposely and actively become informal leaders. They seek, enjoy, and cultivate the role. Others emerge simply because their followers have great respect for them. In some cases, informal leaders may even be uncomfortable about the influence that they have on others. Nonetheless, they do have that influence.
2. **Informal leaders have some capabilities that formal leaders don't.** According to Bacal, that's because they do *not* hold a position of designated authority. For example, informal leaders can say things to coworkers that a person in a formal leadership role can't say, Bacal suggests.
3. **Informal leaders can be excellent followers.** Formal leaders often can mentor informal leaders. When that happens, informal leaders may eventually develop into formal leaders. That is, in fact, how many new formal leaders are developed.

4. **Informal leaders often are excellent advocates.** They are on the front lines and therefore tend to be closer to the employees' perspectives and their issues than a formal leader. They are able to assess the situation well and stand up for and speak on behalf of their followers.
5. **They may or may not make effective formal leaders.** Bacal[3] suggests that some informal leaders would be excellent if they were hired into positions of formal authority. However, others may become ineffective if promoted because formal authority may alter the relationships of new formal leaders with their former peers, Bacal warns. In other words, some informal leaders lose their influence when they step into a formal leadership role because they're perceived as having become "one of them."
6. **Informal authority allows leaders to focus on one issue.** According to Sam Rainer,[4] formal leaders typically deal with a number of issues simultaneously within an organization. For example, a healthcare administrator may be concerned about HR, scheduling, the patient experience, supplies and equipment, cash flow, marketing and public relations, public perception, and much more. An individual with informal authority in the organization, however, is free to focus on more nuanced and narrow issues, or even a singular issue, Rainer says.
7. **Informal leaders routinely have great communication skills, but they don't necessarily talk all the time.** Crow[5] suggests that employees generally listen to an informal leader because they feel they are listened to consistently by that person, not necessarily because the informal leader does a lot of talking.

IDENTIFYING THE REAL INFORMAL LEADERS IN YOUR ORGANIZATION

According to Ilan Mochari,[6] the biggest mistakes managers make when dealing with informal leaders is that they miss who the real informal leaders are. They go down through the hierarchy or identify good performers or high-potential employees, but that doesn't necessarily tell you who the informal leaders are, Mochari warns.

The outstanding informal leaders in your healthcare organization will be relatively easy to identify because everyone knows who they are. But if you need more information than that (and you may), get the informal leaders you've already identified to help you think about who the others may be. You can also construct and administer a short confidential survey to see who your staff identifies as its informal leaders, Mochari suggests.

HOW TO DEAL EFFECTIVELY WITH INFORMAL LEADERS WHO OPPOSE YOU

When informal leaders exert a less-than-positive influence, it's important to gain control of the situation quickly. Although a healthcare leader can't co-opt or manipulate an informal leader without risking a rebellion, here's what you can do:

- **Try to work with, not against the informal leader.** Attempting to bribe, coerce, or otherwise pressure an informal leader may end up backfiring. Resist the temptation to put informal leaders in their place. Edwin Ebreo[7] warns that in many instances, that not only doesn't work, it makes things worse.
- **Look for common ground.** Deborah Krueger[8] suggests that you seek areas of agreement and enlist the informal leader's support for those things on which you agree. This endorsement often positively affects the rest of your discussions, she says.
- **Don't provide informal leaders with more information than you would provide to another employee in the same position.** In fact, Bacal[9] warns that treating informal leaders differently may backfire. Some members of your team may resent the informal leader having privileged or perceived favored status over them. Share privileged information about your healthcare organization only with those who have a need to know because of their jobs, not because of their informal influence on others.
- **Meet regularly.** Regular, well-managed meetings will narrow the gap between you and an informal leader and the rest of your staff, especially if the informal leader is highly resistant to and blocking change. Involve your staff as appropriate, focusing on developing the team and serving your patients as well as you can.
- **Keep the lines of communication open.** Provide relevant and needed information. Create an environment in which it is safe for informal leaders to ask questions, take risks, and challenge you (respectfully) by providing different perspectives. When you don't agree, explain the

rationale for your position and ask for suggestions. Give informal leaders frequent feedback, being careful not to shut down the communication.

- **Respect the informal leader's right to disagree.** Describe your vision, the rationale for your decisions, your goals, and your plans. Then, leave it up to your informal leaders to decide where they stand. If you've done everything you can and an informal leader still disagrees with you, agree to disagree.
- **Ask for the informal leader's support.** Explain what you need from them and why you need it, whether the informal leader agrees with you or not. Express your desire to work together amicably.
- **Offer your support.** Show yourself to be compassionate, concerned, and supportive of your staff. Bacal[9] suggests that one of the best ways to engender support from informal leaders is to offer support to them and their peers.
- **When all else fails, render the informal leader useless by leveling up your own leadership.** According to Ebreo, informal leaders emerge because some elements of leadership are missing in the workplace. When team members become afraid or do not trust the formal leader to listen to their concerns and suggestions, an informal leader surfaces and assumes that role. If you're not being what Ebreo calls a "complete leader," there's opportunity for an informal leader to emerge. What can you do? Become a better, more complete leader. Ebreo says, "Informal leaders have no choice but to let go of their roles when the manager takes full leadership responsibility. This is done by opening all channels of communication, by recognizing their concerns, by giving [staff] second chances when they make mistakes, [and] by helping them succeed rather than demanding it from them." This is consistent with Crow, who says that people "yearn" for leadership and will take it in "whatever mode they can get it." As Ebreo sums it up, "Who needs an informal leader when the formal leaders work great?"

HOW TO COUNSEL A RELUCTANT INFORMAL LEADER

Some staff members may find themselves in the leadership role even though they never applied for official leadership positions and don't particularly want to lead others. According to Kathryn Vercillo,[10] "These employees tend to be smart, charismatic, likeable people who are empathetic enough to relate to big groups." If you identify reluctant informal leaders in your healthcare organization, here's what Vercillo recommends that you tell them:

- **Being chosen as a leader is a positive thing.** It means that you are a strong character within a group and that people like and respect you. You may not want the burden or responsibility, but it's really an honor.
- **You aren't obligated to play this role.** Don't let the rest of the team pressure you into any activities or choices you don't want to make. Although they may see you as the best leader for the group, that doesn't mean you have to do anything special in your role as an informal leader.
- **Working with your boss will make things easier.** There will be less conflict, less pressure, and fewer demands on your time. Stay in close communication with your boss and bring small concerns to the forefront before they become bigger ones.

DEVELOPING INFORMAL LEADERS IN YOUR HEALTHCARE ORGANIZATION

Bacal[11] suggests that there are three scenarios in which you may be tempted to develop an informal leader in your healthcare organization:

1. The informal leader already exists and you want them to remain in that role. Your goal is to help that person become a more successful and effective informal leader.
2. The informal leader already exists and you want to promote them into a formal leadership position in your organization. While you recognize that not all informal leaders want formal power and authority, you know that this one does. Also, you have determined that the informal leader has the potential to succeed in formal leadership.
3. You want to develop a staff member into a new informal leader. Bacal says this is "probably unwise," "likely to fail," and not recommended. Informal leaders are not created, he warns. They emerge organically, usually because informal leaders come to be respected by their peers based on their performance, demeanor, and attitude. Trying to create an informal leader when one doesn't exist smacks of manipulation and creates the opposite of what is needed for informal leaders to thrive. Bacal[1] warns, "It's more likely that attempting to develop and create an informal leader will result in that person being seen as a 'pawn of management,' which, of course, is probably true."

If you decide to groom informal leaders as in scenarios 1 and 2 above, Bacal offers some useful tips:

- Groom an informal leader for promotion to a formal leadership role informally through a mentoring and communication process. Modeling and discussing your leadership thinking can be very powerful.
- Develop informal leaders gradually and without being intrusive. Otherwise, you run the risk that your informal leaders will lose their informal influence.
- Let your informal leaders decide if they want to be developed. Many informal leaders don't want to be in the spotlight or don't see themselves as leaders. Offer to help but don't oversell it. Make sure your attempts to develop the individual aren't seen as pushy, negative, or intrusive.
- Be a strong role model. One of the biggest influences on the development of informal leaders is proper role models. Your informal leaders will be watching you critically to see how you behave, treat others, and communicate. Your actions as a leader, therefore, are much more powerful than your words.

CHAPTER 15 BONUS FEATURE

INFORMAL LEADERS: AN ANSWER FOR ORGANIZATIONS THAT NEED TO DO MORE WITH LESS

Has your healthcare organization restructured, downsized, or undergone budget cuts? If so, and you find yourself having to accomplish more with less, informal leaders may be the answer you're looking for. According to Marcia Smart,[12] "You are sitting on a hidden gold mine of talent and skills." Informal leaders are a creative way to improve your team's performance, work smarter, and produce more with fewer resources.

Smart further argues that informal leaders are often the unsung heroes who work behind the scenes within groups to get the job done. She suggests that you can increase your success by learning how to tap into their abilities. In so doing, you'll be able to increase innovation and performance, stay ahead of the game, make changes that have a greater impact, and exceed expectations, even in economically challenging times.

Cultivating and developing your informal leaders should be top of mind during economically turbulent and stressful times in your healthcare organization. Therefore, if you ever are asking yourself, "How much more can I squeeze from my people?" and "What else can I do right now?," look first to the informal leaders in your organization.

Smart suggests that informal leaders will be "the shortest, most effective route" to mobilizing your people and to delivering outstanding results. Smart adds, "You have an untapped asset hidden in your organization that can greatly assist you to be more successful. They are the informal leaders—untapped human capital—and they want to partner with you."

CHAPTER 16

Motivating Employees Without Carrots and Sticks

Carrot-and-stick management is a long-standing approach to motivating others that relies on the promise of rewards and punishments. It is a simple, straightforward strategy that has been used to motivate employees, to motivate children to eat their vegetables, and to encourage puppies not to have potty accidents in the house. Some workplaces continue to use carrots and sticks today, but is carrot-and-stick management a tool that healthcare leaders should use to motivate their good employees to improve? Probably not. There are better ways to motivate healthcare employees than to dangle carrots in front of them and threaten them with sticks. But before we get into those, let's explore how carrot-and-stick management works and why it may not be the most effective management strategy.

WHAT IS CARROT-AND-STICK MANAGEMENT?

Carrot-and-stick management is an employee-motivation strategy that involves offering a "carrot" (a reward for a desired behavior) or a "stick" (a negative consequence for an undesired behavior). It is based on the belief that employees will be motivated by hope and fear — hope of earning rewards and fear of being punished. Sarah Robinson[1] explains, "The carrot and stick approach has long referred to how we motivate people at work...with the assumption being that people are like donkeys who love carrots and hate getting smacked on their behind by a stick."

Rewards alone are not sufficient in carrot-and-stick management; the threat of punishment also is necessary. Apoorva Mehta[2] says, "If people fail to respond to carrots in a desired manner, sticks can be administered to do the trick." In fact, in the business world, carrot-and-stick management is sometimes called "velvet glove" and "iron fist" management, suggesting that leaders must have both a soft and hard strategy in their toolkit and that they must know when and with whom to use each one.

For carrot-and-stick management to work, the reward and the punishment must both be compelling. Tim McMahon[3] suggests, “Reward and punishment are significant motivators only if the reward is large enough or the punishment sufficiently severe.” That means that employees will not be motivated by inconsequential rewards, rewards they don’t personally value, punishments that lead to mild inconveniences, and demerits that have no consequences. However, as the Indeed editorial team[4] argues, “As long as your reward is attractive enough and your consequence is undesirable, this method can help motivate employees to achieve your preferred outcomes.”

Carrot-and-stick management often is used in learning and behavior modification. For example, B.F. Skinner famously demonstrated a carrot-and-stick approach to learning in his experiments with rats. Skinner found that a laboratory rat will learn to press a bar to receive a food pellet (carrot), but it will also learn to press a bar to stop an unpleasant electrical current (stick).

Skinner’s approach, called *operant conditioning*, suggests that behavior that is reinforced (rewarded) will likely be repeated, and behavior that has no consequence or that is punished will occur less frequently. Saul McLeod[5] explains, “Operant conditioning can be used to explain a wide variety of behaviors, from the process of learning, to addiction, to language acquisition.” It also has practical applications that can be used in classrooms, prisons, and psychiatric hospitals, he says.

WHAT’S WRONG WITH CARROT-AND-STICK MANAGEMENT?

If carrot-and-stick management can motivate desired behaviors, why would healthcare leaders choose *not* to dangle carrots and threaten sticks when trying to motivate their employees? Unfortunately, operant conditioning fails to take into account the role of inherited and other factors in human behavior. The use of carrots and sticks in a laboratory with rats fails to provide a complete explanation of what we can predict will work best in the real world with human beings. McLeod says, “Some psychologists argue that we cannot generalize from studies on animals to humans as their anatomy and physiology is different from humans, and they cannot think about their experiences and invoke reason, patience, memory or self-comfort."

But even if carrots and sticks *can* motivate employees to behave as we like, there is a serious downside to carrot-and-stick management; it doesn't work when we want employees to use their problem-solving, creativity, critical-thinking, and analytical skills.

In fact, carrots and sticks can thwart self-motivation and discourage the very higher-order thinking and behaviors we desire in good healthcare employees. The approach offers extrinsic reasons for behavior change rather than encouraging intrinsic motivators. Hannah Price[6] suggests that carrots and sticks don't trigger the "true motivator" of an individual. This can lead to myriad issues and often, "the motivation method is not sustainable," Price says. Phyllis Pollack[7] concurs, "Recent studies indicate that this approach simply does not work," citing several research findings to support this assertion. Pollack concludes from her survey of research, "While this approach [carrot-and-stick management] may work temporarily, it will not have lasting effect and may make things worse."

Paul Marciano[8] paints an even grimmer picture, saying, "Forty years' worth of research tells us not only that traditional reward and recognition programs aren't effective, but they actually *decrease* the overall morale of a workforce. And yet companies continue to spend their money and time investing in the worst." The absolute worst recognition strategy, in Marciano's opinion, is employee-of-the-month programs. "If you really want to do something to demotivate your team, go ahead and put that one into place."

Carrot-and-stick management may demotivate good employees for good reason. To understand, we must go back to the origins of the approach in the American workplace and consider what has changed since then.

Arguably, employers have used rewards and punishments to motivate people's behaviors since the beginnings of human history. However, carrot-and-stick management became popular in the American workplace during the Industrial Revolution as a means to motivate faster, higher, and more accurate outputs in factories and on assembly lines. Carrots and sticks motivated better performance for limited, specific, and often repetitive tasks —typical work tasks of the early 20th century that were "routine, unchallenging, and highly controlled," according to A Lean Journey. For tasks in which the process is straightforward and lateral thinking is not required, rewards and punishments provided a small motivational boost without harmful side effects, A Lean Journey argues.

However, jobs, workplaces, and employees in the later 20th and early 21st centuries have changed dramatically. Many jobs today, and certainly those in healthcare, often require employees to work with intangibles and to deal with great complexity. Healthcare employees need to see the bigger picture, anticipate and head off myriad problems, juggle multiple tasks and stakeholders, and think on their feet to solve problems they've never before encountered. They work in the arena of human services with all its complexities and challenges, not the production and assembly of consumer goods.

Managers cannot watch healthcare employees all the time the way floor managers watched factory workers 100 years ago. In healthcare today, we want and need employees who are self-motivated to do what is best or right even when no one is watching them or measuring their minute-by-minute output. Unfortunately, carrots and sticks can be a turnoff to the best and brightest employees who do not need or want to submit to a bean-counting reward and punishment strategy.

Another drawback of carrots and sticks is that they shine a spotlight only on what is being measured, rewarded, and punished, not on the full job. They can encourage your employees to hyperfocus on the one thing that will get them their reward or avoid punishment, to the detriment of other important aspects of their jobs. A Lean Journey warns, carrots and sticks "reduce creativity and foster very short-term thinking at the expense of long-term results. They extinguish intrinsic motivation; diminish performance; crush creativity; crowd out good behavior; encourage cheating, shortcuts and unethical behavior; become addictive; and foster short-term thinking."

The bottom line is that carrot-and-stick management doesn't work unless it's applied to simple tasks with simple outcomes, A Lean Journey says. The more complex the task, the less successful the carrot-and-stick method becomes. Today's problems in healthcare organizations are certainly complex and many of them have multiple solutions, some better than others.

A Lean Journey adds, "Rewards [and punishments] will narrow our focus and limit our possibilities and aren't effective with today's problems."

Much has changed since carrot-and-stick management arrived on the management scene. Today, we believe that motivation can be fostered, but it comes from within. We also believe that leaders can help their good employees become and stay motivated by creating and sustaining the conditions that help their employees bring their best selves to work every day. Respect, proactive communication, feedback, and capable and engaged leadership work far better than narrowly focused punishments and rewards. For these reasons, carrot-and-stick management cannot and should not be the primary or sole tool healthcare leaders use to motivate their employees, if they use it at all. Fortunately, there are better strategies.

12 MOTIVATORS THAT WORK BETTER THAN CARROTS AND STICKS

Leaders usually have good reasons for asking good employees to change their behavior. However, most employees do what they do for their own reasons, not for ours. This is true even when our reasons are logical, our arguments are well supported, and our intentions are good. As long as employees have free will and do not feel coerced, they must be self-motivated before they will do what we ask of them.

Leaders can motivate their good employees by talking with them about the relevance of the work they do every day. They can be proactive in identifying and solving problems for their employees and recognize employee contributions in meaningful ways. They also can share their own sources of motivation with their employees. These and other strategies can help healthcare leaders find out what motivates their employees and foster, reinforce, and remove obstacles to their employee's motivation.

If you're looking for ways to create an environment where your employees are highly motivated to do their best work, the 12 strategies below will work far better than rewards and punishments. Lai[9] suggests, "Put away the carrots and sticks and have meaningful conversations instead. You'll be well on your way to leading a highly motivated team."

1. **Focus on your own motivation.** A good place to begin is by exploring what motivates you to excel in your own work. Obviously, you are in

your leadership position today for a reason. What is that reason? What motivated you to do what you did throughout your career to get you to where you are now? Where did that motivation come from? And what might your life be like now if you did not have those motivations?

2. **Model and talk about your sources of motivation.** Good employees are highly attuned to whether their leaders have a genuine connection to the work. Lai suggests, "Employees feel motivated when their leaders are motivated." Share with them: What aspects of your role do you enjoy? What makes you proud to lead your team? What impact can you and your team have on others both inside and outside the organization? How can you adapt your role to increase your energy and enthusiasm?
3. **Find out what makes your employees tick.** Consider that not everyone is going to be like you. Some of your good employees may be looking for recognition, work-life balance, and respect. Others may be seeking opportunities for personal growth and learning, increased responsibility, promotions, and raises. Still others may be looking for ways to exercise their creativity, have fun at work, feel part of a team, or spend their time and energy helping others. And, of course, there will be good employees who are motivated by a combination of these desires or others. Once you've considered your own motivations, create opportunities that allow you to learn more about what motivates each of your employees. One-on-one conversations and surveys can help. So, too, can well-designed team-building exercises that get employees to share with you and with one another what's most important to them. Don't assume that you know what will motivate your good employees. Spend time with them and create opportunities for them to tell you. Lai says, "I'd like to suggest a new dialogue that embraces the key concept that motivation is less about employees *doing great work* and more about employees *feeling great about their work*. The better employees feel about their work, the more motivated they remain over time." Ask your employees: What makes you feel great about your work right now? What would make you feel even better about it? Then remember that there is no one right answer to these questions. Bernard Marr[10] suggests, "One size does not fit all when it comes to workplace motivation." For one employee, getting to leave early for a job well done is a powerful motivator, but for another, it's

simply a handshake with a genuine "Thank you! Your contribution was essential to our success," Marr says.

4. **Listen to your employees with your ears, eyes, and gut.** Pay attention to what your good employees tell you, how they tell you, what they don't say, and how you feel both emotionally and physically while you're listening to them. Ask your employees follow-up questions to draw them out and to get them to elaborate. Explore your employees' ideas and consider their suggestions carefully, as they may provide additional clues about what motivates them.
5. **Check your own biases.** If you find yourself resisting or negatively judging good employees who tell you what motivates them, take time to figure out what's going on. Do you trust that the employees are telling you the truth? Or, could they just be telling you what they think you want to hear? Do you feel that their motivators are inherently petty, selfish, shallow, unrealistic, or just plain wrong? It will be very hard to motivate your employees if they are keeping the truth from you or if you are biased against what motivates them. Work through this until you believe your employees are being sincere about what motivates them and you can think about their motivators without negativity and bias.
6. **Help your employees understand how their work matters.** It's sometimes hard for good employees to see that the quality of their work makes a difference. As well, good employees may believe that anyone could do their job, or that they have nothing special or unique to contribute. Share the context of each job and help your employees see and appreciate the relevance of their roles and what they bring to them. Lai suggests, "There is no stronger motivation for employees than an understanding that their work matters and is relevant to someone or something other than a financial statement." Start by sharing context about the work you're asking them to do. Why do you do what you do? What is the employee doing as a member of your healthcare organization and team that others rely upon? Who benefits from the work and how? What does success look like and mean for your team and for each employee? What role does the employee play in delivering on that promise? What do you see in this employee that is special and valuable? Stories, even hypothetical ones, can help you illustrate the importance of how much the work matters or who would suffer if the work were not done well. Marr suggests, "People

with a purpose are more resilient and focused, so it's important for companies to be sure their employees understand how the work they do improves people's lives."

7. **Build or rebuild trust.** Trust is a foundational component to any relationship, one that is essential for employees to be motivated. Marr explains, "When employees feel that they aren't trusted to do the jobs they are getting paid to do because they continue to be micromanaged, it squelches any motivation they have." Likewise, employees who do feel trusted to do their jobs and who believe they can trust their leaders are likely to be much more highly motivated, Marr says. If you detect that you have a breach of trust or a problem with micromanagement in your healthcare organization, work to correct the problem before you expect your employees to feel highly motivated. Admit the problem and be transparent with your employees about what you are doing to regain their trust and why. That will be a positive and powerful first step toward rebuilding trust.
8. **Anticipate roadblocks.** Your employees will undoubtedly encounter roadblocks and challenges whenever you undertake bold new initiatives or ask anything of them that will be significant, scary, and difficult. That's when their motivation can wane. Lai explains, "Employees are motivated when they can make progress without unnecessary interruption and undue burdens." Recognize that challenges can materially impact their motivation, then be proactive in identifying and addressing them. Talk with your employees about what they believe may make their work difficult, frustrating, or cumbersome. Ask them: What can we do to ease the burden? What roadblocks may surface? How can you/I/we knock them down? How can I help you to see trouble coming and pave the way for your success, without my becoming a nuisance or interfering with your work?
9. **Create a healthy, collaborative work culture.** Good employees who feel that they are part of a team and who get to build collaborative working relationships with others are likely to feel highly motivated. Marr explains, "This sense of belonging to a tribe where you depend on others, and they depend on you, keeps the motivation high." Spend time, energy, and resources to foster teamwork and to reinforce excellent collaborative work. In addition, foster a culture of self-care. Organizations that have the personal health and well-being of their

employees at the top of their list attract self-motivated job applicants, Marr says.

10. **Provide supportive feedback.** Good employees are often motivated by the quest to be the best versions of themselves. Marr says, "They don't want to be complacent, but want to continually grow and face new challenges." Their motivation is likely to increase when they receive helpful and supportive feedback that will help them to improve. Marr explains, "Most employees want to get better and progress in their careers and when a supervisor shows interest and shares ideas on how to improve, most are highly motivated." Become masterful at highlighting your good employees' excellent work and what they can do better. It will also be important for your employees to see a path to career advancement within your organization and to have your feedback and guidance about what they can do to position themselves well on that path. However, don't overplay that card. Doing so will turn the possibility of a promotion into just another carrot. Marr says, "If they view their job as a pit stop on the road to another opportunity elsewhere, their motivation will deflate for the job they're doing now." Talk about the future, but don't let that be the employee's only source of motivation. Focus also on the positives of the position the employee has today.
11. **Recognize and appreciate contributions.** Nearly everyone likes to be recognized and praised. Nonetheless, Lai says, leaders consistently underestimate the power of acknowledgment to bring forth employees' best efforts. Lai says, "Far more powerful [than carrots and sticks] is your commitment to recognizing and acknowledging contributions so that employees feel appreciated and valued." What milestones have been achieved? What unexpected or exceptional results have been realized? Who has gone beyond the call of duty to help a colleague or to meet a deadline? Who has provided great service or support to a patient in crisis? Who "walked the talk" on your values in a way that sets an example for others and warrants recognition? Lai suggests, "Employees are motivated when they feel appreciated and recognized for their contributions." Don't gush and don't overuse praise and recognition or it will lose its sincerity and punch. Be selective and appropriately highlight great work that merits the spotlight.
12. **Be curious.** Being curious about your good employees is the most powerful tool you have to keep them highly motivated —especially when you disagree with the employee, when you have disagreed

in the past, or when you feel that the employee has not lived up to expectations or let you down. Marciano suggests, "It's one thing to say, 'Hey, you should actively listen.' But if you take it to the point of, 'I'm curious about the next words coming out of this person's mouth,' this really changes the way you listen to others." Let your curiosity take you to wherever the employee wants to go. If you can remain curious and keep your biases and prejudices in check, you will have the best chance of uncovering and resolving problems, teasing out nuances of meaning, and finding the most effective ways to heighten employees' motivation. In fact, curiosity may even help you to turn a lackluster, jaded, turned off employee into one who is highly motivated to excel.

CHAPTER 16 BONUS FEATURE

HOW TO MOTIVATE GENERATION Z AND MILLENNIAL EMPLOYEES

Recognition at work is an effective motivator for good employees of every generation, including those who are the youngest members of your team. Ryan Jenkins[11] suggests, "Even though Millennials and Generation Z may expect a different pace and medium for recognition than other generations, recognition is still universally expected across generations."

Yet employee recognition is not universally practiced, at least not sufficiently for Generation Z and Millennial employees, Jenkins warns. In fact, there is often a disconnect between how often leaders believe they are recognizing their employees and how often employees believe that they are being recognized. Jenkins, citing a survey of research studies, says, "More than 80 percent of supervisors claim they frequently express appreciation to their subordinates, while less than 20 percent of the employees report that their supervisors express appreciation more than occasionally." Jenkins refers to this disconnect as a "recognition gap" and warns that it is likely to widen especially as more and more Generation Z employees enter the workforce. These younger employees have new appetites and expectations for how, when, and why their managers should recognize their efforts, Jenkins says.

In the past, employees' expectations for recognition were yearly, quarterly, or at best monthly. However, thanks to the convergence of mobile technology and on-demand information, Generation Z employees expect their recognition to be more personal, helpful, and frequent, putting it closer to weekly. Generation Z employees more so than older employees are likely to measure their success based on the recognition they receive from their managers and coworkers, Jenkins says. Frequent and specific recognition is very important to their motivation, performance, and loyalty.

Considering the influx of more and more Generation Z employees into the workforce, leaders should be mindful of how often they recognize their employees and beef up their efforts. Jenkins suggests that leaders "fill the air" of their organizations with gratitude and appreciation and that they reward their employees frequently for their loyalty and high performance. Then, when they do recognize their employees, Jenkins suggests, they will want to be sure to communicate the following three things, which will resonate especially well with Generation Z and Millennial employees:

1. **I recognize your good work.** Employees want to know that you see what they are doing. Don't assume that they know that you see them. Tell them. Be very specific about what you are recognizing.
2. **I value you.** Of course, you can communicate that your organization values the employee's contributions. However, as a leader, valuing employees personally can help them feel more of a connection, which is very important. Jenkins reports that Generation Z employees are more likely to work harder and stay longer at an organization if they have a supportive manager with whom they feel a connection.
3. **We're going places together.** Help employees believe they are working well with you and that they're also part of a team that has an exciting, bright future. That feeling of going to worthwhile places together may be the single most important key to unlocking Generation Z and Millennial loyalty and performance, Jenkins says.

CHAPTER 17

Creating an Exceptional Onboarding Experience for Your New Employees

Retention is one of the most pressing issues on the minds of C-suite leaders in all industries today — not just in the United States, but around the world. Yet many healthcare organizations are dropping the ball when it comes to onboarding, one of the most effective retention tools at their disposal.

Ron Carucci[1] warns, "Companies often spend very little time onboarding new hires." Claire Moloney[2] agrees, reporting that a whopping 88% of organizations "don't onboard well" and that only 1 in 10 of employees believe that their organizations did a great job of onboarding them.

Healthcare organizations that craft exceptional onboarding experiences are much more likely to retain new hires than those that don't. Exceptional onboarding also results in higher new employee productivity. Numerous metrics support these arguments. For example, Apollo Technical[3] reports, 69% of employees who have had a great onboarding experience are likely to stay for at least three years. SHRM[4] reports that organizations that use a standard onboarding process can expect 50% greater new hire productivity than those that don't. And Apollo Technical reports that 1 in 10 employees who leave an organization do so because of a poor onboarding experience, and that 37% of employees report that their manager did not play a critical role in their onboarding experience. That's a significant gaffe in the onboarding experience, according to Apollo Technical.

The first days and months with a new hire are critical in the life cycle of that employee. Carucci describes the entire first year of employment as employees' most vulnerable period and reports that up to 20% of staff turnover occurs in the first 45 days of employment. Starting new employees on the right foot can stack the deck in your favor for better retention and productivity because, as Arlene Hirsch[5] suggests, onboarding fosters better employee engagement and job satisfaction. For this reason, Hirsch urges, "Onboarding is a prime opportunity for employers to win the hearts and minds of new employees. Don't waste it."

WHAT IS ONBOARDING?

Onboarding refers to the processes through which new hires are integrated into the organization. It includes activities that allow new employees to complete an initial new-hire orientation process and to learn about the organization and its structure, culture, vision, mission, history, and values. For some organizations, the onboarding process consists of one or two days of activities; for others, onboarding may involve a series of activities spanning one or many months, or even a full year. During onboarding, the organization provides new employees with training, knowledge, and resources that will help them to succeed in their new positions, but as you'll see, onboarding usually has a social component, too.

Onboarding is often confused with orientation, but there is a difference. SHRM explains, "While orientation is necessary for completing paperwork and other routine tasks, onboarding is a comprehensive process involving management and other employees and can last up to 12 months." Orientation is usually a one-time event welcoming new employees to your organization. Onboarding is a series of events (including orientation) that helps new hires understand how to be successful in their jobs and the culture of the organization, and how their work contributes to the greater good.

Generally, the longer the onboarding process, the better. As Apollo Technical explains, "Longer onboarding programs are associated with stronger talent and business outcomes such as employee engagement, business reputation, quality hires, and the percentage of diverse hires."

All new employees are onboarded, even if that means that they are left to their own devices to observe what's going on and to figure things out on their own. However, a high-quality, structured onboarding experience designed by the organization will yield the best results. SHRM warns, "Too often, onboarding consists of handing a new employee a pile of forms and having a supervisor or HR professional walk the employee around the premises, making introductions on an ad hoc basis." That is not a quality onboarding program, according to SHRM.

Onboarding that is formalized and thoughtfully structured lays a foundation for long-term success for both the employee and the employer. Exceptional onboarding can improve productivity, build loyalty and engagement, and help employees succeed with the new organization early in their careers. It can positively influence the way they think about their jobs more broadly. Moloney says, "70% of team members who had exceptional onboarding experiences say they have 'the best possible job.'" Conversely, Hirsch warns, new hires who experience badly planned and executed onboarding may conclude that the organization is "poorly managed" and may wonder if it was a mistake to take the job. Such doubts do not bode well for employee satisfaction, confidence, loyalty, productivity, or retention, Hirsch says.

WHO DOES ONBOARDING?

Typically, the responsibility for onboarding falls to the HR department. Toby Graham[6] says that depending on the size of the organization, "HR could be one person, a team of people, or a department across multiple locations." In larger organizations, HR personnel who lead or take part in onboarding may have specialized recruiting and learning roles. As well, several non-HR employees will share responsibility for onboarding by introducing new hires to different aspects of the organization. Even so, there is usually one person in HR who oversees the new hire's onboarding, schedules onboarding activities, troubleshoots, and serves as the point person for the new hire and others throughout the onboarding process.

The new hire's direct supervisor should play an active role in the onboarding process. Graham explains, "Given that most people stay at (or leave) a job due to their relationship with their immediate boss, organizations should pay close attention to the roles of managers and supervisors during onboarding."

It's important that managers establish one-on-one relationships with their direct reports as soon as possible. For some organizations, this occurs on the new hire's first day. For others, it happens when new employees are handed off to their managers after completing basic orientation activities. Graham says, "One primary responsibility for managers and supervisors is to illustrate the link between a new employee's job and the organization's larger mission." In addition, managers are best equipped to set expectations and to teach new employees about what their jobs entail. Onboarding also is the best time for managers to discuss job and performance expectations. Graham suggests, "The faster employees understand the components of the job and expected performance levels, the shorter their time to productivity."

The healthcare organization's leaders, too, should be involved in onboarding new hires. HR Cloud[7] suggests, "Leaders can be called upon to share stories and the narrative of the organization." They are in the perfect position to describe the organization's history and culture and its overall business strategy, mission, vision, and values. The presence of leadership in onboarding reinforces the importance of the content to new employees. More importantly, it demonstrates that the leaders have a firm grasp on where the organization has been and where it is going and that they are accessible, not locked away in a C-suite and never seen. As George Bradt[8] suggests, "You get the employee engagement you deserve. If leaders don't engage with their workers, the workers won't engage with the organization."

Peer mentors also can be part of the onboarding process. Apollo Technical suggests that a peer mentor eases the learning process by serving as the new hire's go-to person for questions, a sounding board for their concerns, and a supportive peer who can guide them in their early days with the organization. Ideally, peer mentors will be employees who exemplify the characteristics that would be desired in the new hire, Apollo Technical says. Therefore, choose your peer mentors carefully. Negative peers can do more harm than good by sharing gossip, unsavory stories, and negative opinions. Don't allow negative influencers to serve as peer mentors, or they will poison your new hires before they have had an opportunity to form their own opinions.

Finally, some organizations include other stakeholders in the onboarding process. A member of a governing board, for instance, can play a role in onboarding, depending on the new hire's responsibilities. So, too, can a representative of a contracting firm with whom the new hire will interface. Likewise, one or more patients can help with onboarding by providing new hires with their own perspectives about the organization.

BEGIN WITH PRE-BOARDING

Onboarding does not have to begin on the employee's first day on the job. It can and should begin the moment your job candidate accepts your offer, because early onboarding is extremely effective. According to Aberdeen Strategy Research,[9] "Companies that use pre-boarding retain 81% of first-year hires." Furthermore, organizations that pre-board new hires are 11% more likely to retain their first-year employees than those that don't.

The goal of early onboarding, or pre-boarding, is to get new hires excited while affirming that they've made the right choice to take a chance on a new job. If pre-boarding is done well, it will link new employees to the organization in a positive way before they report for their first day of work. Rosie Greaves[10] suggests, "The focus [of pre-boarding] should be preparing your new hires and drumming up some excitement as their first day approaches."

The weeks between offer acceptance and the start date present a crucial engagement opportunity. Ashley Bell[11] suggests that organizations make the most of that time, adding, "Trust us, your new hires will appreciate it." Here are several examples of effective pre-boarding activities:

- **Facility tour.** Invite new hires (and perhaps their families) to tour your healthcare facility. SHRM suggests that this visit may include a house-hunting trip and community tour if a new hire will be relocating for the job.
- **Helpful documents and literature.** Mail or email helpful information about the organization to new hires, including benefits options, your organizational chart, and literature for employees and patients.
- **Gifts.** Send a welcome gift to new hires such as cookies, coffee, a coffee mug with the organization's logo, or other logo wear.
- **Peer mentor.** Match the new hire with a peer mentor or buddy who connects with them before the new hire's first day to offer a warm welcome and to answer basic questions.
- **Communication.** Send new hires their new email address and phone number, along with access details for using your communication tools.
- **First-week schedule.** Provide new hires with an itinerary for their first week (at least). Greaves says, "This simple gesture is a fabulous way to help them combat their first-day nerves!"

- **Paperwork.** Ask new hires to complete routine paperwork prior to their first day. "It's clear that no one wants to spend their first day wading through paperwork," Greaves says. Encourage new hires to complete and submit documents like their W-4 and I-9 forms before their first day.
- **Feedback.** Ask new hires for their feedback about the hiring process. Greaves suggests that doing so can go a long way in strengthening their impression of what kind of organization you are. Yet, according to Moloney's research, only 26% of new employees recall being asked for feedback on their candidate journey and the hiring process before their start date. "But when employers ask for feedback," Moloney says, "new hires are 91% more willing to increase their relationship out of the gate. This is crucial for reducing 90-day turnover and bolstering long-term retention." New team members who were asked to provide feedback prior to their start date also had a 79% increase in willingness to refer others to the organization, Moloney reports.
- **First-day instructions.** Provide detailed instructions for the new hire's first day. Greaves says that about 50% of new hires worry that they will be late to their first day at work or show up to the wrong place. Help nip that anxiety in the bud by making sure they know where they will need to be: the address, the department, and the person they need to report to. Provide instructions if the office is difficult to locate or if it typically takes more than a few minutes to walk from the parking lot to the office. Provide information about your dress code, parking, and check-in, as well as any materials new hires should review before their first day.

Additionally, look for opportunities to engage your current employees in the pre-boarding experience. For example, the new hire's team can send them a welcome email with quotes about why they love working in the organization or why they are excited to work with their new team member. Or, as Bell suggests, the team can make and send a welcome video. That may be even better than an email because new hires can begin to put names and faces together before meeting everyone in person.

Bell also suggests that you share the new hire's LinkedIn profile with their new colleagues and encourage them to connect. Greaves suggests that you ask the new hire's manager to congratulate the new hire on making the cut and to welcome them to the team.

Be mindful, however, that although these are all great ideas, you don't want to bombard new hires with too many pre-boarding emails, packages, gifts, or calls. Choose a few and schedule them optimally. Greaves suggests, "Opt for strategic communication about things that will matter in their employee journey," but don't overwhelm them.

FIRST-DAY ONBOARDING ACTIVITIES

Most new hires arrive to their first day filled with high hopes and excitement. Yet, Aberdeen Strategy Research reports, 50% of organizations say that their onboarding program is focused on routine processes and paperwork. The best and most effective employee onboarding programs focus on "people, not paperwork," Aberdeen Strategy Research says. Therefore, carefully plan first-day onboarding activities so that the very first things new hires experience at work are engaging and uplifting, not a pile of boring paperwork and lists of do's and don'ts. Keep the day upbeat and interesting to avoid what Hirsch describes as "death by orientation." Reinforce your new hires' enthusiasm by demonstrating that they made a wise decision in choosing to work for your healthcare organization.

If possible, "bookend" the new hires' first day by having them meet with their new manager before and after group onboarding activities. These would be two 30-minute meetings with their manager, the first one first thing in the morning for a welcome, the second at the end of the day for a debrief. Bookending provides a chance for a warm and personalized one-on-one welcome, begins your new hires' relationship with their manager well, and demonstrates the manager's role as a resource, guide, and helper.

After the morning meeting with the manager, welcome new hires as a group and tell them what to expect of the day. Then, focus at least the morning of Day 1 on your healthcare organization's culture and on forming connections. This is the perfect time to tell stories about your organization's history, values, and big-picture vision for the future. An inspiring presentation by one of your leaders can be an effective kickoff.

Then, spend some time focusing on the new hires by facilitating an engaging icebreaker activity that connects them to your organization. For example, if service to others or trust or respect are some of your organization's core values, encourage new hires to share how those values are important in their personal lives. Break larger onboarding groups into smaller groups of four to six so everyone will have a chance to speak and connect.

If possible, plan a lunch for Day 1 new hires so they have a chance to socialize and form bonds with one another. Invite a few peer mentors and other stakeholders to the lunch to interact with your new hires and to get to know them in an informal way. Dedicate the lunch to "informal small talk," Greaves says, not to work details. To help, give each table a list of interesting conversation questions to stimulate their discussion.

Moloney reports that career development is a leading reason that employees leave their jobs, and that addressing development during onboarding increases new hires' onboarding satisfaction by a factor of 3.5. Therefore, dedicate some time after lunch to the topic of career development. Moloney urges, "Let your new team members know how important learning and development are at your organization." Describe opportunities for training, career advancement programs, credentialing, mentorship programs, and tuition reimbursement. If possible, ask one of your most successful current employees to describe their career path and how they took advantage of your various development opportunities.

You may take care of some necessary processes and paperwork after you've discussed career advancement. However, don't end the day with that. Instead, end the first day of onboarding on a high note with another engaging and uplifting activity. Do your best to send your new hires home pumped up about their new jobs and your organization. Then send them back to their managers for their bookended 30-minute debrief.

THE REMAINING ONBOARDING EXPERIENCE

Human beings, by nature, like to look ahead. Greaves says, "We like to plan for, anticipate, and straight-up daydream about what's coming and what might be." You will be well on your way to high retention if you can get your new employees excited about their future in your healthcare organization. Therefore, after the first day or days of onboarding, provide your employees with a schedule of their remaining onboarding experience. Show them everything they are going to do in the weeks and months ahead, and when. That will give them a roadmap to their learning and put to rest any concerns they may have about having to figure out everything on their own.

Moloney reports that the entire new-hire onboarding experience typically consists of 54 discrete activities, both large and small. The average new hire will be assigned three documents to sign, upload, or acknowledge and 41 administrative tasks to complete, Moloney says. They will also have 10 learning outcomes to strive for — the learning goals they must achieve within topics such as organizational culture, market knowledge, and role alignment.

They also will encounter a variety of instruments to assess their learning. Exceptional onboarding programs vary the learning tasks so that they appeal to various learning styles. For example, an onboarding program may ask new hires to read articles or books, watch videos, listen to podcasts, explore websites, observe or shadow someone, engage in live or virtual conversations, attend live or online classes, journal, role play, interview someone, or solve hypothetical problems, among other learning tasks. Moloney says, "This variety of activities ensures the new hire is fully acclimated and integrated into their new role."

Make sure your new hires know that completing your onboarding program is mandatory and that positive performance reviews will depend on them doing so.

An onboarding overseer, typically someone in HR, must facilitate the remainder of the new hire's onboarding. That individual must monitor and assess the new hire's progress toward learning outcomes and bring the new hire back on track if their onboarding efforts decline.

Managers also will want to stay in frequent contact with their new hires throughout the onboarding process. Moloney suggests that they check in at specific times, such as on days 1, 7, 14, 30, 60, and 90, at a minimum. Moloney says, "When the manager takes an active role in onboarding, team members are 3.4 times as likely to feel like their onboarding process was successful."

Design your onboarding program so that it ends with a bang, not a whimper. For example, design an onboarding capstone project in which new hires write a paper or deliver a presentation to peers about what they've learned through onboarding. Then, share feedback one-one-one with each graduate of your onboarding program. Also ask your graduates to provide you with feedback so you can identify ways to improve your onboarding program.

Congratulate them with a certificate or a small gift. Then, encourage and guide your graduates to continue their learning by developing individualized learning plans with their managers that include new learning goals, activities, and assessment instruments. Point them to programs and tools both inside and outside your healthcare organization that can help them to continue to learn as they move forward in their careers.

REBOARDING

Reboarding is a process of reintroducing existing employees to the workplace after an extended absence. It refers to a formalized program for good employees who are returning from a furlough, medical leave, or temporary assignment; returning to the physical workplace after working virtually; or in some cases, experiencing an internal transfer or promotion.

According to Ed Beltran,[12] "The goal of reboarding is to reassimilate employees into their positions successfully." Therefore, reboarding should update employees on current and new projects, help them acclimate to new team cultures and relationships, and share with them expectations, policies, and other changes that have occurred in their absence. SHRM says, "Investing in reboarding can lead to increased productivity in a shorter time frame and allow employees the time to reconnect socially and emotionally to their teams and work, resulting in stronger engagement and job satisfaction."

Employees you are reboarding already have significant knowledge of the organization's culture, benefits, and administrative processes, so their reboarding generally takes less time than their initial onboarding. In most instances, the employee's manager will integrate the employee into their role and the new culture of the team, while an HR professional will help the employee complete necessary paperwork and/or administrative tasks and learn about changes in the organization's structure, benefits, development opportunities, governance, and policies.

Of course, reboarding provides needed information to the employee, but more importantly, it offers the opportunity for the employee to feel confident, motived, and refocused. It addresses individual well-being, positivity, and productivity as employees become accustomed to the changes that have occurred in their absence or that go hand-in-hand with their transfer or promotion. Most importantly, reboarding should have a social component.

Beltran explains, "A reboarding process should restore camaraderie, communication, and community, as well as strengthen ties to the business and among team members."

It can be scary to return to work after a long absence or to take on new responsibilities. There may be new team members the employee won't know, new technologies and ways of doing things, and shifts in staff or policy. Even veteran employees may feel anxious at such a tender moment in their careers. A structured reboarding program can be a great comfort and allay concerns or fears about returning to work or stepping into a new role.

CHAPTER 17 BONUS FEATURE

THE THREE DIMENSIONS OF ONBOARDING

A well-designed, structured onboarding program is not an event, but an experience that is strategic and scalable. Specifically, Carucci suggests that effective onboarding addresses three dimensions of the employee's experience:

1. **Organizational onboarding.** Exceptional organizational onboarding programs address how basic things work in your organization, yet they don't overwhelm new hires by throwing too much at them at once. These programs generally begin with an orientation that focuses on what new hires need to know to succeed in the first few weeks on the job. Carucci explains, "These include where to get an ID card, how to navigate the building, and how to enroll in health benefits and educate themselves on regulations and policies." Organizational basics also include clocking in and out, where to stow personal items and lunches, where to find coffee and restrooms, and location of the break room. Organizational onboarding also provides a crash course in your workplace lingo. Carucci says, "There's almost always a litany of cryptic acronyms that companies use for key processes or roles — decoding them can be one of the most distressing challenges for new hires." The more often a new hire must awkwardly ask, "Sorry, I'm new. What does SSRP stand for?" the more they feel like an outsider. Simple tools like glossaries of terms and acronyms can help new hires get up to speed quickly, Carucci suggests. Organizational onboarding

also includes activities that help new employees assimilate and adapt to organizational values and norms. Therefore, Carucci suggests, "At key intervals — three, six, and nine months — hiring managers should formally engage [new hires] in conversations about the organization's history and brand, how performance is measured and rewarded, and how growth opportunities arise."

2. **Technical onboarding.** New hires may have been hired for their capabilities and experience, yet not know how to deploy them in your healthcare organization. Even those with areas of deep expertise may become insecure and anxious when they suddenly feel like beginners. They will often cite past successes to prove their competence, which can quickly exhaust their new colleagues, who will tire of hearing the new hire start each sentence with, "In my last job." Technical onboarding will boost new hires' confidence. To start, provide new hires with job descriptions that include well-defined accountabilities and boundaries. Help them understand where their autonomy begins and ends. Provide opportunities for early wins. Carucci reports, "An astounding 60% of companies report that they do not set short-term goals for new hires." Yet, they should, Carucci says, to boost their confidence. Schedule weekly coaching sessions. Assign tasks with an expectation that they be completed at the three-, six-, and nine-month marks, starting with targets you are confident your new hires can meet. Then gradually increase the level of responsibility associated with each task. Discuss gaps in new hires' skill sets and work to close them; discourage new hires from faking it. Most importantly, help new hires understand why their contributions matter. Carucci says, "New hires that feel grounded in their contribution and understand how it fits into the larger organization gain confidence and feel loyal faster."
3. **Social onboarding.** Carucci reports that 40% of adults report feeling lonely. This sense of isolation is amplified for new hires, who often feel like strangers in a foreign land. Unfortunately, their loneliness can increase the chances of them leaving the job. That is why social onboarding is important; it helps new hires build relationships quickly so they feel a sense of belonging. Specifically, Carucci says, new hires, in partnership with their manager, should identify 7–10 people (superiors, peers, direct reports, and internal and external customers) whose success they will contribute to, or who will contribute to their success. Then,

new hires should craft plans to connect with each of these stakeholders one-on-one during their first year. Carucci explains, "This can be a short meeting over coffee or lunch—an opportunity to learn and ask for guidance." In addition, building social capital with teammates daily will help to build camaraderie and trust. Therefore, social onboarding should include planned and structured opportunities for socializing with coworkers. For example, one of the best ways to start things off well is to ask a friendly employee on your staff to have lunch with the new hire during his first few days on the job, and to make sure that the new hire knows in advance that this will be happening. Another is to facilitate ice-breaker activities that enable new hires to become known quickly by teammates and for them to get to know their new coworkers, Carucci says.

BONUS CHAPTER

Creating a Core Beliefs Statement: 25 Guiding Truths for Your Employees

Taking your good employees to the next level requires training, motivation, policies, procedures, and strategies like the ones we have explored in this book. However, in addition to these specifics, I urge you to give all of your employees the proper perspective about their own development, as well as their importance and place in your organization. Doing so will help them become better learners and will ultimately make them more motivated, better-informed employees. It also will make them more receptive to your efforts to help them to improve.

The best tools for establishing that perspective in your good employees will be your organization's mission, vision, and values statements. Ideally, these statements should be much more than a sign on your wall or some words printed in your employee handbook. They should be living, breathing documents that guide your organization's culture and provide your employees with direction and purpose.

- **Mission statement.** Your mission statement articulates your identity. As the Indeed editorial team[1] explains, "Mission statements help employees see the meaning and purpose of their work by giving them clear reasons their job benefits a larger goal."
- **Vision statement.** Your organization's vision statement defines where you are going. It reveals what your organization most hopes to be and to achieve in the long term and the kind of world it hopes to create. For this reason, Sean Peek[2] explains, a vision statement has a relatively lofty purpose and is an "aspiration."
- **Values statement.** Your values statement articulates the core principles that guide and direct your organization and its culture by creating a

moral compass for your employees. According to SHRM,[3] "[A values statement] guides decision-making and establishes a standard against which actions can be assessed."

Together, your mission, vision, and values statements can provide a firm foundation on which to create a shared culture of excellence for your good employees. These statements can help your employees make good decisions and keep their heads when their patience is tested.

In addition, a core values statement is another tool that will help good employees become excellent ones. David Darmann[4] suggests that examples of values described in a values statement are loyalty, honesty, trust, accountability, respect, curiosity, inclusion, courage, and innovation.

A core beliefs statement, on the other hand, defines much more specifically for employees how to apply those values to the work they do every day. Anna Katharina Schaffner[5] says, "Core beliefs are our most deeply held assumptions about ourselves, the world, and others. They are firmly embedded in our thinking and significantly shape our reality and behaviors." In fact, nothing matters more than our core beliefs, Schaffner says. They are the root causes of many of our problems, including our automatic negative thoughts. However, our core beliefs, both personal and professional, are also at the root of our successes. Unfortunately, they are often overlooked in most workplaces.

Every employee in your healthcare organization holds core beliefs, sometimes very deeply. These beliefs may be based on childhood experiences or formative experiences in their careers. Sometimes they are accurate, sometimes not. They also can be self-perpetuating. Schaffner explains, " Like magnets, [core beliefs] attract evidence that makes them stronger, and they repel anything that might challenge them. But it is possible to change them."

Of course, you cannot hope to know or change the core beliefs of every employee in your organization. However, a carefully crafted core beliefs statement for your organization can help you realign any negative values your employees have and illustrate for them how to apply your values every day.

Below is a statement of core beliefs that you can use with your employees. Each of these 25 beliefs is crucial to the success of any healthcare organization. I encourage you to reference it as a starting point for creating your own core beliefs statement. Review it with your employees and ask them to help you revise it, adding beliefs that are specific to your organization, community, or specialty. Finalize your core beliefs statement and include it in your employee handbook. Then require all of your employees to read and sign it.

More importantly, return to your core beliefs statement again and again when you assess employee performance, and offer suggestions for improvement. For example, ask your employees to read aloud the belief in your core belief statement that applies to the situation at hand and explain to you how the behavior you observed fell short of that belief. That will take the sting out of your criticism, help your employees see what they have done that could have been better, and help them aspire to higher and higher levels of performance.

Finally, use your core beliefs statement as a teaching tool. For example, you can make each of the 25 beliefs below the topic of a staff training program. Your good employees will enjoy connecting the belief to their job tasks and discussing the challenges they face applying it every day. Engage them in guided conversation and role plays. Or highlight one of the beliefs and ask your employees how they can live that belief through their behaviors every day. Encourage them to envision fulfilling that belief even better than they do now. Help them to anticipate challenges that can derail them from behaving in concert with that belief. Give them hypothetical challenges and ask them to apply one of your beliefs to the situation.

Through this kind of work, your core beliefs statement can begin to change the way your employees think. Eventually, they may be able to incorporate your organization's core beliefs into their own beliefs system. Ultimately, you can use your core beliefs statement to help bring new employees into the fold and to guide your good employees to becoming stellar ones.

CORE BELIEFS STATEMENT: 25 TRUTHS WE BELIEVE

1. Each of us is an important and valuable part of our team. No one person on our staff can single-handedly be responsible for our healthcare organization's success. One of our most important

responsibilities at work is to get along with our coworkers and to welcome new staff members to our team.

2. We highly value our donors, volunteers, board of directors, practitioners, and every employee who works here. However, the most important person in our healthcare organization is the patient.
3. Every patient in this healthcare organization deserves to be treated with the utmost respect and as a welcomed guest. We must be courteous to our patients — always — and do our best to make every patient as comfortable as possible.
4. We provide the best possible professional care for our patients. We do not cut corners or skimp. We insist on doing a first-rate job in everything we do.
5. We are a professional organization and as such, each of us must look professional and act professionally at all times. There is no room for carelessness in our appearance, conduct, manner, speech, workstation, work, or habits.
6. Each of us represents our profession and our healthcare organization to the public. This is true when we are both inside and outside of our organization.
7. Our patients' questions are important. We have an obligation to regard all questions and concerns as serious and valid. We do not belittle or ignore a patient's questions or feelings, no matter how obvious, trivial, or irritating they may seem.
8. Our patients' fears and pain are real to them. If a patient is apprehensive about treatment or complains of experiencing pain or fear, those feelings deserve our respect. We do not minimize or deny the way a patient feels.
9. Everything that we see and hear that is confidential does not leave our organization and should be discussed appropriately and only when necessary. We are mindful of what we say and who is around us whenever we speak.
10. Our healthcare organization needs our complete loyalty. We do not talk negatively about a coworker, patient, or other stakeholder in our organization inside or outside of work. If we do not like something that's happened here, we tell our managers, HR representatives,

or other appropriate persons in our organization so they can do something about it.

11. The way we say things matters and can make a tremendous difference in the way others will react to us. We must be especially careful when we talk to patients. Our language can either calm or aggravate their fears and concerns. When we speak with them, we use the most positive, professional, constructive, and sensitive language we possibly can.
12. Our professional development never stops. We seek worthwhile educational opportunities such as courses, seminars, conferences, lectures, training programs, and meetings of our professional associations. We read publications and books and consume other media that will help us grow professionally. We learn new skills and are curious about and open to new ideas and technologies.
13. Staff meetings are important to us. We participate in them to keep ourselves informed of opportunities, problems, new policies, and plans that are vital to continuing and expanding the success of our healthcare organization. We prepare for meetings as needed and arrive to them on time.
14. We are individually responsible for the tasks assigned to us. This is true even if we delegate part of a job to someone else.
15. Our healthcare organization needs our positivity, confidence, and enthusiasm. If we are positive and confident, our patients and coworkers will pick up on that attitude. If we are negative, complain, and carry a frown on our faces, our negative attitude will be reflected here as well.
16. We will make mistakes. That is understandable. However, we have two goals. First, we do our best to anticipate and prevent mistakes whenever we can. We seek the help of others when we need it. Second, when we do make a mistake, we admit it, take steps to correct it, and learn from it so we won't repeat it. We apologize when that is warranted. Then, we share what we've learned so others don't make the same mistake.
17. Healthcare may seem costly to us and to the patient. Nonetheless, we put a lot of thought into our fees and they are fair and reasonable. Our fees are based on much more than the cost of the materials and

the equipment alone. If we are ever in doubt about the reasonableness or fairness of a particular fee, we ask the appropriate person in our organization for an explanation. We must feel confident about our fees so we can discuss them confidently with patients and feel good about the cost of their care.

18. A highly productive day in our healthcare organization doesn't happen by accident or luck. It depends on careful planning and tight control of the appointment schedule. In addition, our productivity relies on our staying focused and on schedule.
19. We avoid negative assumptions about our patients. For example, we do not assume that a patient has financial difficulties, is not intelligent, is irresponsible, or is a troublemaker based on appearance or first impression. We give our patients the benefit of the doubt until they prove to us otherwise.
20. Each practitioner's time is one of the most valuable resources of our healthcare organization. Support staff is here in large part to free our practitioners so they can spend as much time as possible providing their services to our patients. Therefore, we must do everything in our power to prevent unnecessary interruptions of our practitioners' work.
21. We control the tasks we undertake, not the other way around. For example, we control the appointment schedule, conversations with patients, financial arrangements, our time, and our own career development. These will not control us unless we let them.
22. We present information to our patients so they will give us the response we want. Generally, that means that we give our patients choices. For example, we ask them, "Would you like to hold for a few minutes or would you prefer me to call you back?" rather than, "Can you hold?"
23. We compliment our patients whenever we can do so honestly to communicate that we care about them. We thank our patients for their patience and understanding. We apologize if we have kept them waiting.
24. We appropriately share anything a patient tells us that conveys negative thoughts about their experience. For example, patients may complain about having to wait, difficulty finding a parking

space or getting through on the telephone, a painful procedure, not understanding their treatment, the temperature in the office, or even the office location. We tell the appropriate person in our organization, even when we see no apparent remedy for the complaint or if it seems to us that the complaint is unjustified. We believe that patients' complaints are right to them, even if they are wrong to us, and that they deserve our response. Therefore, we share how we respond to patient complaints in case more is needed to be done for them. We also believe that sharing complaints can uncover or highlight problems that exist in our organization and that knowing that they exist will be the only way we can ever solve them.

25. What we do has an impact on our patients, coworkers, organization, and on the quality of care our patients receive. We put forth our best effort every day, even when it seems that no one is watching us or will notice the difference. We believe that someone inevitably will and that we will take pride in ourselves when we give our work our best effort.

References

PART 1
Next Level Healthcare Employees: The Big Picture

1. Call M. Why is Behavior Change so Hard? University of Utah Accelerate Learning Community blog, January 31, 2022. https://accelerate.uofuhealth.utah.edu/resilience/why-is-behavior-change-so-hard. Accessed May 9, 2023.
2. eLearning Partners. 9 Reasons Why Your Employees Are Your Company's Most Valuable Asset. blog. www.e-learningpartners.com/blog/why-employees-are-your-companys-most-valuable-asset. Accessed May 9, 2023.
3. McKinnon T. Here Are 3 Ways To Take Your Team From Good to Great. Entrepreneur, July 21, 2015. www.entrepreneur.com/article/248583.
4. Hppy. 5 simple ways to make good employees great employees. Get Hppy blog. https://gethppy.com/talent-management/5-simple-ways-make-good-employees-great-employees. Accessed May 9, 2023.
5. Skhmot N. 5 Benefits of Continuous Improvement. The Lean Way blog, August 5, 2017. https://theleanway.net/5-Benefits-of-Continuous-Improvement.
6. Nye KA. How 14 Benefits of Continuous Improvement Are Connected. Kevin A. Nye blog, August 5, 2019. www.kevinanye.com/how-14-benefits-of-continuous-improvement-are-connected/.
7. Milsom J. 10 Benefits of Continuous Improvement. i-Nexus blog, October 20, 2020. https://blog.i-nexus.com/10-benefits-of-continuous-improvement.
8. Indeed Editorial Team. What Is Quality? Definition, Importance, and Tips. Indeed blog, September 27, 2021. www.indeed.com/career-advice/career-development/quality-working.
9. Greco A. Why I Love Continuous Improvement. Continuous Improvement International blog, May 20, 2020. https://continuous-improvement.com/why-i-love-continuous-improvement/.
10. Krashen SD. *Explorations in Language Acquisition and Use*. Portsmouth, New Hampshire: Heinemann; 2003.
11. Western P. What Is the i+1 Principle? Oxford Open Learning blog, July 20, 2020. www.ool.co.uk/blog/what-is-the-i1-principle/.
12. Ali M. *The Soul of a Butterfly: Reflections on Life's Journey*. New York: Simon & Schuster; 2004.
13. Goldsmith O. *The Miscellaneous Works of Oliver Goldsmith*. London: Allen Bell; 1832.
14. Webster M. How To Be a Good Leadership Role Model. The Lazy Leader blog, July 1, 2021. https://thelazyleader.co/how-to-be-a-good-leadership-role-model/.
15. Horlick A. Involving Employees in Change: 5 Quick Tips. Navigo blog, January 20, 2020. www.navigo.ca/blog/involving-employees-change-5-quick-tips.
16. Keogh O. Hard Skills Get You Hired, Poor Soft Skills Could Get You Fired. *The Irish Times*, November 11, 2016. www.irishtimes.com/business/work/hard-skills-get-you-hired-poor-soft-skills-could-get-you-fired-1.2859688.

17. Reynolds M. Three Reasons Strategic Leaders Use Quick Wins To Drive Long-Term Performance. Vistage blog, November 13, 2013. www.vistage.com/research-center/business-leadership/3-reasons-strategic-leaders-use-quick-wins-to-drive-long-term-performance/.
18. Young SH. 22 Tips for Effective Deadlines. Lifehack blog, Updated March 9, 2023. www.lifehack.org/articles/featured/22-tips-for-effective-deadlines.html.
19. Amabile TM, Kramer SJ. The Power of Small Wins. *Harvard Business Review*, May 2011. https://hbr.org/2011/05/the-power-of-small-wins.
20. Hearn S. 10 Barriers to Employee Engagement. Clear Review blog, March 6, 2017. www.clearreview.com/5-reasons-employees-arent-engaged/.

PART 2
How to Take Your Good Employees to the Next Level

Chapter 1: Customer Service 101: An Introduction for Healthcare Employees

1. Practice Builders. Customer Service Excellence. Practice Builders blog. https://practicebuilders.com/build-your-practice/customer-service-excellence. Accessed July 18, 2018.
2. Tutorials Point. Customer-service Introduction. Tutorials Point tutorial. https://tutorialspoint.com/customer_service/customer_service_introduction.htm. Accessed July 18, 2018.
3. Root, GN. Features of Good Customer Service. Chron. https://smallbusiness.chron.com/features-good-customer-service-2076.html. Accessed May 10, 2023.
4. EA Consulting. 6 Characteristics of Great Customer Service. Errol Allen Consulting blog, June 3, 2013. https://errolallenconsulting.com/6-characteristics-of-great-customer-service/.
5. Marta. The 5 Crucial Characteristics for People in Customer Service. User Like blog, October 30, 2014. https://userlike.com/en/blog/the-5-crucial-characteristics-for-people-in-customer-service.
6. Ciotti G. 15 Customer Service Skills That Every Employee Needs. World-Wide Business Centres blog, June 9, 2015. https://wwbcn.com/15-customer-service-skills-that-every-employee-needs/.
7. Hills L. Teaching Your Staff To Reframe Negatives Into Positives. *Journal of Medical Practice Management*. 2018;34:95–99.
8. Lorette K. Customer Service Characteristics. Chron. https://smallbusiness.chron.com/customer-service-characteristics-756.html. Accessed July 24, 2018.
9. Landsman I. The Top Personality Traits for Successful Customer Service. Help Spot blog, August 24, 2021. www.helpspot.com/blog/customer-service-personality-traits.
10. Business Training Works. Top Customer Service Tips. Business Training Works blog. www.businesstrainingworks.com/training-resource/21-tips-for-excellent-retail-customer-service/. Accessed May 10, 2023.
11. Bacal R. What Is the CARP System for Defusing Angry Customers? Customer Service Zone blog. http://customerservicezone.com/faq/angercarp.htm. Accessed May 10, 2023.

Chapter 2: How to Create an Ownership Mentality within Your Team

1. Bock H. 3 Ways to Create An Ownership Mentality Within Your Team. The Muse blog,

2. June 19, 2020. www.themuse.com/advice/3-ways-to-create-an-ownership-mentality-within-your-team.
3. de Haaf M. 9 Ways To Help Your Employees Take Ownership of Your Business. Medallia blog. https://blog.medallia.com/customer-experience/9-ways-help-employees-take-ownership-business/. Accessed May 8, 2017.
4. Ducoff N. How To Get Employees To Embrace Ownership Thinking. Strategies blog. https://strategies.com/how-to-get-employees-to-embrace-ownership-thinking. Accessed May 9, 2017.
5. Efron L. Four Ways To Get Your Employees To Care Like Owners. *Forbes*, July 15, 2013. www.forbes.com/sites/louisefron/2013/07/15/four-ways-to-get-your-employees-to-care-like-owners/#18cf22ad1a70.
6. Oglethorpe A. Six steps To Help Your Employees Take Ownership and Responsibility. HRZone blog, August 27, 2010. www.antoinetteoglethorpe.com/six-steps-to-help-your-employees-take-ownership-and-responsibility/.
7. Charpentier W. How to Motivate Staff To Take Ownership. Chron. http://smallbusiness.chron.com/motivate-staff-ownership-42309.html. Accessed May 9, 2017.
8. Erb M. How to Inspire an Ownership Spirit Among Employees. *Entrepreneur*, March 15, 2011. www.entrepreneur.com/article/219328.
9. Busse R. Cultivate an Attitude of Ownership Among Your Employees. Business Know-How blog, March 13, 2014. www.businessknowhow.com/manage/ownershipattitude.htm.
10. Coleman J. Take Ownership of Your Actions By Taking Responsibility. *Harvard Business Review*, August 30, 2012. https://hbr.org/2012/08/take-ownership-of-your-actions.
11. Tye J. *The Cultural Blueprinting Toolkit Workbook*. Solon, IA: Values Coach, Inc.; 2013.
12. Spence, J. How to Create an "Ownership Mentality" On Your Team. John Spence blog, September 24, 2009. http://blog.johnspence.com/2009/09/how-to-create-an-ownership-mentality-on-your-team/.
13. Shannon E. Stop Whining–Take Ownership. Diversity Jobs blog. https://www.diversityjobs.com/career-advice/career-advice/stop-whining-take-ownership/. Accessed May 9, 2023.

Chapter 3: Improving Your Workplace Experience to Increase Employee Productivity and Engagement

1. Meister J. The Future of Work: Airbnb CHRO Becomes Chief Employee Experience Officer. *Forbes*, July 21, 2015. https://www.forbes.com/sites/jeannemeister/2015/07/21/the-future-of-work-airbnb-chro-becomes-chief-employee-experinece-officer/?sh=11264e3e4232.
2. Accenture. Designing a Workplace Experience to Drive Growth. Accenture blog, October 24, 2019. www.accenture.com/us-en/insights/cloud/designing-workplace-experience-drive-growth.
3. Fitoussi V. 8 Stats To Persuade Your Team That Employee Experience Matters. Tanmayah Consultancies blog. https://www.tanmyah.net/post/8-stats-to-persuade-your-team-that-employee-experience-matters. Accessed May 10, 2023.
4. Lane. Emerging Definition of Workplace Experience. Lane blog. October 30, 2019. https://joinlane.com/blog/the-emerging-definition-of-workplace-experience/. Accessed November 9, 2021.
5. Godfrey N. The Origins of Employee Experience. Stewart Leadership blog. https://blog.stewartleadership.com/origins-employee-experience. Accessed May 17, 2023.

6. Suszko D. The Case for the Chief (Employee) Experience Officer. Work Design blog, June 14, 2019. www.workdesign.com/2019/06/the-case-for-the-chief-employee-experience-officer/.
7. Cavanaugh K. The Rise of the Workplace Experience Manager. Robin Powered blog. September 11, 2019. https://robinpowered.com/blog/workplace-experience-manager-role.
8. Kaemingk D. 10 Ways to Improve Employee Experience at Work. Qualtrics blog, May 21, 2019. www.qualtrics.com/blog/10-ways-to-improve-employee-experience/.
9. van Vulpen E. How Employee Journey Mapping Can Change the Employee Experience. Academy to Innovate HR blog. www.aihr.com/blog/employee-journey-mapping/. Accessed May 17, 2023.
10. First Up. Employee Experience: What It Is and How To Improve It. First Up blog. May 20, 2021. https://firstup.io/blog/employee-experience-what-it-is-and-how-to-improve-it/#improve.
11. HR Morning. 5 Ways to Improve Employee Experience Post-COVID. HR Morning blog, September 22, 2021. www.hrmorning.com/articles/employee-experience-post-covid/.
12. Face2FaceHR. Seven Ideas to Improve Your Workplace Environment. Face2FaceHR blog, November 26, 2018. https://face2facehr.com/seven-ideas-to-improve-your-workplace-environment/.
13. Palmer T. 5 Ways To Ensure a Terrible Workplace Experience. Decision Wise blog. https://decision-wise.com/5-ways-ensure-terrible-employee-experience/. Accessed November 19, 2021.

Chapter 4: Going Above and Beyond for Your Patients

1. Kelly C. Why Going Above and Beyond in Business Makes all the Difference. *Forbes*, January 7, 2016. https://www.forbes.com/sites/theyec/2016/01/07/why-going-above-and-beyond-in-business-makes-all-the-difference/?sh=32818d971ef3.
2. Brown MS. Cultivating a Culture of Extraordinary Customer Service. Unique Venues blog, February 6, 2019. https://www.uniquevenues.com/blog/cultivating-culture-extraordinary-customer-service/.
3. Fleming W. Want Your Employees to Go Above and Beyond To Serve Your Customers? Humana blog, February 21, 2019. https://www.humananews.com/news-details/2019/want-your-employees-to-go-above-and-beyond-to-serve-your-customers/default.aspx#gsc.tab=0
4. Matti E. The Differentiated Customer Experience: What Makes Employees Go Above and Beyond? LinkedIn blog, May 8, 2017. https://www.linkedin.com/pulse/differentiated-customer-experience-what-makes-employees-matti
5. Spinoza JD. 5 Traits That Will Make for an Employee That Will Go Beyond the Basics. Zoomshift blog, May 17, 2019. www.zoomshift.com/blog/great-employee-traits.
6. UPMC St. Margaret Above-and-Beyond Recognition Form. University of Pittsburgh Medical Center St. Margaret website. www.upmc.com/-/media/upmc/locations/hospitals/st-margaret/careers/nursing-school/documents/above-and-beyond-nomination-form-revised-10-11.pdf?la=en&hash=CC819CEBFC FE71C99A381A8DA46CA8040BBA89D4. Accessed March 21, 2019.
7. Lesonsky R. 5 Things That Motivate Employees to Go Above and Beyond. Small Business Trends blog, May 23, 2017. https://smallbiztrends.com/2017/05/motivate-employees-to-go-above-and-beyond.html.

Chapter 5: How to Assess, Recognize, and Reward Teamwork

1. Irvine D. A Workplace Truism to Remember: You Get What You Reward. EREMedia blog, November 5, 2012. www.eremedia.com/tlnt/a-workplace-truism-to-remember-you-get-what-you-reward/. Accessed May 23, 2016.
2. Schrage M. Reward Your Best Teams, Not Just Star Players. *Harvard Business Review,* June 30, 2015. https://hbr.org/2015/06/reward-your-best-teams-not-just-star-players.
3. Geraghty S. The Basics of a Successful Employee Rewards Program. Talkdesk blog, March 29, 2013. www.talkdesk.com/blog/the-basics-of-a-successful-employee-rewards-program/.
4. Gallo A. How To Reward Your Stellar Team. *Harvard Business Review,* August 1, 2013. https://hbr.org/2013/08/how-to-reward-your-stellar-tea/.
5. Mitchell B. Individual vs. Team Rewards: The 75/25 Rule. Snowfly White Paper, February 2013. https://snowfly.com/white-paper-individual-vs-team-rewards-the-75-25-rule/. Accessed May 24, 2016.
6. Bell A. 33 Amazing Employee Recognition Ideas You Need To Be Using. SnackNation blog, August 21, 2015. www.snacknation.com/blog/employee-recognition-ideas/. Accessed May 31, 2016.
7. Krotz JL. Reward Employees for Teamwork. Groco blog. https://groco.com/?s=Reward+Employees+for+Teamwork. Accessed May 19, 2023.
8. Bares A. Rewarding Teamwork. Upsize blog. www.upsizemag.com/business-builders/rewarding-teamwork. Accessed May 26, 2016.
9. Williams K, & Karau S. Social Loafing and Social Compensation: The Effects of Expectations of Coworker Performance. *J Pers Soc Psychol.* 1991;61:570–581.
10. American Psychological Association Center for Organizational Excellence. Making Teamwork Rewarding. Good Company blog, July 16, 2008. www.apaexcellence.org/resources/goodcompany/newsletter/article/48.
11. Klubnik J. *Rewarding and Recognizing Employees: Ideas for Individuals, Teams, and Managers.* New York: McGraw Hill; 1996.
12. Lurie SJ, Schultz SH, Lamanna G. Assessing Teamwork: A Reliable Five-Question Survey. *Family Medicine.* 2011;43:731–734. www.stfm.org/fmhub/fm2011/November/Stephen731.pdf.

Chapter 6: Increasing Employee Commitment: 25 Strategies

1. Eaton R. Why Commitment Matters So Much to Leaders and Teams. Bizcel blog July 15, 2014. http://bizxcel.com/blog-post/why-commitment-matters-so-much-leaders-and-teams. Accessed September 17, 2015.
2. Vance RJ. *Employee Engagement and Commitment: A Guide to Understanding, Measuring, and Increasing Engagement in Your Organization.* SHRM Foundation's Effective Practice Guidelines. Alexandria, VA: Society for Human Resources Management; 2006. https://www.shrm.org/hr-today/trends-and-forecasting/special-reports-and-expert-views/documents/employee-engagement-commitment.pdf.
3. Beck M. Compliance vs. Commitment. Eliciting Excellence blog, January 9, 2020. https://www.elicitingexcellence.com/employee-engagement/8515/amp/..
4. Rogers JR. Enabling Others to Act — Inspiring Commitment. The Leadership Challenges. www.leadershipchallenge.com/resource/enabling-others-to-act-inspiring-commitment-aspx. Accessed September 28, 2015.

5. Dessler G. How To Earn Your Employees' Commitment. *Academy of Management Perspectives*. 1999;13(2):58–67. https://journals.aom.org/doi/10.5465/ame.1999.1899549.
6. Leheney M. The Five Commitments of Leadership. BA Times for Business Analysts blog, July 21, 2009. www.batimes.com/articles/the-five-commitments-of-leadership.html.

Chapter 7: Using Morning Huddles to Build Your Team

1. Vrabie A. Why the Morning Huddle Is the Best Meeting You'll Ever Have. Sandglaz blog, May 15, 2014. http://blog.sandglaz.com/how-to-run-a-morning-huddle-with-your-team/.
2. Stewart EE, Johnson BC. Huddles: Improve Office Efficiency in Mere Minutes. June 14, 2007. *Fam Pract Manag*. 2007 June;14(6):27–29. .http://www.aafp.org/fpm/2007/0600/p27.html.
3. Fisher-Day M. Morning Huddles Help Improve Dental Team Morale, Productivity. Dentistry IQ blog, September 19. 2013. www.dentistryiq.com/articles/2013/09/morning-huddles-help-improve-dental-team-morale-productivity.html.
4. DuCharme B. What Is a Morning Huddle? Sally MacKenzie's e-Management Newsletter. http://mckenziemgmt.com/managementtips/print/belle/PrintBelleArticle323.html. Accessed July 20, 2016.
5. Fluence. Putting on Your Game Face: Dental Practice Morning Huddle. Fluence blog, May 19, 2011. www.fluenceportland.com/consulting/putting-on-your-game-face.
6. Paige A. Topics for Morning Huddle in the Workplace. Chron blog. http://smallbusiness.chron.com/topics-morning-huddles-workplace-18001.html. Accessed July 20, 2016.
7. Anderson SJ. No More Morning Huddle. Henry Schein Dentrix blog, October 12, 2010. www.henryschein.com/us-en/dental/SalesCon/article_NoMoreMorningHuddle.aspx.
8. Banta L. The Secret to a Dynamic Morning Huddle. Henry Schein Dentrix blog. April 30, 2013. www.dentrix.com/articles/content/id/474. Accessed July 19, 2016.
9. Jamison L. 10 Ways to Ensure That Morning Huddles Will Positively Impact the Dental Practice. Dental IQ blog, July 15, 2013. https://www.dentistryiq.com/practice-management/article/16354638/10-ways-to-ensure-that-morning-huddles-will-positively-impact-the-dental-practice.
10. Levitt MA. Expectations from Your Morning Huddle. Jodena Consulting blog. www.jodena.com/expectations-from-your-morning-huddle.html. Accessed October 5, 2016.

Chapter 8: Developing Your Staff's Empathy

1. Stillman J. 3 Habits That Will Increase Your Empathy. *Inc*. August 22, 2014. www.inc.com/jessica-stillman/3-habits-that-will-increase-your-empathy.html.
2. Krznaric R. Six Habits of Highly Empathetic People. *Greater Good Magazine*. November 22, 2012. at https://greatergood.berkeley.edu/article/item/six_habits_of_highly_empathic_people1.
3. McNamara C. How to Develop Skills in Empathy. Management Help Free Management Library blog, December 16, 2010. https://management.org/blogs/personal-and-professional-coaching/2010/12/16/developing-your-skills-in-empathy.
4. Beirne B. 4 Relationship-Building Activities That Emphasize Empathy. Ovation Communication blog, December 10, 2013. www.ovationcomm.com/blog-1/bid/358611/4-Relationship-Building-Activities-That-Emphasize-Empathy. Accessed September 20, 2018
5. Fowler C. Why Empathy Is Your Most Important Skill (And How To Practice It). LifeHacker blog, January 20, 2014. https://lifehacker.com/why-empathy-is-your-most-important-skill-and-how-to-pr-1505011685.

6. Krznaric R. *Empathy: Why It Matters, and How to Get It*. New York: Perigee; 2014.
7. Orloff J. 10 Traits Empathetic People Share. *Psychology Today*. February 19, 2016. www.psychologytoday.com/us/blog/emotional-freedom/201602/10-traits-empathic-people-share.
8. Zuniga O. 5 Characteristics of Empathetic People. Step to Health blog, April 16, 2017. https://steptohealth.com/5-characteristics-empathetic-people/.
9. Pressley D. The Importance of Empathy in the Workplace. Smart Business blog, November 16, 2012. www.sbnonline.com/article/the-importance-of-empathy-in-the-workplace/.
10. Winter J. Three Exercises to Teach Your Team Empathy. UX Booth blog, July 11, 2017. www.uxbooth.com/articles/three-exercises-to-teach-your-team-empathy/.

Chapter 9: Helping Your Employees Become Better Actors

1. Ciotti G. 16 Customer Service Skills That Every Employee Needs. NCMA blog. https://ncmagroup.com/2020/08/13/16-key-customer-service-skills-and-how-to-develop-them/. Accessed May 21, 2023.
2. Stevenson D. Acting for Non-actors. Doug Stevenson blog. www.storytelling-in-business.com/keynotes-training/story-theater-method/acting-for-non-actors/. Accessed May 21, 2023.
3. Robbins JM. *Acting Techniques for Everyday Life: Look and Feel Confident in Difficult Real-Life Situations*. New York: Marlowe & Company; 2002.
4. Open Mind. Acting Skills for Your Customer Service. Open Mind blog, June 21, 2022. http://www.openmind.in/acting-skills-for-your-customer-service/..
5. Frawley R. How Improv Can Enhance Scripted Acting. Casting Network blog, September 15, 2022. https://www.castingnetworks.com/news/how-improv-can-enhance-scripted-acting/.
6. These Are Their Stories. The Sam Waterston Hair Part Mystery Solved! These Are Their Stories blog, May 23, 2008. https://thesearetheirstories.blogspot.com/2008/05/sam-waterston-hair-part-mystery-solved.html.
7. Scinto J. Why Improv Training Is Great Business Training. *Forbes*. June 27, 2014. www.forbes.com/sites/forbesleadershipforum/2014/06/27/why-improv-training-is-great-business-training/#75b97a4b6bcb.
8. Wallace C. 3 Reasons Why Listening Is the Most Important Part of Acting. *Backstage*. July 18, 2014. www.backstage.com/magazine/article/reasons-listening-important-part-acting-12768/.
9. Price L. "What Did You Say?" Active Listening in the Drama Classroom. Theaterfolk blog, July 23, 2016. www.theatrefolk.com/blog/say-active-listening-drama-classroom/.
10. WhatCulture. 10 Actors Who Conducted Insane Research for Iconic Movie Roles. WhatCulture blog, July 18, 2021. http://whatculture.com/film/10-actors-who-conducted-insane-research-for-iconic-movie-roles.
11. Elizabeth. Actors Who Went to the Extreme to Prepare for a Role. The Chive blog, June 30, 2018. http://thechive.com/2018/06/30/actors-who-went-to-the-extreme-to-prepare-for-a-role-15-photos/.
12. Zemler E. 15 Actors Who Went To Seriously Extreme Measures for a Role. *Elle*. February 5, 2016. www.elle.com/culture/movies-tv/a33861/extreme-role-prep/.
13. Backstage. Successful Actors Talk About Their Training. *Backstage*. April 25, 2016. https://www.backstage.com/magazine/article/successful-actors-talk-training-55312/.
14. The Fitzmaurice Institute. Fitzmaurice Voicework Technique. Fitzmaurice Institute website. www.fitzmauriceinstitute.org/fitzmaurice-voicework/. Accessed May 21, 2023.

15. Kingman V. How to Make Your Voice Deeper: A Definite Approach. Wingman blog. https://get-a-wingman.com/how-to-make-your-voice-deeper-a-definite-approach/. Accessed May 21, 2023.
16. Wright KC. 7 Movement Techniques for Actors. *Backstage.* April 21, 2023. www.backstage.com/magazine/article/movement-techniques-actors-study-8763/.
17. Sherwin L. *All the Workplace Is A Stage: Acting Techniques To Create Award-Winning Business Performance.* Northwest Territories: Inukshuk Publications; 2015.
18. Stephson A. Acting 101 for Managers. Workplace Insiders blog, November 28, 2012. https://workplaceinsiders.com/tag/acting-skills-for-managers/. Accessed December 2, 2018.

Chapter 10: Teaching Your Staff to Reframe Negatives into Positives

1. Newburg A, Waldman M. Why This Word Is So Dangerous to Say or Hear. *Psychology Today.* August 1, 2012. https://www.psychologytoday.com/us/blog/words-can-change-your-brain/201208/why-this-word-is-so-dangerous-to-say-or-hear.
2. McNamara C. Basic Guidelines to Reframing — To Seeing Things Differently. Management blog, February 2, 2012. Https://Management.Org/Blogs/Personal-And-Professional-Coaching/2012/02/02/Basic-Guidelines-To-Reframing-To-Seeing-Things-Differently/.
3. Hooper B. The Awesome Communication Tool – Reframing. Brenda Hooper blog. July 6, 2016. http://brendahooper.com/the- awesome-communication-tool-reframing/. Accessed May 24, 2018.
4. Conversational Receptionists. 5 Ways Positive Words Can Make Customer Service Easier. Conversational Receptionists blog. www.conversational.com/5-ways-positive-words-make-customer-service-easier/. Accessed May 29, 2018.
5. Polacyzak J. The Art of Positive Communication in Customer Service. Ecwid blog. August 31, 2016. www.ecwid.com/blog/the-art-of-positive-communication-in-customer-service.html.
6. Gao K. 40+ Positive Phrases to Create Positive Scripting for Customer Service. Comm 100 blog, September 15, 2017. www.comm100.com/blog/positive-customer-service-phrases.html. Accessed May 29, 2018.
7. Pinnacle. Why You Should Teach Employees Reframing Skills. Pinnacle blog. https://pinnacle.jobs/blog/why-you-should-teach-employees-reframing-skills/. Accessed May 21, 2023.
8. Scott E. 4 Steps to Shift Perspective and Change Everything. Very Well Mind blog. September 28, 2020. www.verywellmind.com/cognitive-reframing-for-stress-management-3144872.
9. Call Centre Helper. Top 25 Words, Phrases, and Empathy Statements. Call Centre Helper blog, January 27, 2023. www.callcentrehelper.com/the-top-25-positive-words-and-phrases-1847.htm.
10. Conversational Receptionists. 50 Positive Words and Phrases To Use in Customer Service. Conversational Receptionists blog. www.conversational.com/50-positive-words-phrases-use-customer-service/. Accessed May 21, 2023.

Chapter 11: Fostering a Culture of Gratitude in Your Healthcare Organization

1. *Psychology Today*. Gratitude. *Psychology Today*. www.psychologytoday.com/us/basics/gratitude. Accessed May 22, 2023.
2. Harvard Health Publishing. Giving Thanks Can Make You Happier. Harvard Health Publishing blog, August 14, 2021. www.health.harvard.edu/healthbeat/giving-thanks-can-make-you-happier.

3. Ducharme J. 7 Surprising Benefits of Gratitude. *Time*, November 20, 2017. https://time.com/5026174/health-benefits-of-gratitude/.
4. Thompson, SP. The Science of Gratitude. Bright Line Eating blog, November 23, 2016. https://www.brightlineeating.com/blog/the-science-of-gratitude/.
5. Economy P. 14 Scientifically Proven Ways Gratitude Can Bring You Success and Happiness. *Inc*. November 3, 2016. www.inc.com/peter-economy/14-powerfully-beneficial-effects-of-gratitude.html.
6. Riordan CM. Foster a Culture of Gratitude. *Harvard Business Review*, April 23, 2013. https://hbr.org/2013/04/foster-a-culture-of-gratitude.
7. Siegel K. How Cultivating a Culture of Gratitude Can Improve Your Workplace for All. *Forbes*, June 12, 2018. https://www.forbes.com/sites/forbeshumanresourcescouncil/2018/06/12/how-cultivating-a-culture-of-gratitude-can-improve-your-workplace-for-all/?sh=356f52f52264.
8. Smith JA. Five Ways to Cultivate Gratitude at Work. *Greater Good Magazine*, May 16, 2013. https://greatergood.berkeley.edu/article/item/five_ways_to_cultivate_gratitude_at_work.
9. Sun K. How to Create a Culture of Gratitude in the Workplace. *Forbes*, December 18, 2017. www.forbes.com/sites/karlsun/2017/12/18/how-to-create-a-culture-of-gratitude-in-the-workplace/#62156ae27a18.
10. Academy of Management. How Gratitude Benefits Employees and Organizations. *Insights Journal*. January 14, 2019. https://journals.aom.org/doi/10.5465/amr. 2014.0374.summary.
11. Ludden D. Why Expressing Gratitude Can Be so Hard to do. *Psychology Today* blog, September 7, 2018. www.psychologytoday.com/us/blog/talking-apes/201809/why-expressing-gratitude-can-be-so-hard-do.
12. Gaille B. 39 Thank-You Messages for Employees. Brandon Gaille blog, June 12, 2017. https://brandongaille.com/37-thank-you-messages-for-employees/. Accessed November 19, 2019.
13. Murchison C. When to Express Gratitude at Work. Greater Good Science Center video, May 1, 2019. https://www.youtube.com/watch?v=D4vsF6ihL8I.

Chapter 12: How to Develop Your Employees' Patience

1. Root GN III. Examples of Excellent Customer Service Skills. Chron. http://smallbusiness.chron.com/examples-excellent-customer-service-skills-2082.html. Accessed May 22, 2023.
2. Bolton J. Four Steps to Developing patience. *Psychology Today*, September 2, 2011. www.psychologytoday.com/us/blog/your-zesty-self/201109/four-steps-developing-patience.
3. Operation-Meditation. Having Patience Benefits You and Those Around You. Operation-Meditation blog. http://operationmeditation.com/discover/having-patience-benefits-you-and-those-around-you/. Accessed March 20, 2018.
4. Corleone J. Irritability and Diet. Livestrong blog, October 3, 2017. www.livestrong.com/article/249937-irritability-and-diet/. Accessed March 21, 2018.
5. Stone J. How to Calculate How Much Water You Should Drink. University of Missouri System. https://www.umsystem.edu/totalrewards/wellness/how-to-calculate-how-much-water-you-should-drink. Accessed May 22, 2023.
6. Sasson R. How to Be Patient in the Workplace. Success Consciousness blog. https://www.successconsciousness.com/blog/personal-development/how-to-be-patient-in-the-workplace/. Accessed May 22, 2023.

7. Huhman HR. Employees Don't Get Enough Sleep, and It's Your Fault. *Entrepreneur*, April 25, 2016. www.entrepreneur.com/article/274277.
8. Gaines M. How to Motivate Employees to Exercise. Chron. https://www.nawhc.org/resources/All%20Documents/How%20to%20Motivate%20Employees%20to%20Exercise%20_%20Chron.com.pdf. Accessed May 21, 2023.
9. Stone J. Understanding Impatience. *Psychology Today*, November 4, 2014. www.psychologytoday.com/us/blog/clear-organized-and-motivated/201411/understanding-impatience.
10. Lively KJ. Affirmations: The Why, What, How, and What If? *Psychology Today*, March 12, 2014. www.psychologytoday.com/us/blog/smart-relationships/201403/affirmations-the-why-what-how-and-what-if.
11. 7 Mindsets. 6 Keys to Developing Patience. 7 Mindsets blog. http://7mindsets. com/developing-patience/. Accessed May 22, 2023.
12. Brenner. How to Deal with Grumpy and Impatient Co-Workers. Chron. http://work.chron.com/deal-grumpy-impatient-coworkers-5333.html.
13. Llopis G. 5 Powerful Ways Leaders Practice Patience. *Forbes*, June 3, 2013. https://www.forbes.com/sites/glennllopis/2013/06/03/5-powerful-ways-leaders-practice-patience/?sh=75f68223421a.

Chapter 13: Using Rituals to Strengthen Your Team

1. Gino F, Norton MI. Why Rituals Work. *Scientific American*, May 14, 2013. www.scientificamerican.com/article/why-rituals-work/.
2. Colan L. Rituals Are a Way to Reinforce the Fabric of High-performing Teams. The Business Journals. April 30, 2007. https://www.bizjournals.com/houston/stories/2007/04/30/smallb4.html.
3. King SK. Rituals and Modern Society. Huna International blog. www.huna.org/html/skritual.html. Accessed May 22, 2023.
4. Carrico K. Ritual. Cultural Anthropology blog. www.culanth.org/curated_collections/4-ritual. Accessed May 22, 2023.
5. Neale L. *The Power of Ceremony.* Rio Rancho, NM: Eagle Spirit Press; 2011.
6. Lagare CH, Souza AL. Searching for Control; Priming Randomness Increases the Evaluation of Ritual Efficacy. *Cognitive Science*, August 13, 2013. http://onlinelibrary.wiley.com/doi/10.1111/cogs.12077/abstract.
7. Hahn M. Corporate Culture as Rites and Ceremonials. Articles Gratuits blog, April 21, 2007. http://en.articlesgratuits.com/corporate-culture-as-rites-and-ceremonials-id1519.php. Accessed May 28, 2015.
8. Warrillow J. The Secret Rituals and Traditions That Bring Teams Together. CBS News. December 23, 2010. www.cbsnews.com/news/the-secret-rituals-and-traditions-that-bring-teams-together/.
9. Neal J. *Enlightened Organizations: Four Gateways to Spirit at Work.* New York: Palgrave MacMillan; 2013.
10. The Matrix Group. Matrix Group's X-Men Team Wins 2014 Pumpkin Carving Contest. Matrix Group blog. October 31, 2014. www.matrixgroup.net/news-events/news/2014/10/31/matrix-group%27s-x-men-team-wins-2014-pumpkin-carving-competition. Accessed May 28, 2015.

Chapter 14: Staff Coaching: Using Active Listening and Powerful Questions to Unleash Your Staff's Potential

1. Green H. Know When to Manage and When to Coach. *Forbes,* May 1, 2012. www.forbes.com/sites/work-in-progress/2012/05/01/know-when-to-manage-and-when-to-coach/#5806995223be.
2. Stack L. Managing vs. Coaching: In Today's Workplace, You Really Need Both. TLNT blog, July 7, 2014. www.tlnt.com/managing-vs-coaching-in-todays-workplace-you-really-need-both/.
3. Harski C. Why the Coach Approach Beats the Manager Mentality. *Entrepreneur*, February 18, 2014. www.entrepreneur.com/article/231568.
4. Hills L. *They'll Eat Out of Your Hand If You Know What To Feed Them: The 30 Essential Communication Skills That Give Highly Successful Career Professionals Their Edge.* Fairfax, Virginia: Blue Pencil Publishing; 2014.
5. Aguilar E. Active Listening: The Key To Transforming Your Coaching. *Education Week* Teacher blog, April 27, 2014. https://www.edweek.org/education/opinion-active-listening-the-key-to-transforming-your-coaching/2014/04.
6. International Coaching Federation. ICF Core Competencies. ICF website. https://coachingfederation.org/credentials-and-standards/core-competencies. Accessed May 22, 2023.
7. Lee HT. The Most Important Coaching Competency: Active Listening. Coaching Journey's Journey to Your Next Level blog. http://coaching-journey.com/the-most-important-coaching-competency-active-listening/. Accessed November 28, 2017.
8. Vogt E. The Art and Architecture of Powerful Questions. *MicroMentro Corporate Learning Journal.* 1994. http://www.cashflow88.com/decisiones/powerfulquestions.pdf.
9. Miglino M. Powerful Questions. International Coach Academy blog. August 18, 2014. https://coachcampus.com/resources/powerful-questions/.
10. The Coaching Tools Company. 549 Powerful Coaching Questions. The Coaching Tools Company ebook. www.thecoachingtoolscompany.com/wp-content/uploads/2015/04/549-Powerful-Coaching-Questions-FREE_u.pdf. Accessed May 23, 2023.

Chapter 15: Working Well with the Informal Leaders in Your Organization

1. Grimsley S. Informal Leadership: Definition, Lesson, & Quiz. Study.com lesson transcript, Updated September 14, 2021. https://study.com/academy/lesson/informal-leadership-definition-lesson-quiz.html#lesson.
2. Bacal R. What Is an Informal Leader? Bacal and Associates blog. http://leadertoday.org/faq/informalleader.htm. Accessed May 23, 2023.
3. Bacal R. Understanding Informal Leaders in an Organization (and Benefiting from Them.) Bacal and Associates blog. http://leadertoday.org/articles/informalleadersunderstanding.htm. Accessed May 23, 2023.
4. Rainer S. The Advantages of Informal Authority. Church Executive blog, November 28, 2012. http://churchexecutive.com/archives/the-advantages-of-informal-authority.
5. Crow P. Strategy for Informal Leadership. Peak Operational Strategies. February 27, 2014. http://operational-strategies.com/strategy-of-informal-leadership/. Accessed July 13, 2014.

6. Mochari I. Why You Need To Develop "Informal Leaders" Among Your Employees. *Inc.* February 27, 2014. www.inc.com/ilan-mochari/informal-leaders-culture.html.
7. Ebreo E. How Do You Deal with Informal Leaders in the Workplace? Anything HR blog, November 21, 2006. http://anythinghr.blogspot.com/2006/11/how-do-you-deal-with-informal-leaders.html.
8. Krueger DL. Informal Leaders and Culture Change. American Nurse Today blog, August 11, 2013. www.americannursetoday.com/article.aspx?id=10646&fid=10604.
9. Bacal R. Benefiting from Informal Leaders in Your Organization: Communication Is the Key. Bacal and Associates blog. http://leadertoday.org/articles/informalleadershipbenefits.htm. Accessed May 23, 2023.
10. Vercillo K. Best Leadership: Formal vs. Informal. Tough Nickel blog, September 7, 2022. https://toughnickel.com/business/Formal-vs-Informal-Leaders.
11. Bacal R. Some Pitfalls to Think About When Developing an Informal Leader. Bacal and Associates blog. http://leadertoday.org/articles/developinformalleaders.htm. Accessed May 23, 2023.
12. Smart M. *The Hidden Power of Informal Leadership: What You Need To Know To Identify Your Hidden Leaders, Built Trust, Inspire Action, and Get Results.* Idaho Falls: Xulon Press, 2010.

Chapter 16: Motivating Employees without Carrots and Sticks

1. Robinson S. What's Wrong with the Carrot and Stick Approach? Fresh Concepts blog, October 17, 2017. https://www.freshconceptsonline.com/whats-wrong-carrot-stick-approach/.
2. Mehta AN. What Is Carrot and Stick Policy? The Times of India. July 15, 2007. https://timesofindia.indiatimes.com/what-is-carrot-and-stick-policy/articleshow/2204414.cms.
3. McMahon T. Carrots and Sticks Don't Motivate in a Thinking Environment. A Lean Journey blog, July 14, 2014. www.aleanjourney.com/2014/07/carrots-and-sticks-dont-motivate-in.html.
4. Indeed Editorial Team. Carrot and Stick Motivation: Definition and Examples in the Workplace. Indeed blog, December 17, 2020. www.indeed.com/career-advice/career-development/carrot-and-stick-motivation.
5. McLeod S. What Is Operant Conditioning and How Does It Work? Simply Psychology blog, May 12, 2023. www.simplypsychology.org/operant-conditioning.html.
6. Price H. How to Be a Motivational Leader — Without Carrots and Sticks. Jostle blog. https://blog.jostle.me/blog/how-to-be-a-motivational-leader-without-carrots-and-sticks. Accessed May 23, 2023.
7. Pollack P. Forget the "Carrot and Stick" Approach! Mediate blog, November 12, 2018. www.mediate.com/articles/pollack-carrot-stick.cfm. Accessed March 23, 2021.
8. Kruse K. This Yale Psychologist Says Carrots and Sticks Don't Motivate. *Forbes*, March 27, 2017. https://www.forbes.com/sites/kevinkruse/2017/03/27/this-yale-psychologist-says-carrots-and-sticks-dont-motivate/?sh=40ea0742222d.
9. Lai L. Motivating Employees Is Not About Carrots and Sticks. *Harvard Business Review,* June 27, 2017. https://hbr.org/2017/06/motivating-employees-is-not-about-carrots-or-sticks. Accessed March 24, 2021
10. Marr B. What Really Motivates Employees (Hint: It's Not Carrots or Sticks). Bernard Marr & Co. blog, July 2, 2021. www.bernardmarr.com/default.asp?contentID=1147.

11. Jenkins R. This Has Been a Top Employee Motivator for Over 46 Years. *Inc*, June 10, 2019. https://www.inc.com/ryan-jenkins/this-has-been-a-top-employee-motivator-for-over-46-years.html.

Chapter 17: Creating an Exceptional Onboarding Experience for Your New Employees

1. Carucci R. To Retain New Hires, Spend More Time Onboarding Them. *Harvard Business Review*, December 3, 2018. https://hbr.org/2018/12/to-retain-new-hires-spend-more-time-onboarding-them.
2. Moloney C. 10 Employee Onboarding Statistics You Must Know in 2022. Kallidus blog. https://www.kallidus.com/resources/blog/10-employee-onboarding-statistics-you-must-know-in-2022/. Accessed May 23, 2023.
3. Apollo Technical. Why Onboarding Is Important and a Key To Success. Apollo Technical blog. February 16, 2023. www.apollotechnical.com/why-onboarding-is-important/.
4. SHRM. Understanding Employee Onboarding. SHRM Toolkit. www.shrm.org/resourcesandtools/tools-and-samples/toolkits/pages/understanding-employee-onboarding.aspx. Accessed May 23, 2023.
5. Hirsch AS. Don't Underestimate the Importance of Good Onboarding. SHRM website. August 10, 2017. www.shrm.org/resourcesandtools/hr-topics/talent-acquisition/pages/dont-underestimate-the-importance-of-effective-onboarding.aspx.
6. Graham T. Employee Onboarding as a Shared Responsibility. KPA blog, June 16, 2020. www.kpa.io/blog/employee-onboarding-as-a-shared-responsibility.
7. HR Cloud. The Onboarding Process: Who Is Responsible for What? HR Cloud blog, May 19, 2014. www.hrcloud.com/blog/onboarding-whose-job-is-it-anyway/.
8. Bradt G. Leaders Must Take Onboarding Personally. Association for Talent Development blog, May 13, 2014. www.td.org/insights/leaders-must-take-onboarding-personally.
9. Aberdeen Strategy Research. Perfecting the Onboarding Funnel. Aberdeen Strategy Research blog, September 22, 2016. www.aberdeen.com/hcm-essentials/perfecting-onboarding-funnel/.
10. Greaves R. 7 Best Practices for a Killer Pre-Boarding Experience. Harver blog. December 11, 2019. https://harver.com/blog/pre-boarding/.
11. Bell A. 7-Steps to Perfect Employee Onboarding Process for New Hires & Best Onboarding Software Platforms in 2023. SnackNation blog. https://snacknation.com/blog/onboarding-process/. Accessed May 24, 2023.
12. Beltran E. A Guide to Reboarding Employees During and After the Pandemic. *Forbes*, October 29, 2021. www.forbes.com/sites/forbesbusinesscouncil/2021/10/29/a-guide-to-reboarding-employees-during-and-after-the-pandemic/?sh=5d6a40e71033.

Bonus Chapter: Creating a Core Beliefs Statement: 25 Guiding Truths for Your Employees

1. Indeed Editorial Team. Why Is a Company's Mission Statement Important? Indeed blog, February 23, 2023. https://www.indeed.com/career-advice/career-development/why-mission-statement-is-important.
2. Peek S. What Is a Vision Statement? *Business News Daily*, February 21, 2023. https://www.businessnewsdaily.com/3882-vision-statement.html.

3. SHRM. What Is the Difference Between Mission, Vision, and Values Statements? SHRM HR Q & As. https://www.shrm.org/resourcesandtools/tools-and-samples/hr-qa/pages/isthereadifferencebetweenacompany%E2%80%99smission,visionandvaluestatements.aspx. Accessed October 4, 2022.
4. Darmann D. 70+ Examples of Core Company Values & How They Shape Your Culture. Hotjar blog, October 31, 2022. https://www.hotjar.com/blog/company-values/.
5. Schaffner AK. Core Beliefs: 12 Worksheets to Challenge Negative Beliefs. Positive Psychology blog, June 26, 2020. https://positivepsychology.com/core-beliefs-worksheets/.

www.ingramcontent.com/pod-product-compliance
Lightning Source LLC
Chambersburg PA
CBHW060405220326
41598CB00023B/3027
9781960762030